Professional Values and Practice

Meeting the Standards

Third Edition

 Edited by **Mike Cole**

David Fulton Publishers

David Fulton Publishers Ltd
The Chiswick Centre, 414 Chiswick High Road, London W4 5TF

www.fultonpublishers.co.uk

David Fulton Publishers is a division of Granada Learning Limited, part of ITV plc.

British Library Cataloguing in Publication Data
A catalogue record for this book is available from the British Library.

ISBN 1 84312 384 3

10 9 8 7 6 5 4 3 2 1

Typeset by Servis Filmsetting Ltd, Manchester
Printed and bound in Great Britain

Contents

About the authors

Dr Maud Blair was a lecturer at the Open University from 1991–2002, where she was based in the Faculty of Education and Language Studies. Her main areas of teaching and research related to issues of race, ethnicity and gender. In 2001 she was seconded as an advisor on ethnicity to the Department for Education and Skills (DfES). She joined the DfES on a permanent basis and works in the Schools' Directorate on issues of ethnicity and education. She is co-author of the DfES report *Making the Difference: teaching and learning in successful multi-ethnic schools* published in 1998. She has written and published widely on issues of gender and ethnicity.

Dr Mike Cole is Senior Lecturer in Education, and Co-ordinator of the Inclusion and Social Justice Research Group in the Faculty of Education and Sport at the University of Brighton. He has written extensively on equality issues. Forth-coming books include a second, completely revised edition of the highly successful, *Education, Equality and Human Rights* (originally published by Routledge/Falmer in 2000; new edition Routledge 2005) and *Marxism, Postmodernism and Education: pasts, presents and futures*, to be published by Routledge in 2006.

Valerie Coultas worked in several London comprehensive schools, as Head of English and Assistant Head Teacher, until recently taking up a post as Senior Lecturer in English in the School of Education at Kingston University. She has recently helped to establish a new education journal, *Radical Education*, published by Blueprint, Cambridge.

Kate Daly joined the DfES in January 2003, working within the Ethnic Minority Achievement Project to lead the EAL (English as an Additional Language) strand of the Ethnic Minority Achievement Strategy. This work entails developing a national framework for EAL which includes training and support for mainstream staff, training and support for EAL specialist staff and a national approach to EAL assessment. For the previous seven years, she was Senior School Improvement Officer in the London Borough of Lewisham, responsible for equalities and liter-acy. She has led teams of specialist EAL teachers in Lewisham and Bexley.

Linda Hurley was a classroom teacher for 20 years before working as a literacy consultant for East Sussex LEA. While in this role she wrote *What About Reception*, which gave practical advice to teachers on implementing the Literacy Strategy in Reception classes. She is now Senior Lecturer in Early Years at the University of Brighton, teaching Advanced Early Years and Education Studies. She has also been working in Mauritius on a British Council project to tackle underachievement through literacy.

Jeff Nixon began his teaching career in a boys' secondary modern school in 1972. He then worked in the Community Studies department of a 13–18 community college in West Yorkshire, where he became Head of Department and then Head of House. Since 1983 he has worked for the National Union of Teachers at the Union's Haywards Heath Regional Office, initially as District Officer and now as Regional Officer. The views expressed in his chapter are his own, rather than those of the NUT.

Joanna Oldham is currently the Co-ordinator of Primary English at Liverpool Hope University College. She was originally a secondary school teacher of English and she then became an educational researcher in primary and secondary schools. She has retained research interests in literacy, media and assessment while working in higher education since 1997.

Linda Rice taught in mainstream, special schools and special facilities within mainstream schools, for 25 years before working as a Local Education Authority teacher advisor for pupils with special educational needs. She is a regional tutor for the Makaton Vocabulary Development Project. For three years Linda was a senior lecturer at the University of Brighton School of Education where she contributed to both undergraduate ITE and Masters level courses. During this time she was a part-time member of the Economic and Social Research Council (ESRC) funded 'SPRinG' research project which worked in collaboration with teachers on effective collaborative group working in Key Stage 1 classrooms. In addition to this she worked over a three-year period with primary and secondary teachers and head teachers in Mauritius. This was part of a British Council Link project in collaboration with the Mauritius Institute of Education.

Dr Krishan Sood is a principal lecturer in education leadership and management at the University of Lincoln, with special interests in educational management, science education, marketing and diversity. In his teaching career spanning 28 years, he has gained a width and depth of experience as a classroom teacher, an advisory teacher and as a lecturer in three universities. He considers it a great privilege to have worked in over 60 primary schools and five secondary schools, small and large, rural and urban, as an advisory teacher in Warwickshire. He has had experience of working collaboratively, in team teaching situations and in planning, leading and monitoring progress when running in service education and training (INSET) or workshops for a large variety of professionals. He has had a depth of experience of community groups in Warwickshire through his work with the local branch of the Race Equality Council and as past governor of a special school and a large comprehensive.

Preface

Those awarded Qualified Teacher Status [QTS] must understand and uphold the professional code of the General Teaching Council [GTC] for England.

(Teacher Training Agency (TTA) 2004: 7 Section 1)

To gain Qualified Teacher Status, a teacher needs to demonstrate eight qualities, numbered S1.1 to S1.8 in *Qualifying to Teach* (see Figure 1). The chapters of this book deal with each of these qualities, each chapter considering one of them. The chapter authors have adopted a broad perspective in considering their themes.

In the Introductory chapter, I set out some conceptual and practical issues with respect to equality and equal opportunity issues. Specifically, I examine the key equality concepts of 'race' and racism; gender; disability; sexuality and social class. I argue that we are not born 'ist/phobic',[1] that 'ism/phobia' is a product of the society or societies in which we live. I suggest six steps that might be taken to check, unlearn, counteract and get beyond 'isms/phobia'. I conclude that while we can make important changes in societies as they are, in order to fully eradicate oppression in all its forms, we need to change society.

Maud Blair and Kate Daly, in Chapter 1, address themselves to S1.1, namely that beginning teachers 'have high expectations of all pupils;[2] respect their social, cultural, linguistic, religious and ethnic backgrounds; and are committed to raising their educational achievement' (TTA 2004: 7). The authors conclude that while technical competencies are important, they are not sufficient in a diverse, class-based, gendered, multi-ethnic, multi-faith, multilingual society. Teachers, they argue, must be constantly reflective about their practice and must be creative in providing a curriculum that is inclusive of all pupils and that provides social justice in the wider society.

In order to be inclusive of all pupils, it is necessary to 'treat [them] consistently, with respect and consideration, and [be] concerned for their development as learners' (TTA 2004: 7). Thus Joanna Oldham in Chapter 2 addresses the issue of how teachers should treat pupils particularly with respect to them as learners. Oldham explores possible tensions between learning styles on the one hand and the nature of curriculum and assessment frames on the other. In a consideration of learning within a cycle of planning, teaching and assessment, Oldham stresses the importance of formative assessment and concludes that consideration for pupils manifests itself in teachers prioritising learning not assessment.

Chapter 3 focuses on the TTA (2004) requirement for beginning teachers to 'demonstrate and promote the positive values, attitudes and behaviour that they expect from their pupils' (S1.3, *ibid.*). Arguing that values are relative, Linda Rice

Those awarded Qualified Teacher Status must understand and uphold the professional code of the General Teaching Council for England by demonstrating all of the following:

1.1 They have high expectations of all pupils; respect their social, cultural, linguistic, religious and ethnic backgrounds; and are committed to raising their educational achievement.

1.2 They treat pupils consistently, with respect and consideration, and are concerned for their development as learners.

1.3 They demonstrate and promote the positive values, attitudes and behaviour that they expect from their pupils.

1.4 They can communicate sensitively and effectively with parents and carers, recognising their roles in pupils' learning, and their rights, responsibilities and interests in this.

1.5 They can contribute to, and share responsibly in, the corporate life of schools*.

1.6 They understand the contribution that support staff and other professionals make to teaching and learning.

1.7 They are able to improve their own teaching, by evaluating it, learning from the effective practice of others and from evidence. They are motivated and able to take increasing responsibility for their own professional development.

1.8 They are aware of, and work within, the statutory frameworks relating to teachers' responsibilities.

*In this document, the term 'schools' includes Further Education and VI form colleges and Early Years settings where trainee teachers can demonstrate that they meet the Standards for Qualified Teacher Status.

Figure 1 Professional values and practice (*Source:* TTA 2004)

examines the impact of teacher values on pupil experiences and teachers' expectations. Values, she concludes, must be seen in the context of global and national economic and political forces. Although education reflects economic and political processes (intensifying globalisation, market forces, privatisation), it can also challenge them. Teachers and others involved in education can utilise the current government insistence on inclusive education to make demands for an education system that firmly promotes equality and social justice.

In addressing herself to the requirement that beginning teachers 'can communicate sensitively and effectively with parents and carers, recognising their roles in pupils' learning, and their rights, responsibilities and interests in this' (S1.4, *ibid.*), Linda Hurley, in Chapter 4, notes that parent/carer support for schools is widely recognised as a crucial determinant of educational performance. Drawing on her own research, Hurley argues against seeing parent/carers as a homogenous group, devoid of social class, culture, sexuality and diversity. Often, she concludes, power differentials mean that teachers have the power and parents[3] the anxiety. To reverse this state of affairs, parents/carers should be seen as 'co-communicators', 'co-supporters', 'co-learners' and 'co-decision makers' in order for them to have an *active*, rather than a passive involvement in the life of the school and Hurley sees it as the teacher's responsibility to facilitate this.

Like the other contributors to this book, Krishan Sood, in Chapter 5, responds to the TTA requirements in a critically analytical manner. Thus in addressing himself to S1.5 which stresses the need for beginning teachers to 'contribute to, and share responsibly in, the *corporate* life of schools'[4] (TTA 2004: 7) (my emphasis), Sood takes the position that schools should be properly thought of as 'communities' rather than corporations, viewing them as acting as catalysts in bringing the community together. The school, he argues, should help develop community skills, knowledge and capacities regardless of age, gender, disability, social status, sexuality or ethnic origin.

Chapter 6, also written by Krishan Sood, examines 'the contribution that support staff and other professionals make to teaching and learning' (*ibid.*). Sood concludes that learning support assistants and other professionals must be considered not just part of the staff, but as part of a team. He suggests that beginning teachers have a decisive role to enable this to happen for the benefit of all pupils.

Requirement S1.7 states that beginning teachers need to be 'able to improve their own teaching, by evaluating it, learning from the effective practice of others and from evidence'. They also need to be 'motivated and able to take increasing responsibility for their own professional development' (*ibid.*). Thus, argues Valerie Coultas in Chapter 7, an effective teacher is someone who sees himself or herself as a learner. The teacher who is a learner can always contribute to the development of other colleagues. However, it is essential that this is combined with a commitment to teaching and education as a source for building a more egalitarian society, a commitment that will motivate *all* colleagues and pupils.

In order for teachers to function effectively in schools, they need to be 'aware of, and work within, the statutory frameworks relating to teachers' responsibilities' (S1.8, *ibid.*). Thus, in Chapter 8, Jeff Nixon begins by discussing the concept of a teacher's duty of care. He then examines the statutory framework relating to teachers' conditions of service. Nixon then provides an overview of regulations/guidance on the welfare of the child, special needs and health and safety. He concludes with a discussion of legislation concerned with equality and equal opportunities issues.

Mike Cole

Notes

1   'Ist/phobic' is a short-hand term to cover racist; sexist; disablist; classist; and homophobic/ Islamophobic/xenophobic. Individuals may exhibit one or more 'isms' and/or be phobic.

2   'Pupils' is used throughout the book to refer to pupils and students. It is acknowledged that in secondary schools and beyond, the common nomenclature is 'student'. However 'pupils' is used in order to avoid the rather clumsy nomenclature of 'pupil/student'. Where chapter authors are referring specifically to the secondary school, they may use 'student'. In addition, the contributors have generally adopted the nomenclatures 'beginning teacher' and 'teacher education', as opposed to the TTA's 'trainee teacher' and 'teacher training'. This reflects our collective belief that achieving QTS involves much more than mere 'training' (Cole 1999).

3   The role of parent, carer and guardian is referred to in different chapters variously as 'parent', 'parent/carers', 'parents/carers'. It is recognised of course that a child may live with a single parent, guardian or carer or indeed may not live in a domestic unit.

4   In the TTA document, the term 'schools' includes further education and sixth form colleges, and early years settings where beginning teachers can demonstrate that they meet the standards.

References

Cole, M. (1999) 'Professional issues and initial teacher education: what can be done and what should be done', *Education and Social Justice*, 2 (1), 63–6.

Teacher Training Agency (TTA) (2004) *Qualifying to Teach: professional standards for Qualified Teacher Status and requirements for initial teacher training*. London: TTA.

Introductory chapter: education and equality – some conceptual and practical issues

Mike Cole

Learning objectives

To raise awareness of:

- conceptual issues relating to 'race' and racism; gender; sexuality; disability and social class
- practical issues related to these identities in an institutional context
- practical issues related to these identities on a personal level.

Part one: conceptual issues

Introduction

IN ORDER TO BE AWARDED Qualified Teacher Status (QTS) in England and Wales, teachers must demonstrate that they have high expectations of and respect for *all* pupils (S1.1 of TTA 2004: 7) (my emphasis). If teachers are to do this, then it is self-evident that they are aware of the way that social class, gender, ethnicity, disability and sexuality impact on pupils' lives.[1] Teaching and learning about equality, then, is *not* an optional extra, something to be tagged on to teacher education courses after the important stuff has been dealt with. It is, rather, an integral part of the teaching and learning process.

First of all, however, a distinction needs to be made between equality of opportunity, on the one hand, and equality, on the other. Equal opportunity policies in schools and elsewhere, seek to enhance social mobility within structures that are essentially unequal. In other words, they seek a meritocracy, where people rise (or fall) on merit, but to grossly unequal levels or strata in society – unequal in terms of income; wealth; life-style; life-chances and power. Egalitarian policies, policies to promote equality, on the other hand, seek to go further. First, egalitarians attempt to develop a systematic critique of structural inequalities, both in society at large and at the level of the individual school (or other institution). Second, egalitarians are committed to a transformed economy, and a more socially just society, where wealth and ownership is shared far more equally, and where citizens (whether young citizens or teachers in schools, economic citizens in the workplace or political citizens in the polity) exercise democratic controls over their lives and over the structures of the societies of which they are part and to which they contribute.

Meritocrats seek equality of opportunity.[2] Egalitarians seek equality of outcome. While equal opportunity policies in schools (and elsewhere) are clearly essential, it is the egalitarian view that they need to be advocated within a framework of a longer-term commitment to equality (Cole and Hill 1999: 1–2; Cole 2005a).

Equality and equal opportunity issues have been pertinent through history (Cole 2005b) and they are pertinent now (Hill and Cole 2001). Another of the requirements of TTA (2004) is that those awarded QTS need to 'recognise and respond effectively to equal opportunities issues as they arise in the classroom' (S3.3.14 of TTA 2004: 13). This includes 'challenging stereotyped views', 'challenging bullying or harassment' and 'following relevant policies and procedures' (*ibid.*). In order to do this, it is necessary to understand equality issues *per se* as well as being able to apply them to education. *Theory and practice must be interrelated*. For example, in order for us, as teachers (and other educational workers), to deal with racism in schools, we first of all need to understand what is meant by the concept of racism; to challenge homophobic bullying, we need to be conversant with sexuality issues; to deal with gender differentials in achievement, for example, we need to understand what is meant by gender. In order to deal with social class issues, we need to know about theories of social class, and in order to deal with disability issues, we need to be aware of issues of disability rights.

All of these equality issues are dealt with at length in Cole (2005b) and Hill and Cole (2001). They are dealt with on a subject-by-subject basis, at the primary level in Cole *et al.* (1997); and at the secondary level, in Hill and Cole (1999).

As well as needing to have a sound knowledge of the equality issues both *per se* and in relation to education, beginning teachers and teachers also need to know the current state of play with respect to national and international legislation pertaining to equality and equal opportunity issues (see Chapter 8 for a thorough analysis; see also the regular editions of Natfhe's *Equality News* http://www.natfhe.org.uk/help/EqNews.html).

Clearly, equality and equal opportunity issues are interrelated. For example, every human being has multiple identities. To take a case in point: there are, of course, lesbians, gays, bisexuals and transgendered (LGBT) people in all social classes, among the Asian, black and other minority ethnic communities and among white communities. There are LGBT people with disabilities and special needs. Equality and equal opportunity issues are also discrete. For conceptual clarity, I will deal with each in turn.

'Race' and racism

It is now widely recognised that 'race'[3] is not a valid scientific concept. For example, there are more genetic differences within one so-called 'race' than between different so-called 'races'. Racism, however, is, of course, real enough, and, in order for teachers to deal with it, they need to have a conceptual awareness of what it means. My view is that we should adopt a wide-ranging definition of racism, rather than, for example, a narrow one based, as it was in the days of Empire, for example, on biology. Racism can be institutional or personal; it can be dominative (direct and oppressive) as opposed to aversive (exclusion and cold-shouldering) (Kovel 1988); it can be overt or covert; intentional or unintentional; biological and/or cultural. Attributes ascribed to ethnic groups can also be seemingly positive, as, for example, when whole groups are stereotyped as having strong cultures or being good at sport. Such stereotypes may well be followed up, respectively, with notions that 'they are taking over', or 'they are not so good academically'. The point is to be wary of attributing any stereotypes to ethnic groups. All stereotypes are *at least potentially* racist. There can, of course, be permutations among these different forms of racism (Cole 2004a).

The implications for education are obvious. Education has played a role in reproducing racism (monocultural and much multicultural education), but also has a major role to play in undermining racism (antiracist education). Monocultural education is to do with the promotion of so-called British values; multicultural education is about the celebration of diversity and has often been tokenistic and patronising, and antiracist education focuses on undermining racism. The Stephen Lawrence Inquiry report acknowledged that '[r]acism, institutional or otherwise, is not [only] the prerogative of the Police Service'

(Macpherson 1999: 6.54) and that 'other agencies including for example those dealing with housing and education also suffer from the disease [*sic*]' (*ibid.*). It went on to argue that if racism is to be eradicated, there must be specific and co-ordinated action both within the agencies themselves and by society at large, particularly through the education system, from pre-primary school upwards and onwards (*ibid.*).

Modern technology has major implications for delivering antiracist multicultural education, in that it allows people to speak for themselves. This is not an argument in favour of postmodern multivocality, where all voices are equally valid; but rather the flagging of opportunities to avoid speaking on other people's behalf (for discussions on the way in which racism impacts on schooling and what can be done about it, see Chapter 1 of this volume; see also Cole 1998; Cole 2004a, b; Cole and Blair 2005).

In appearing to mark a retreat from the Government's commitment to the implementation of these most minimalist recommendations, David Blunkett's remarks (Travis 2003) denying the existence of institutional racism have a sinister ring. Blunkett's intervention represents an attempt to turn back the tide; to trivialise institutional racism by describing it as a 'slogan'; indeed to deny its existence and to revert back, in Blunkett's own words, to 'individual prejudice' as being the major problem (for an analysis, see Cole 2004a). I recently did some TTA-funded research with colleagues at Sussex University and University College Canterbury. We found widespread racism and xenophobia in schools in the south-east of England: for example, an Asian beginning teacher was asked by a pupil if she rode on elephants, and a mentor advised another student, 'never tell them you're German'. A report of the research can be found at the following website: www.sussex.ac.uk/usie/rc/final_rep_tta.pdf (see also Cole and Stuart (2005), which is an academic report of the research; and East Sussex County Council (2004), which gives further disturbing evidence of racism in the south-east of England).

To repeat, teachers need a conceptual awareness of what racism is in order to combat the racism endemic in our education system.

Gender

A distinction needs to be made between 'sex' and 'gender'. Essentially, sex is biological and gender is constructed. Most people, though not all, are born essentially male or female. However, gender roles are learned and are relative to time and place. In other words, what is considered 'acceptable modes of dress' or body language for males and females varies dramatically through history and according to geographical location (this is not to say, of course, that everyone in a given society conforms to such norms – there are many examples throughout history of people who have refused to conform). The implications for schools are that they can reproduce sexism, but they can also challenge it. Schools can be non-sexist, or they can be anti-sexist. The curriculum, actual and hidden, can be non-sexist, or it can be anti-sexist. In other words, it can make sure that it does not promote sexism, or it can actively promote anti-sexism. Traditionally, there has been concern among feminists and their supporters about the way in which schooling has reproduced gender inequalities, particularly with respect to female subordination. More recently, now that it has become apparent that many boys are now being out-performed by girls, there has been more general media and government concerns.

If many boys are now being out-performed by girls, this is not to say, of course, that schooling does not continue to reproduce other forms of sexism, of which females are at the receiving end. For example, boys often still dominate in mixed gender classrooms and schools and university education departments suffer from an over-representation of men in higher positions, which is a reflection of the wider society. For discussions on the way in which sexism impacts on schooling, on differential achievement and what can be done about it, see Hirom (2001), Martin (2005) and the Equal Opportunities Commission (http://www.eoc.org.uk).

To repeat, gender roles are not fixed, but are relative to time and place. Boys do not *need* to do badly at school relative to girls. Sexism does not *need* to predominate in schools. Women's structural location in the workforce can be changed and teachers *can* do something about it.

Disability

Richard Rieser has made a distinction between what he calls the 'medical' and 'social models' of disability (see Figures 2 and 3). The 'medical model' views the disabled person as the problem. Disabled people are to be adapted to fit into the world as it is. Where this is not possible, disabled people have been shut away in some specialised institution or isolated at home. Often disabled peoples' lives are handed over to others (Rieser 2005a).

The 'social model' of disability views society as the problem. It is up to institutions in society to adapt to meet the needs of disabled people. This is the model favoured by disabled people.

The educational implications for each of these are the 'fixed continuum of provision' and the 'constellation of services' (see Figures 4 and 5). Under the former, the disabled person is slotted and moved according to the assessment of (usually non-disabled) assessors. This model is based on segregation (Rieser 2005b). With respect to the 'constellation of services', provision is made for the disabled child in mainstream school. The child and teacher are backed up by a variety of support services (*ibid.*).

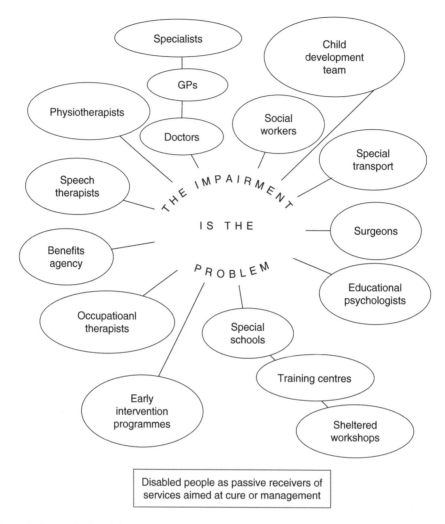

Figure 2 The medical model

Currently, there is a wide consensus among disability activists, many educational institutions and the Government that the way forward is inclusion, which, of course, relates to the 'social model' and the 'constellation of services' (*ibid.*; see also, Chapter 3 of this volume).

Sexuality

Sexuality has often been ignored in education. First, I wish to stress that I believe that it is an issue for every teacher, primary as well as secondary (there is evidence that some children identify as gay or lesbian in the primary years (NUT 1991: 7; Epstein 1994: 49–56). In most schools, lesbians, gay men and bisexuals will be members of the teaching and other staff. In some schools, there will be

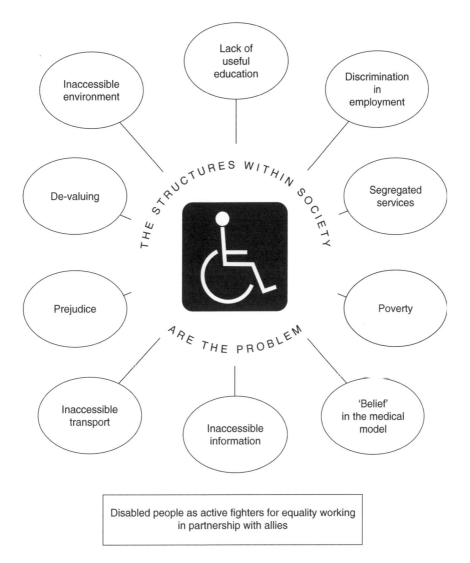

Figure 3 The social model

transgendered members of staff. Some parents/guardians will be LGBT people and some school pupils will be open about their sexuality. Virtually all children will be aware of issues of sexuality.

Section 28 of the Local Government Act of 1988, which discriminated against gays, lesbians and bisexuals by prohibiting local authorities from 'intentionally promoting homosexuality' or promoting 'the teaching in any maintained school of the acceptability of homosexuality as a pretended family relationship', has now been repealed. Pleasingly, delegates at the 2003 Liberal Democrats' annual conference in Brighton welcomed the repeal of Section 28 and called for sex education

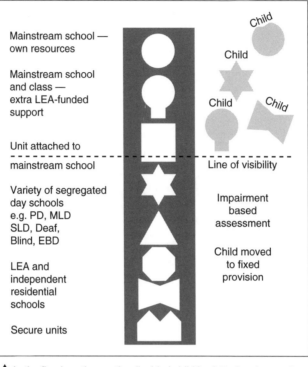

▲ In the fixed continuum the disabled child is slotted and moved according to an impairment based assessment

Figure 4 The fixed continuum of provision (*Source:* Mason and Rieser 1994)

which is 'honest, non-judgemental and thought provoking' and which includes all types of 'sexual orientation' to be made available at Key Stage 2. The Education spokesperson, Phil Willis, also added the important caveat that we should also teach young children about 'the dangers of inappropriate relationships' (the Brighton evening *Argus* 25 September 2003: 6).

The NUT's Code of Professional Conduct deems harassment on the grounds of sexual orientation to be unprofessional conduct. Homophobia is an unacceptable feature of society and there is evidence that lesbian and gay young people experience bullying at school, including physical acts of aggression, name calling, teasing, isolation and ridicule (for details see Forrest 2005; see also the Stonewall website: http://www.stonewall.org.uk/stonewall). There is also evidence that young people who experience homophobic violence are likely to turn to truancy, substance abuse, prostitution or even suicide. Lesbian, gay and bisexual pupils should be listened to and should be encouraged to seek parental/carer advice and/or encouraged to refer to other appropriate agencies for advice. Their experiences of homophobia and harassment should not be

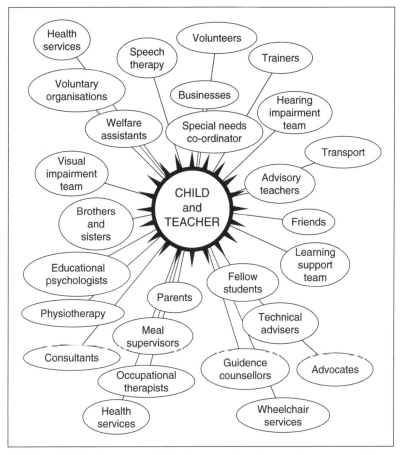

▲ The constellation of services provides what the child and the class teacher need in ordinary schools, from a variety of services, resource and specialist. This conception allows for the development of inclusive schools.

Figure 5 The constellation of services (*Source:* Mason and Rieser 1994)

dismissed as exaggerated or exceptional. Homophobic jokes, remarks or insults should be challenged.

The curriculum should tackle homophobia, as well as other forms of discrimination, and the school's equal opportunities policy should include a section on LGBT equality. Just to give some examples: in order to promote equality for LGBT people, a range of family patterns and life-styles can be illustrated in fiction used in English lessons, while drama can help to examine feelings and emotions. Reference can be made to famous lesbian and gay writers, sports personalities, actors, singers and historical figures (NUT website: www.teachers.org.uk). For fuller discussions of sexuality and education, see Williamson (2001) and Forrest (2005).

Social class and capitalism

Social class defines the social system under which we live. For this reason, among others, social class has tended to be left out of teacher education programmes. There has been general agreement that we should challenge racism and sexism, and, more recently disability discrimination and homophobia. However, social class, except in the narrow, though none the less fundamentally important, sense of more opportunities for working-class children, has been largely ignored. This is because discussion of social class and capitalism poses a threat to the *status quo*, much more profound than the other equality issues.

There are two major ways in which social class is classified. First, there is 'social class' as based on the classification of the Office for Population Census Studies (OPCS), first used in the census of 2001, which updated that of the Registrar General, previously used since 1911. Based on occupation, life-style and status, it accords with popular understandings of social class differentiation; in particular, the distinctions between white-collar workers, on the one hand, and blue-collar workers and those classified as long-term unemployed, on the other. However, it is not without its difficulties: (i) it masks the existence of the super-rich and the super-powerful (the capitalist class); (ii) it glosses over and hides the antagonistic and exploitative relationship between the two main classes in society (the capitalist class and the working class); and (iii) it segments the working class and thereby disguises the ultimate common interests of white-collar, blue-collar and long-term unemployed workers (Hill and Cole 2001: 151–3). Thus, while for sociological analyses in general, it has its uses, its problematic nature should not be forgotten.

Another way to conceive social class is the classic Marxist definition, in which those who have to sell their labour power in order to survive are the working class and those who own the means of production and exploit the working class by making profits from their labour are the capitalist class.

In post-World War II Britain, the economic system was generally described as a mixed economy; that is to say, the economy was partly owned by the state (e.g. the railways, gas, water and electricity and the telephones) and partly owned by private capitalist enterprises. This is no longer the case and capitalism, and particularly globalisation, is openly exalted as the only way the world can be run.

Business is in schools, in the sense of both influencing the curriculum *and* having an increasing financial stake in schools (Allen *et al.* 1999). Schools are encouraged to provide 'better value for money'. Vast numbers of teachers have resisted and continue to resist these processes of 'businessification'. It is my view that it is essential to recreate a view of education that is anti-authoritarian, dialogical and interactive, an education that empowers pupils, rather than one which lies in the hands of capital; an education which, following the great Brazilian educator, Paulo Freire, puts 'social and political analysis of everyday life at the centre of the curriculum' (cited in McLaren 2002: xxix). Young people have a right to know what has gone on and is going on in the world. As Chris Mullard put it, some 15 years ago in a talk at what was then Brighton Polytechnic, education is a meaningless process unless it is concerned with the struggle against all forms of tyranny, whether based on ignorance, oppression, inequality or exploitation.

Instead of commodifying knowledge in the interests of global capitalism, education should be about empowerment, where visions of an alternative way of running the planet become part of the mainstream curriculum. This is not a case for making schools arenas of propaganda (indeed, it could be argued that they resemble this to some extent now), or to move schools into the realm of politics, since, as Freire put it, 'education has always been a political act' (cited in Darder 2002: 56) (prior to Thatcher and Blair, many educationists argued that education is apolitical – not any more). As Peter McLaren (2002) concludes his book, *Life in Schools*, schools should cease to be defined as extensions of the workplace or as frontline institutions in the battle for international markets and foreign competition. Freire urged teachers, to detach themselves and their pupils from the idea that they are agents of capital, where *banking education* (the teacher deposits information into an empty account) is the norm and to reinvent schools as democratic public spheres where meaningful *dialogue* can take place.

To summarise: all equality issues are important, but, in my view, they all need to be considered in the context of, but not *reduced* to, social class and capitalism. Capitalism is in many ways reliant on the other forms of inequality. Education should not exist for the glorification of capital, of consumption, of commodification. Teachers at all levels of the education system need to foster critical reflection, with a view to transformative action.

Part two: practical issues

Introduction

It is the role of educators, in my view:[4]

- to develop the learning of all pupils to the maximum rather than vague notions of 'to their full potential'
- to enable pupils to make rational and informed decisions about their own lives
- to enable pupils to make rational and informed decisions about the lives of others
- to foster critical reflection, with a view to transformative action
- to help empower[5] pupils to be in a position to take transformative action.

Equality and equal opportunity issues have both an institutional dimension and an individual dimension. I will deal with each in turn.

The institutional challenge

The UK Race Relations (Amendment) Act 2000, outlined by Jeff Nixon in Chapter 8, requires each school in England and Wales to eliminate unlawful racial discrimination; to promote equality of opportunity; and to promote good relations between people of different racial groups. Specifically schools must prepare a written 'race' equality policy; implement the policy; and monitor and evaluate its impact on pupils, staff and parents/carers of different ethnic groups, in particular with respect to attainment. All racist incidents, whoever perceives them to be racist, irrespective of whether they are on the receiving end, must be investigated. It is, in my view, the most progressive equality legislation in Europe.

A White Paper, introduced by the Queen's Speech in November 2004 heralded the Commission for Equality and Human Rights (CEHR), which will take over the work of the Commission for Racial Equality, the Equal Opportunities Commission and the Disability Rights Commission. Its brief is to *fight discrimination* on grounds of 'race', gender and disability; but also on grounds of religion, sexual orientation and age.[6] It is envisaged that the CEHR will come into being in 2007.

In addition, the Equality Bill will require the public sector to *promote* gender equality. As I have pointed out, the sector is already required to promote 'race' equality under the Race Relations (Amendment) Act (2000). A separate bill, the Disability Discrimination Bill will do the same for disability. There are no provisions for this requirement to be extended to religion or belief, sexual orientation or age. Regulations outlawing discrimination *at work* on grounds of religion or belief or sexual orientation came into force in 2003, and a ban on ageist discrimination at work will come into force in 2006.[7]

Another bill will outlaw incitement to religious hatred. On the surface, this seems very positive, but there are concerns about how it will be interpreted, and any implications it may have for academic freedom (Natfhe Equality News <http://www.natfhe.org.uk/help/EqNews.html>: accessed January 2005).

As far as the private sector is concerned, a 'lighter touch' would be applied. This means apparently that private companies will be encouraged to follow new codes of practice which might stress the importance of specified holidays for religious staff, of changing the nature of family away days to be more inclusive of lesbian or gay staff, and of recognising the crucial role that older staff can play (*ibid.*).

While these issues are, of course, important, it is important that they are backed up by effective legislation, such as the Race Relations (Amendment) Act, thus making it mandatory for institutions to be pro-active in promoting equality in all its forms. The concern is that the new Commission will be as weak or weaker than the old Commissions. It is important that the Commission 'has teeth'; that is able to act decisively and effectively. I believe that there is a need for new harmonised but diverse equality legislation covering all equality issues, and for such legislation to extend beyond the confines of the world of work. A good start might be to extend the excellent provisions of the Race Relations (Amendment) Act to all issues of equality. With respect to education, this would make it incumbent on educational institutions to:

- be pro-active and to create equality policies for all the equality issues
- to record and monitor all racist, sexist, homophobic, disablist and classist incidents
- to provide termly reports to the Local Education Authority.

As with the specifications of the Race Relations (Amendment) Act, racist, sexist, homophobic, disablist and classist incidents should be deemed as such (until proven otherwise) if any member of the educational community perceives them as such.

For equal opportunities in education to become a reality, there is a need for major institutional changes: for effective legislation to *enforce* and *promote* equal opportunity in all its manifestations.

The personal challenge

It needs to be stressed that people's positions *vis-à-vis* the equality issues outlined in this chapter are not *natural*, but reflect particular social systems. Inequalities are not *inevitable* features of any society; they are social constructs, crucial terrains between conflicting forces in any given society. In other words, societies do not *need* to be class-based; to have racialised hierarchies; to have one sex dominating another. I do not believe that people are *naturally* homophobic or prone to marginalising the needs of disabled people. On the contrary, we are socialised into accepting the norms, values and customs of the social systems in which we grow up. This is a very powerful message for teachers. If we *learn* to accept or to promote inequalities, we can also *learn* to challenge them. Schools have traditionally played an important part in that socialisation process. They have also played a major role in undermining that process (Darder 2002; McLaren 2002).

In the personal challenge it is first important to distance oneself from the notion of 'political correctness', a pernicious concept invented by the Radical Right, and which, to my dismay, has become common currency. The term 'political correctness' was coined to imply that there exist (left-wing) political demagogues who seek to impose their views on equality issues, in particular appropriate terminology, on the majority. In reality, nomenclature changes over time. Thus, in the twenty-first century, terms such as 'negress' or 'negro' or 'coloured', nomenclatures which at one time were considered quite acceptable, and are now considered offensive. Antiracists are concerned with *respect* for others' choice of nomenclature and, therefore, are careful to acknowledge changes in it, changes which are decided by oppressed groups themselves (bearing in mind that there can be differences of opinion among such groups). The same applies to other equality issues. Thus, for example, it has become common practice to use 'working class' rather than 'lower class';[8] 'lesbian, gay, bisexual and transgender' rather than 'sexually deviant'; 'disability' rather than 'handicap'; and 'gender equality' rather than 'a woman's place'. Using current and acceptable nomenclature is about the fostering of a caring and inclusive society, not about 'political correctness' (Cole and Blair 2005).[9]

Haberman (1995: 91–2) suggests five steps which he considers to be essential for beginning teachers to overcome prejudice. I have adapted and considerably expanded Haberman's arguments and replaced his concept of prejudice with ism/phobia,[10] in order to encompass racism, sexism, disablism, classism and homophobia/Islamophobia/xenophobia. I have also provided my own examples of how each step might develop. It is important to point out that these steps apply to all members of the educational community, as well as beginning teachers, as specified by Haberman. I have also created a sixth step.

The first step is a thorough self-analysis of the content of one's ism/phobia. What form does it take? Is it overt or covert? Is it based on biology or is it cultural? Is it dominative (direct and oppressive) or aversive (excluding and cold-shouldering) (Kovel 1988)? Is it intentional or unintentional?[11] Are my attitudes patronising? This is, of course, a *process* rather than an event. In many ways, this step is the most crucial and difficult of the steps.

The second step is to seek answers to the question of source. How did I learn or come to believe these things? Did I learn to be ist/phobic from my parents/carers? Did I become ist/phobic as a result of experiences at primary school or at secondary school? Was it in further education or in higher education? Did I pick up ism/phobia from my peers; from the media; from newspapers; from the Internet? Was it a combination of the above? Why was I not equipped to challenge ism/phobia, when I came across it?

Step three is to consider how do I suffer or benefit from my ism/phobia? How does it demean me as a human being to have these beliefs? On the other hand, how do I benefit psychologically and/or materially from holding these beliefs?

Step four is to consider how one's ism/phobia may be affecting one's work in education. Am I making suppositions about young people's behaviour or attitudes to life based on their social class, ethnicity, impairments, gender, sexuality, religion or nationality? Am I making negative or positive presumptions about their academic achievement? If there is evidence of low achievement, am I taking the necessary remedial actions? Am I making assumptions about the parents/carers of the young people in my care? Am I making assumptions about other members of the school community, based on the above?

Step five is the phase in which one lays out a plan explicating what one plans to do about one's ism/phobia. How do I propose to check it, unlearn it, counteract it and get beyond it? This can involve reading a text or texts and/or websites which address the issues. It should mean an ongoing update on equality/equal opportunities legislation. As mentioned in Part one of this chapter, the trade union, Natfhe, has a very good website on such legislation (http://www.natfhe.org.uk/help/EqNews.html). It must certainly mean acquainting oneself with differential rates of achievements, and a critical analysis of the various explanations for this, centring on the explanations given by those who are pro-equality. It should mean acquainting oneself with various forms of bullying related to isms/phobia and their effects. It might mean going on a course or courses.

It is not being argued that these five steps will necessarily occur in an individual's psyche (although they might) or spontaneously. Indeed, they can often be better addressed in group situations. I am suggesting that, as in this chapter, encouragement should be given for individuals to take these steps. Such encouragement could be done in the form of an introductory lecture to beginning teachers (and educational workers). Also it is not being suggested that this is *merely* an individual process. It could be followed up with the sharing of questions and answers in groups and publicly. This could then progress (in practice) to an exploration of how a shared analysis of the five steps relates to the work of the school and the community; local, national and international.

The personal and the institutional

After or during these five steps, the sixth step should be to connect the personal with the institutional, in order to undermine isms/phobia, and to promote equality. This might involve becoming active in one's school and/or community or becoming a trade union activist. It might involve joining and working for a pro-egalitarian political party. It might involve becoming active in local, national or international lobby groups. It should involve making the combating of isms/phobia and the promotion of equality central to one's work in educational institutions, in both the actual curriculum (what is on the timetable) and the hidden curriculum (everything else that goes on in educational institutions). It might involve writing and lecturing about isms/phobia and equality.

Conclusion

In this chapter, I began by outlining the main conceptual issues with respect to equality opportunity and equality issues in schools. I argued that for equal opportunities in education to become a reality, there is a need for major institutional changes: for effective legislation to *enforce* and *promote* equal opportunity in all its manifestations. In addition, schools and other educational institutions should be places where personal and group reflection on *and action on* equality issues is central, and an integral part of the institutions' ethos. If we are to relate to and empower our pupils, if we are to engage in meaningful and successful teaching, we need to begin with the pupils' comprehension of their daily life experiences, whether in pre-school or university. From their earliest years, children's self-concepts are tainted by cultures of inequality. By starting from *their* description of these experiences, we are able to ground our teaching in concrete reality, then to transcend common sense and to move towards a critical scientific understanding of the world. This is the process by which teachers can support the process of the self-empowerment of tomorrow's children. As Antonia Darder puts it in her book, *Reinventing Paulo Freire*, 'empowerment . . . entails participation in pedagogical relationships in which pupils/students experience the freedom to break through the imposed myths and illusions that stifle [them] and the space to take individual and collective actions that can . . . transform their lives' (2002: 110).

As stressed above, I firmly believe that we are not born ist/phobic. Ism/phobia is a product of the society in which we live.[12] We can make important changes in societies as they are. However, in order to fully eradicate oppression of all forms, we need to change society. At the beginning of this chapter, I made a distinction between equal opportunities and equality. Socialists support all progressive reforms. Thus, what is happening with respect to the promotion of equality and equal opportunities in the UK, the rest of Europe and elsewhere is to be welcomed. But, in order to achieve real equality, there is a need for a transformed world economy – a socialist economy. If this all sounds implausibly idealistic, it might be worth considering which is the more utopian: the continued survival of imperialistic, destructive and anti-democratic world capitalism, or a democratic world, planned for need and not profit (Meiksins Wood 1995).

I will end with a quote from the Hillcole Group. Whatever the twenty-first century has to offer, the choices will need to be debated:

Each person and group should experience education as contributing to their own self-advancement, but at the same time our education should ensure that at least part of everyone's life activity is also designed to assist in securing the future of the planet we inherit . . . Democracy is not possible unless there is a free debate about all the alternatives for running our social and economic system . . . All societies [are] struggling with the same issues in the 21st century. We can prepare by being better armed with war machinery or more competitive international monopolies . . . Or we can wipe out poverty . . . altogether. We can decide to approach the future by consciously putting our investment into a massive drive to encourage participation from everyone at every stage in life through training and education that will increase productive, social, cultural and environmental development in ways we have not yet begun to contemplate.

(Hillcole Group 1997: 94–5)

As Callinicos has argued, challenging the current climate requires courage, imagination and will power inspired by the injustice that surrounds us. However, '[b]eneath the surface of our supposedly contented societies, these qualities are present in abundance. Once mobilized, they can turn the world upside down' (2000: 129).

Acknowledgements

I would like to thank Brian Donovan, Dave Hill, Rose Malone and Glenn Rikowski for their very helpful comments on an earlier draft of this chapter. As always, responsibility for any inadequacies remains mine.

Notes

1   These five equality issues are not spelt out directly in TTA (2004). Instead, the regulations identify 'social, cultural, linguistic, religious and ethnic backgrounds' (p. 6). Since fulfilling TTA requirements clearly requires attention to all of the five equality issues, I would argue that, to fully ensure inclusion for all, the five issues should be made explicit (for a discussion, see Cole 1999).

2   Tony Blair's speech at the Labour Party annual conference on 2 October 2001 was a classic example of the exhaltation of meritocracy and equal opportunities, rather than equality:

> People ask me if I think ideology is dead. My answer is: in the sense of rigid forms of economic and social theory, yes. The 20th century killed those ideologies and their passing causes little regret. But, in the sense of a governing idea in politics, based on values, no. The governing idea of modern social democracy is community. Founded on the principles of social justice. That people should rise according to merit not birth; that the test of any decent society is not the contentment of the wealthy and strong, but the commitment to the poor and weak.
>
> But values aren't enough. The mantle of leadership comes at a price: the courage to learn and change; to show how values that stand for all ages, can be applied in a way relevant to each age. Our politics only succeed when the realism is as clear as the idealism. This party's strength today comes from the journey of change and learning we have made. We learnt that however much we strive for peace, we need strong defence capability where a peaceful approach fails. We learnt that equality is about equal worth, not equal outcomes.
>
> (Blair 2001)

3   I put 'race' in inverted commas because I question its validity as a scientific concept. Robert Miles (1982: 9–16) has argued cogently against the notion that there exist distinct 'races'. After a review of the literature, he gives three reasons for this. First, the extent of genetic variation within any population is usually greater than the average difference between populations. Second, while the frequency of occurrence of possible forms taken by genes does vary from one so-called 'race' to another, any particular genetic combination can be found in almost any 'race'. Third, owing to inter-ethnic heterosexual relationships and large-scale migrations, the distinctions between 'races', identified as dominant gene frequencies, are often blurred (*ibid.*: 16).

4   This section of the chapter is based on my paper, 'Promoting equality in schools' which was a keynote address at a Joint Symposium on *Imagining and Negotiating a Future of Equality in School Practice at Primary and Post-primary Level*, sponsored by The Equality Authority of Ireland and The Educational Studies Association of Ireland, Herbert Park Hotel, Dublin, 2004.

5 'Empowerment' can mean all things to all people. What I have in mind here is something on the lines of Colin Lankshear's (1995) adaptation of Feinberg's notion of 'elliptical' statements. Empowerment, for me, represents far more than psychologistic notions of 'sensing that one has more power'. Empowerment needs to situated structurally. The empowered person needs to know who she or he is; where she or he is coming from; what she or he is up against; how she or he can move forward; and what the end result of empowerment might look like. As Lankshear puts it:

> the full version of elliptical statements about empowerment will require attention to at least four variables. Adequate accounts will be required of (1) the SUBJECT of empowerment; (2) the power STRUCTURES in relation to which, or in opposition to which, a person or group is becoming empowered; (3) the PROCESSES or 'achievement' by which empowerment arguably occurs; and (4) the ENDS or OUTCOMES of becoming thus empowered.
>
> (Lankshear 1995: 303)

6 Social class is not mentioned. For Marxists, social class equality is an oxymoron, since capitalism is fundamentally dependent on the exploitation of one class by another. The end of this exploitation would herald the end of capitalism and its replacement by socialism (see Hickey 2005, for a discussion). However, it is my view that discrimination with respect to social class origin (classism) should be part of the legislation. Thus, it is pleasing to note that, signalling the low achievement of white working-class boys, Trade and Industry Secretary, Patricia Hewitt, has stated that as well as 'disadvantaged Muslim communities' the CEHR will have within its remit such boys growing up

> in families and communities where the old manufacturing jobs have disappeared, many of the parents aren't in work and where if you do apply for a job, many employers will take one look at the post-code and not even offer you an interview.
>
> (Travis 2004)

Whether this is a genuine concern for all deprived people, or more a reflection of the backlash against multiculturalism (Vaz 2004) is another question.

7 Here is not the place for a detailed analysis of the Government's motives in introducing this legislation (but see Cole 2005a). Suffice it to say that, in my view, they have much to do with fostering an inclusive workforce that uses all its talent in sustaining the economy and making profits. The New Labour Government, of course, is a 'modernising' party that has fully distanced itself from its socialist roots, and totally embraced neo-liberal global capitalism. Having said that, for socialists, the reforms embraced by the new Commission and the new bills are, of course, to be welcomed. While socialist commitment is to a transformed world (see below) any progressive reforms should be supported in principle.

8 As a Marxist, I recognise, of course, that the working class are structurally located in a subordinate position in capitalist societies, and, *in this sense*, are a 'lower class'. However, the nomenclature 'working class' is used to indicate respect for the class as a whole, a class which sells its labour power to produce surplus for capitalists in an exploitative division of labour (see, for example, Cole 2005c, Hickey 2005).

9 The term has recently been extended to include anything that the Radical Right finds not to its liking. Thus, for leader of the British Conservative Party, Michael Howard, 'political correctness' has blurred the difference between 'right' and 'wrong'. As he puts it, '[t]he clear distinction between right and wrong has been lost in sociological mumbo-jumbo and politically correct nonsense' (http://politics.guardian.co.uk/conservatives/story/0,9061,1280083,00.html). Can one assume that Howard is aware that using the term, 'mumbo-jumbo' is racist? Its actual origin is 'the protective spirit of the Khassonkee tribe of Senegal' (Green 1998: 815).

10 For grammatical clarity, I have put 'ism/phobia' in the singular. Clearly, for many people it will be 'isms/phobia'. I also recognise that there are a number of positive 'isms' – socialism; feminism; trade unionism among them.

11 These considerations are adapted from my definition of racism (see ' "Race" and racism' section of this chapter and also, for example, Cole 2004a: 37–8).

12 Having visited Cuba on three occasions, I became even more convinced of the importance of socialisation. Forty-five years of socialisation in socialist values has had a dramatic effect all over

the island. The selfish Thatcherite values abundant in the West are generally not apparent. They are creeping in, however, mainly in the areas surrounding, but not in, the tourist resorts and hotels, and in some of the *casas particulares* (private rented accommodation).

References

Allen, M., Benn, C., Chitty, C., Cole, M., Hatcher, R., Hirtt, N. and Rikowski, G. (1999) *Business, Business, Business: New Labour's education policy*. London: Tufnell Press.

Blair, T. (2001) Speech at the Labour Party annual conference. http://www.newecon.org/blairspeech10-02-01.html (accessed January 2005).

Callinicos, A. (2000) *Equality*. Oxford: Polity.

Cole, M. (1998) 'Racism, reconstructed multiculturalism and antiracist education', *Cambridge Journal of Education*, 28 (1), 37–48.

Cole, M. (1999) 'Professional issues and initial teacher education: what can be done and what should be done', *Education and Social Justice*, 2 (1), 63–6.

Cole, M. (2004a) ' "Brutal and stinking" and "difficult to handle": the historical and contemporary manifestations of racialisation, institutional racism, and schooling in Britain', *Race, Ethnicity and Education*, 7 (1).

Cole, M. (2004b) ' "Rule Britannia" and the new American Empire: a Marxist analysis of the teaching of imperialism, actual and potential, in the English school curriculum', *Policy Futures in Education*, 2 (3).

Cole, M. (2005a) 'Human rights, equality and education', in Cole, M. (ed.) *Education, Equality and Human Rights: issues of gender, 'race', sexuality, disability and social class*, 2nd edn. London: Routledge.

Cole, M. (ed.) (2005b) *Education, Equality and Human Rights: issues of gender, 'race', sexuality, disability and social class*, 2nd edn. London: Routledge.

Cole, M. (2005c) 'New Labour, globalization and social justice: the role of education', in Fischman, G., McLaren, P., Sunker, H., and Lankshear, C. (eds) *Critical Theories, Radical Pedagogies and Global Conflicts*. Lanham, Maryland: Rowman and Littlefield.

Cole, M. and Blair, M. (2005) 'Racism and education: from Empire to New Labour', in Cole, M. (ed.) *Education, Equality and Human Rights: issues of gender, 'race', sexuality, disability and social class*, 2nd edn. London: Routledge.

Cole, M. and Hill, D. (1999) 'Equality and secondary education: what are the conceptual issues?', in Hill, D. and Cole, M. (eds) *Promoting Equality in Secondary Schools*. London: Cassell.

Cole, M. and Stuart, J. M. (2005) ' "Do you ride on elephants?" and "never tell them you're German": the experiences of British Asian and black, and overseas student teachers in south-east England', *British Educational Research Journal*.

Cole, M., Hill, D. and Shan, S. (eds) (1997) *Promoting Equality in Primary Schools*. London: Cassell.

Darder, A. (2002) *Reinventing Paulo Freire: a pedagogy of love*. Cambridge, MA: Westview Press.

East Sussex County Council (2004) *One of Us* (Videotape). Lewes: East Sussex County Council.

Epstein, D. (1994) 'Introduction', in Epstein, D. (ed.) *Challenging Lesbian and Gay Inequalities in Education*. Buckingham: Open University Press.

Forrest, S. (2005) 'Difficult loves: learning about sexuality and homophobia in schools', in Cole, M. (ed.) *Education, Equality and Human Rights: issues of gender, 'race', sexuality, disability and social class*, 2nd edn. London: Routledge/Falmer.

Green, J. (1998) *The Cassell Dictionary of Slang*. London: Cassell.

Haberman, M. (1995) *Star Teachers of Children in Poverty*. West Lafayette, Indiana: Kappa Delta Pi.

Hickey, T. (2005) 'Class and class analysis for the twenty-first century', in Cole, M. (ed.) *Education, Equality and Human Rights: issues of gender, 'race', sexuality, disability and social class*, 2nd edn. London: Routledge/Falmer.

Hill, D. and Cole, M. (eds) (1999) *Promoting Equality in Secondary Schools*. London: Cassell.

Hill, D. and Cole, M. (eds) (2001) *Schooling and Equality: fact, concept and policy*. London: Kogan Page.

Hillcole Group (1997) *Rethinking Education and Democracy: a socialist alternative for the twenty-first century*. London: Tufnell Press.

Hirom, K. (2001) 'Gender', in Hill, D. and Cole, M. (eds) (2001) *Schooling and Equality: fact, concept and policy*. London: Kogan Page.

Kovel, J. (1988) *White Racism: a psychohistory*. London: Free Association Books.

Lankshear, C. (1995) 'Afterword: some reflections on "Empowerment"', in McLaren, P. and Giarelli, J. (eds) *Critical Theory and Educational Research*. Albany, NY: State University of New York (SUNY) Press.

HM Government (1988) *Local Government Act*. http://www.legislation.hmso.gov.uk/acts/acts 1988/Ukpga_19880009_ en_5.htm (accessed February 2005).

Martin, J. (2005) 'Gender, education and the new millennium', in Cole, M. (ed) *Education, Equality and Human Rights: issues of gender, 'race', sexuality, disability and social class*, 2nd edn. London: Routledge/Falmer.

Mason, M. and Rieser, R. (1994) *Altogether Better*. London: Comic Relief.

McLaren, P. (2002) *Life in Schools*, 4th edn. Boston, MA: Pearson Education.

Macpherson, W. (1999) *The Stephen Lawrence Inquiry, Report of an Inquiry by Sir William Macpherson*. London: The Stationery Office.

Meiksins Wood, E. (1995) *Democracy Against Capitalism*. Cambridge: Cambridge University Press.

Miles, R. (1982) *Racism and Migrant Labour*. London: Routledge and Kegan Paul.

National Union of Teachers (NUT) (1991) *Lesbians and Gays in Schools: an issue for every teacher*. London: National Union of Teachers.

Home Office (2000) *Race Relations (Amendment) Act*. http://www.homeoffice.gov.uk/comrace/race/ raceact/ amendact.html (accessed February 2005).

Rieser, R. (2005a) 'Disability discrimination, the final frontier: disablement, history and liberation', in Cole, M. (ed.) *Education, Equality and Human Rights: issues of gender, 'race', sexuality, disability and social class*, 2nd edn. London: Routledge/Falmer.

Rieser, R. (2005b) 'Special educational needs or inclusive education: the challenge of disability discrimination in schooling', in Cole, M. (ed.) *Education, Equality and Human Rights: issues of gender, 'race', sexuality, disability and social class*, 2nd edn. London: Routledge/Falmer.

Teacher Training Agency (TTA) (2004) *Qualifying to Teach: professional standards for Qualified Teacher Status and requirements for initial teacher training*. London: Teacher Training Agency.

Travis, A. (2003) 'Blunkett: racism tag is aiding racists', *Guardian*, 15 January.

Travis, A. (2004) Minister defends new equality body. http://www.guardian.co.uk/ guardianpolitics/story/0,,1215402,00.html (accessed January 2005).

Vaz, K. (2004) 'Divided we stand, united we fall', *Guardian*, 21 May.

Williamson, I. (2001) 'Sexuality', in Hill, D. and Cole, M. (eds) *Schooling and Equality: fact, concept and policy*. London: Kogan Page.

High expectations, respect and commitment

Maud Blair and Kate Daly

Those awarded Qualified Teacher Status must understand and uphold the professional code of the General Teaching Council for England by demonstrating . . . [that] they have high expectations of all pupils; respect their social, cultural, linguistic, religious and ethnic backgrounds; and are committed to raising their educational achievement.

(TTA 2004: 7 Section 1.1)

Learning objectives

To raise awareness of:

- the need for cultural sensitivity in the school context
- different learning needs of pupils from diverse backgrounds
- the need for readers to reflect on their own development needs in relation to 'race' and ethnicity.

Introduction

THE PHRASE, 'EDUCATION FOR ALL' became a slogan for 1980s' multiculturalism in schools. In Britain, this new ethos, which was heralded by the Rampton (1981)/Swann Report (1985), was a recognition that society needed to face up to the challenges of rapid cultural change that had taken place in the post-war years. The Report (the inquiry was first chaired by Lord Rampton) was an important milestone in the education system. For the first time a major official inquiry highlighted the degree of racism that was affecting a significant number of British children in schools. Although multicultural education had been a feature of many schools in the 1970s, this was the first time that an official report recognised the importance of preparing teachers to acknowledge and cater for diverse cultural needs in the classroom. This led to the setting up in local education authorities of centres for multicultural education and the subsequent implementation of antiracist training initiatives for teachers. Although many mistakes were made in the name of multicultural education (Cole 1989, 1998; Cole and Blair 2005) and antiracist education (McDonald *et al.* 1989) and severe critiques were levelled at some of the training initiatives (see Sivanandan 1985), the Swann Report could be said to have been the first official document to set standards for a more inclusive system of education.

The Standards for the Award of Qualified Teacher Status (TTA 2004) can be seen as building on the Swann agenda. 'Under the new Standards, beginning teachers must provide evidence that: "They have high expectations of all pupils; respect their social, cultural, linguistic, religious and ethnic backgrounds; and are committed to raising their educational achievement"' (p. 7). There is of course an assumption behind the setting of standards that teaching is a moral enterprise underpinned by a set of commonly accepted truths. Although there are some who would question the validity of such an assumption (for a discussion, see Chapter 3 of this volume) and ask whether it is desirable to set standards and indeed whether there can ever be agreement about what these standards should be, an increasing number of writers and commentators endorse the need to identify a set of working principles which guide teachers and other professionals in their work, especially in relation to work with children (Soltis 1986; Halpin 2000; DfES 2004a). The relativism that surrounds debates about ethics, values and standards has been dismissed as ignoring the real need that teachers have for guidance in an increasingly complex profession (Campbell 2000). Teachers, it is argued, need to work by a set of common principles not only to safeguard their own professional identities, but in order also to protect children.

It could be argued that standards are particularly important in an ethnically diverse and changing context. The historical experiences of pupils from minority ethnic groups within the British school system would indicate that a code of practice is essential. The last 50 years have not delivered the educational successes on which Asian, black and other minority ethnic families had built their hopes when they left their homes in various parts of the diaspora to come to Britain. At the time of writing, black (Caribbean heritage) pupils and pupils of Pakistani and Bangladeshi heritage as a whole, still straddle to a large extent the bottom end of achievement tables (Gillborn and Gipps 1996; Gillborn and Mirza 2000; Bhattacharyya *et al.* 2001; Ison 2005). The over-representation of black pupils in exclusions from school highlights the tenacity of problems faced by black pupils and the official malaise in dealing with them. The picture is made more complex by the presence of children from diverse refugee and asylum seeking families

(Myers and Grosvenor 2001). Then there are local education contexts which reveal difficulties faced by certain white minority ethnic groups such as Turks and Portuguese (Peters 2002).

How are teachers and in particular beginning teachers to fulfil these requirements in the face of such complexity? This chapter is written for them and is an attempt to provide some pointers as to how best one can translate these abstract requirements into practice. In discussing the standards set out by the DfES/TTA above, we explicitly accept their validity, but do not shy away from acknowledging the difficulties faced by beginning teachers in their attempt to comply with them as a basis for obtaining their teaching qualifications.

Self-reflection – coming to grips with professional values

The first step in any attempt for the (beginning) teacher to understand ways of putting the above standards into practice needs to be a thorough examination of oneself as a teacher – 'Who am I, what do I think of children and what do I think of teaching?' Teaching has sometimes been considered a second career option, something one does because other options are closed, or because it fits in with family commitments, or what one does until one has made up one's mind about what one really wants to do (Maylor 1996). There are many, of course, who enter teaching because it is a vocation for them, they are inspired to teach and that is what they have always wanted to do. A close examination of one's motives for taking up teaching as a career is useful in helping the teacher to understand his or her experience of it. Often we look outside ourselves, to external causes when things do not work for us as we would wish. The idea that one is entirely controlled by external forces is disempowering and stymies efforts to address what the real problems could be. Some reflection of why one is in teaching, particularly where a teacher's experience is negative in relation to others in the same environment, might reveal areas of potential change that might help the individual take control of their situation. The thinking might go something like this:

> I came into teaching by default. The result may be that at some level I am not as fully committed as I ought to be. The consequences are that I do not give of myself completely and my pupils can sense this. This is leading to a deterioration in their behaviour and adding frustration and stress to my life.

This is of course a very simplistic example given only to provide an idea of the direction such thinking might take. It is not assumed that all negative experiences can be traced back to the individual, but that each individual must take responsibility by at least reflecting on where they may themselves be contributing to the situation (Halpin 2000).

The idea that teachers need to reflect on what they do is by no means new (Stenhouse 1983). However, more often than not, this reflection is about methods of teaching and not about the 'being' of teaching. The 'being' of teaching requires an examination of one's values in relation to a range of factors to do with one's world view and whether one is equipped mentally and emotionally for the job.

In the Introductory chapter Mike Cole adapts and expands, at length, Haberman's (1995) five steps in overcoming our 'isms/phobia'. He explains that 'step five is the phase in which one lays out a plan explicating what one plans to do about one's ism/phobia. How do I propose to check it, unlearn it, counteract it and get beyond it?' In the following sections, we take this last sentence, 'How do I propose to check it, unlearn it, counteract it and get beyond it?' to examine the various elements of the teaching standards given above and on which this chapter is based.

High expectations

It is widely accepted that underachievement in pupils is related, among other things, to the level of expectation the teacher has of them (Blair 2001; Blair and Bourne 1998). How does a teacher check his/her own expectations of pupils? It is important to know the social class, ethnic, gender and special needs profile of one's pupils and to ask questions, such as:

- What attitudes do I have towards people of this or that background?
- What do I know about them?
- Where did I get my knowledge?
- On what are my beliefs and attitudes based?

Dependent on age and disclosure, this also applies to sexuality.

The history of racism, social class, gender, disability and sexuality is imbued with notions of inferiority (Cole 2005). That teachers are no less affected by racist and/or prejudicial attitudes than other members of society is stating the obvious. In order to check such attitudes one has to acknowledge them. One method in this process is to ask the question: What are the common-sense understandings or stereotypes about this group and to what extent do I take these stereotypes for granted? Feeding one's guilt about these feelings is at best pointless and at worst counterproductive. It would be better to acknowledge the presence of normative and often unsubstantiated beliefs in society and in oneself, and resolve to move on from there. What in practical terms does that mean? It means getting to know pupils as individuals and not assuming that their behaviour or performance is somehow caused by their particular class, gender or minority status. Various aspects of their experience may be caused by the social and political circumstances or dominant understandings of 'race' or ethnicity or gender, disability, sexuality and social class, namely, the way they are positioned in the society, but not by the fact of difference.

Secondly, teachers need to know each pupil well by knowing the circumstances of their lives and the extent to which these circumstances affect them on a day-to-day basis. What could be going on in the child's life that is leading to fluctuations in behaviour or in performance? Thirdly, the teacher needs to set challenges for him- or herself by setting targets for each pupil, reflecting on why he or she has set those targets for that particular pupil and then devising an individual programme to help that pupil reach those targets. Important questions to ask are:

- To what extent am I influenced by that pupil's ethnicity, or gender, or class or disability etc. in setting that target?
- To what extent is my action influenced by realistic knowledge of the individual child and not by 'prior knowledge' of the ethnic group, special needs, gender or economic status/social class of the child?

In some cases one's expectations of pupils are influenced by the culture and ethos of the school in which one works. In one school which had changed from a white middle-class grammar school to a comprehensive school catering for a largely working-class Pakistani and Bangladeshi population, the head teacher realised that the only way to tackle the culture of low expectations of the staff was to create a system of accountability which made each teacher responsible for the level of achievement of their pupils. Teachers had to explain to the head of their department why pupils performed at particular levels, and heads of departments in turn had to explain the performance of their department to a deputy head. Teachers were thus forced to look closely at the nature of their explanations and to re-think their methods of supporting their pupils. This itself became a system of support for the teachers who were able to identify areas of personal and professional development. Departments that followed this conscientiously experienced a large shift in the performance levels of their pupils (Blair and Bourne 1998). The difference was that instead of teachers blaming the pupils' cultures, or languages or social class positions for their performance, they asked a different set of questions, namely, 'What do I know about this pupil and what am I doing to help and support him or her?'

This practice of looking inwards rather than outwards towards the child and his/her family for explanations of failure or low performance, is an important step in unlearning previously held assumptions. The teacher's concerns must be for *all* pupils so that one is motivated, not by a charitable attitude which in effect renders different ethnic groups 'Other', but by a professional approach which recognises, via honest self-reflection, one's responsibilities towards all pupils.

Respecting the social, cultural, linguistic, religious and ethnic backgrounds of pupils

We often take the meaning of the term 'respect' for granted. Do teachers and pupils share the same meanings? Among the most widely reported concerns of black pupils, especially in secondary schools, is the concern that teachers do not respect them (Blair 2001; Blair and Bourne 1998; Sewell 1997; Wright *et al.* 2000). All pupils wish to be treated with respect, but how do teachers demonstrate this? It is by understanding and then putting into practice the ways in which pupils wish to be respected. A simple questionnaire about what pupils like and do not like about the school will soon reveal many areas in which they do not feel respected. A small study conducted with 200 Year 10 students in a London school exposed widespread unhappiness with the way they felt they were treated by teachers. Statements such as:

> 'Their body language. It's just rude. And the way they talk to you, man, it's just so rude.'
> 'It's the tone of voice which they use in front of the whole class.'
> 'Say you're talking, yeah, and they say things like, "shut up".'

(Blair 2001: 54)

These are hardly revolutionary insights. They also apply to all humankind and should be treated just as seriously coming from children and young people as they would do coming from adults. This is, of course, not to deny that pupils are rude to teachers, but what is being underlined here is the importance of teachers always setting the example and being role models for pupils.

Cultural

When the term 'respect' is extended to cultural differences, this poses a particular challenge to teachers and to schools. Misunderstandings can occur very easily, and are an increasing challenge to schools the more diverse the society becomes. Given this situation, what should the teacher do? What is clear is that when parents do not respond to situations in expected ways, for example they respond negatively or do not turn up to a meeting about the behaviour of a child, this is a sign that the school or the teacher needs to delve deeper in order to understand where miscommunication or misunderstanding may have taken place. It is not a sign that the parents are not interested in their children's education. It is often the case that schools do not take the initiative to open up avenues of communication with parents because they feel hampered by language differences, or by a negative interaction with parents from a particular ethnic group, which then translates into suspicion or lack of trust for the whole group. An important question to consider is: What was the tone and manner of the initial communication? Language differences do not necessarily denote different values or different human needs. They may only denote a different way of understanding the same issues, or a simple miscommunication of an issue. Equally, where negative interactions have occurred, it is important that the school or teacher find out what went wrong and re-establish positive channels of communication. It is after all, the school, or it could be the individual teacher, who is providing a service, and not the other way around.

This is a basic understanding of 'respect' – namely, not operating on the basis of stereotypes, being able to put things right with parents when they go wrong, finding ways of communication which are based on an assumption that parents, whatever their background, are interested and concerned about the education of their children. This is an important starting place before one can hope to introduce initiatives which take into account different cultural backgrounds. Without this acceptance that differences are *different* and not inferior, any such initiatives are not only likely to be superficial, and therefore easy to see through, but likely to be counterproductive and not gain the support of the parents or the pupils. Parents and pupils are the best resource available and once they see that the school or the teacher is interested in them and in their cultures, they will go out of their way to help with time, ideas, and resources (Blair and Bourne 1998). The ethos of the school must therefore be one in which parents and pupils feel comfortable, and have a sense of belonging.

Having established this kind of ethos, it becomes easier to introduce activities that are inclusive of the different cultural heritages of the pupils. In one school, the English department collected folk tales from the children (and this, of course, meant that the parents were involved) and with the rich source of tales from diverse countries, they were able to draw parallels with stories around the world and show the commonalities that exist in humankind and to draw on these parallels in their teaching of literature. It is, however, important not to single out minority students for this information, but to involve all pupils, including those from dominant cultures. People around the world, show, through their stories, that they share the same concerns, the same desires, the same ambitions.

Social

'Social' can cover a number of different areas from social class to peer group cultures. Social class has played a significant part in educational provision in Britain.

From the introduction of mass education in the 1870s to the present day, educational provision has reflected divisions of class in different ways, but generally in ways which have benefited those with middle-class cultural capital (Bowles and Gintis 1976). Social class is, as a result, one of the significant indicators of pupil performance (Hatcher 2005; Hill and Cole 2001).

Social class interacts with ethnicity, gender and other indicators of identity in the experiences that pupils have. An important watchpoint for the teacher is not to assume that ethnicity is the sum total of the identities of pupils from minority ethnic groups. This may appear to be stating the obvious. However, research evidence shows that teachers do sometimes seek remedies for problems based on pupils' ethnicity alone, disregarding other factors that make up the pupils' identities such as their social class position, gender or their age (Blair 2001). This has the effect of blocking the teacher's ability to think through imaginative ways of helping them (Wright *et al.* 2000). There are many areas of disadvantage which working-class pupils from minority ethnic groups might share with their white working-class counterparts and which need to be considered in conjunction with issues of gender and ethnicity. To what extent might a problem be the outcome of poverty or poor living conditions, or domestic disruption? To what extent might the fact of being working class, and black and male be leading to unfair treatment of some pupils and therefore to behavioural and academic difficulties? Individual difficulties have been known to have been attributed to a pupil's 'racial' or cultural background and not to the fact of, for example, racism or adolescence, leading inevitably to mishandling of problems to the detriment of the pupils concerned.

An area of social interaction that has been the subject of much discussion and debate is that of black boys and teachers. Black boys of Caribbean heritage have been and are, at the time of writing, over-represented among those who are excluded from school. Explanations proffered vary from racism (Gillborn 1990, 1995), the strong pull of the peer group on black boys (Sewell 1997), to the over-representation of middle-class white women in primary schools and the absence of black male role models (Abbott 2002).

How is the teacher to understand this and what lessons can be drawn from these various explanations? Again the importance of reflecting on one's own attitudes cannot be overemphasised. Gillborn (1990) writes that black boys are sometimes regarded by white teachers as threatening. The result has been either an unfair level of discipline imposed on black boys, or a fear of reprimanding them leading to an absence of clear boundaries for the pupils in question and consequent deterioration in their behaviour. Every teacher therefore needs to examine his or her fears and anxieties about 'race'. What are these fears and where do they come from? How can they be overcome? How are they affecting relationships in the classroom or in the school?

The peer group is where young adolescents have their identities affirmed and where they feel their sense of belonging confirmed (Cullingford and Morrison 1997; Hargreaves *et al.* 1996). It is a time in a young person's life that teachers need to properly understand. This is particularly important in situations where young people from particular groups feel alienated and/or rejected by the society. The peer group in these circumstances is for young people a refuge and place of safety. It is easy, in circumstances where the peer group constitutes a powerful alternative culture for young people, for teachers to feel that their efforts are in vain, to conclude that the fault lies in the young people themselves and that there is no more that they can do. However, research shows that some teachers succeed with even the most difficult of pupils if one attempts to understand them and their world views, to empathise with what they are going through, to include them in decisions and to take account of their interests and concerns in one's teaching so that what they learn has relevance in their lives (Fine 1991; Ladson-Billings 1994).

Relevant questions to reflect upon here might be:

- How much do I understand the need for children and in particular young people to establish a sense of their own identity?

- How is this process manifesting itself among the young people of (this) school?

- What is the ethos and social environment of the school and how does it support pupils?

- What can I do to change things?

- What is my own relationship with pupils and how far do I attempt to communicate with them in ways that confirm their sense of self?

Linguistic background

Respect is about recognising our common humanity and accepting our differences. The history of racism and of colonialism is a history of hierarchy where people's languages, among other things, were placed both implicitly and explicitly, in order of importance. The languages of colonised countries were inevitably placed in positions of least importance (Cole and Blair 2005). This situation was often perpetuated in British schools where children who spoke one or more languages from non-European countries were in some schools regarded as having 'language problems' while the teaching of languages such as German or French to English speakers was considered as improving children's language skills. This often led to children who spoke non-European languages being forbidden to speak their home languages and for these to be considered an impediment to learning English. Research evidence contributed in large part to a re-assessment of this approach. Evidence that use of the child's mother tongue enhanced the acquisition of a second language, helped to shift the perception that these languages were a hindrance rather than a help (Cummins 1991).

However, the acceptance of the logic of language acquisition is not necessarily a sign of respect for other languages. The teacher needs to demonstrate in other ways his or her acceptance and regard for languages other than his or her own, and in particular those languages which have been subject to inferiorisation.

Schools use a range of strategies for including the languages of the pupils they teach. At a simple level, schools can display signs and greetings in a variety of languages to reflect the school population. It is simple, and on its own, tokenistic, but is nevertheless appreciated by parents and by pupils who are able to feel welcomed and appreciated by the school. Other displays which depict the histories and achievements of different peoples around the world are also effective and important in challenging normative assumptions about 'Others' (Blair and Bourne 1998). The effective school or teacher goes further to find out about the various displays and what they mean to the communities whose histories they tell and to incorporate this into the teaching and learning process.

Some schools try to be inclusive of both pupils and parents. In the English department of one school, students wrote stories and poetry in their home languages and these were translated and then recited in both the original language and English. Students were also asked to write short plays in both languages so that parents who did not speak English were able to attend performances and understand what was going on. Students' language work was displayed around the school and all languages were seen to be equally valued (*ibid.*).

Displays and other forms of inclusion of diverse languages and cultures are in themselves not enough unless they are accompanied by fundamental reflection and evaluation of one's taken-for-granted assumptions, and pupils are themselves taught to engage in similar processes of reflection.

Religion

At the time of writing, there is a lot of debate in the media and in society about whether or not the State should support Faith schools. The argument against has been that Faith schools are divisive; to support them is to encourage ghettoisation of minority ethnic and religious groups and so threaten social cohesion. The popular belief is that the taxpayer should not be supporting such a move especially in the period post-September 11 and the attacks on economic and civilian structures in the USA. These beliefs are reinforced by social divisions and violent strife between specific ethnic groups such as those that occurred in Bradford and Oldham between South Asian and white people in the summer of 2000. They are also endorsed by political statements about the need to integrate minorities in order to avoid such problems in the future.

At one level, these beliefs constitute good common sense. They also have a wide popular appeal, thus giving them greater legitimacy. But in order to truly learn to respect pupils' diverse religious affiliations, the teacher needs to understand the global and political context in which these ideas are expressed. Had the discussions about Faith schools been taking place in a society in which such schools were unknown and this was a new idea that the public was being asked to support, and through taxation, the arguments could be debated objectively. However, Faith schools have existed in Britain since before the introduction of mass education, and have often been extolled for the positive service they render both educationally and morally to the society. What then is the basis of the objection to more schools of this kind today?

The fact that the schools in question are mainly Islamic (notwithstanding September 11) would have to be considered very carefully as a reason for such objections. The teacher needs first of all to examine the historical relationship between Christianity and Islam, the political context of Islamophobia in the West specifically and in Britain in particular (Commission on British Muslims and Islamophobia 2002), and the hierarchical positioning of religions within the education system and in society generally. Secondly, one needs to ask, in the context of Britain today, the questions:

- What, in principle, do I think about Faith schools regardless of which faith it is? and

- Now that I understand the debate in its wider context, what position do I take and why?

The importance of these questions lies in the practice of thinking critically and reflectively about issues that affect one's attitudes and beliefs and by extension, one's relationships with pupils of different faiths. It is only on the basis of such critical understanding and questioning that one can assess whether one *accepts* and not merely *tolerates* different faiths (Bhavnani 2002), and can properly respond to the needs of pupils of faiths other than one's own.

English as an Additional Language (EAL)

Nationally, more than ten per cent of school pupils are learning English as an additional language (DfES 2004b). Many UK born pupils learn to hear and speak a language other than English at home and in their community during the first few years of their life. Although they may be exposed to some English at preschool age from watching television or from older siblings, their extensive exposure to English effectively begins when they enter the education system.

Early exposure to more than one language has been found to provide a cognitive advantage (Petitto *et al.* 2001), yet, as we note above, teachers have not always approached the teaching of English as an additional language in this way. It is important that teachers ensure that bilingual pupils understand that their first language is valued. Negative attitudes towards a young child's first language will quickly lead to discontinuation of usage in academic contexts and for some pupils, this will eventually lead to a plateau of achievement. Teachers should therefore find opportunities to celebrate the diversity of pupils' languages and encourage pupils to use their first language for learning where possible. It is not necessary for teachers to share the first language to do this; in some cases pupils can discuss with peers in their first language and then report back to the teacher in English. This allows pupils to develop concepts in their strongest language without being limited by their lack of proficiency in English.

Within the context and language rich curriculum of the Foundation Stage and the physical context of playground games, many EAL learners quickly develop the ability to communicate verbally in English with their peers. Within two years, most pupils learning EAL have acquired a good level of conversational fluency in English.

However, as the language demands of the curriculum increase in complexity, higher order skills such as the language of hypothesising, evaluating, predicting and classifying are fundamental to the development of thinking skills and progress in the National Curriculum. Exposure to target language alone without explicit teaching of the academic language required will not usually be sufficient to ensure continued progress in English beyond the initial stages (Ofsted 2003a; DfES 2004c). Teachers of all subjects need therefore to consider the language demands of the curriculum and employ specific strategies to ensure access for EAL learners including those who appear orally fluent.

There is also a large group of pupils who arrive in school at any age, apparently new to English. It is important that the teacher finds out as much as possible about the new pupil in order for appropriate educational arrangements to be made. Late-arriving pupils are faced with the task of acquiring English and learning curriculum content at the same time. Language support is best provided within the curriculum wherever possible, as time out of subject lessons for additional language tuition will ultimately cause the learner to fall further behind in the curriculum. Rather, teachers of all subjects should employ strategies to enable access for these pupils such as the use of visual cues to promote understanding, allowing opportunities for oral rehearsal of concepts and providing templates as a support for writing.

As comprehension usually precedes production of language, it is useful to identify progress of pupils new to English by looking for signs of language use which indicate understanding, such as gestures, pictures and short verbal responses. Tasks requiring formal recording are not likely to be indicative of ability or understanding.

While teachers are often understandably concerned about meeting the needs of pupils relatively new to English, many such pupils are highly motivated, make rapid progress within the curriculum and in some cases exceed the educational performance of UK born pupils within a few years (Ofsted 2003b).

For both UK born EAL learners and recent arrivals, accurate identification of cognitive ability as well as language proficiency is vital. The dilemma which faces education professionals when assessing EAL learners is the danger of diagnosing a learning difficulty when none is present, or the failure to identify a learning difficulty because poor progress is wrongly attributed to language development needs (Hall 2001). Teachers should take great care in interpreting the results of standardised tests since the results have invariably been standardised for a monolingual population (Cline and Shamsi 2000). Hall (2001) describes a model of hypothesis testing where it is necessary to consider a range of complex social, linguistic and medical factors involved in making an accurate diagnosis of special educational needs for pupils learning English as an additional language.

Commitment to raising achievement

It would probably be unusual to find a teacher who was not committed to raising the achievement of his or her pupils. Why then would such a condition exist in the standards for Qualified Teacher Status? The probable reason lies, once again, in the racial and ethnic dimensions of academic achievement. Reviews of research by Gillborn and Gipps (1996), Gillborn and Mirza (2000), Bhattacharyya *et al.* (2001) and Ison (2005) have shown the persistence of underachievement among some minority ethnic groups over the years. There is no single explanation for this. Writers have variously pointed to issues of language acquisition, to social class, gender, racism and to an interplay of all these, as significant factors in pupil achievement. An important point made by many social analysts and educators is that teaching is a middle-class profession perpetuating middle-class values and therefore excluding in its processes and underlying assumptions, pupils from working-class backgrounds (Sharp and Green 1984). Furthermore, in a society where the bulk of the teaching profession is white, then the interaction of 'race' and class mediates in a powerful way the relationships between minority ethnic group pupils and their teachers (Sleeter 1993).

The exhortation that teachers should be committed to the achievement of their pupils is rooted in an implicit acknowledgement of the role of stereotypes in influencing teachers' beliefs, attitudes and actions. Research shows that such stereotypes affect teachers' relationships with very young children. Connolly (1995), for example, detailed the ways in which six-year-old boys of Caribbean background were labelled and the effects of this labelling on teachers' attitudes towards them. Stereotypes of black men prevalent in the wider society were just as likely to be used against these boys so that they were constructed not only as sexually deviant, but as behaviour problems needing and deserving more stringent control than their white and/or Asian peers.

Individual teachers and schools use many strategies for raising achievement generally and some have developed imaginative and innovative ways to engage their pupils from different social and ethnic backgrounds. Researchers have found that an important method for motivating and encouraging students is to investigate the social and cultural interests of pupils and to incorporate these into one's teaching. Teachers use folk tales, histories, pop and football stars, hip hop music and whatever is topical among pupils or in their communities to bring relevance to points they wish to illustrate in their teaching of various subjects (Ofsted 2002; Blair and Bourne 1998; Ladson-Billings 1994). Important too is the need to understand the barriers to learning for one's pupils. For example, having an afternoon homework club or revision class may be an important strategy. However, unless one monitors take-up of such provision, there is no guarantee that those who need such provision make the most of such opportunities. Boys will often not take advantage of these resources for fear of being labelled swots, or 'nerds'. The teacher or school needs to engage with these fears and find ways of encouraging boys to take up such opportunities. Where particular pupils never seem to take advantage of extra resources provided by the school, it is worth investigating the personal circumstances of the pupil to see whether there are factors in the home or in the school which might be creating difficulties for the pupil. Where a pupil's homework is consistently poor, is it possible they do not have facilities at home for homework? This can be a real issue for refugees or asylum seekers who might live in inadequate temporary homes where a simple item such as a table is a luxury (Virani 2002).

There could be many other factors. For example:

- Is it possible that the pupil is being bullied?
- Are pupils of Gypsy/Traveller background afraid to come to after-school activities for fear of harassment?
- Do some pupils live too far from the school to take advantage of what is on offer?
- Do such opportunities clash with other community or religious activities such as visits to the Mosque?

Commitment to raising achievement is therefore about going one step further in one's efforts to make sure that all pupils are given an equal chance to succeed. Providing equality of opportunity is not only about neutral provision of access but ensuring that the outcomes are also fair.

It is becoming increasingly accepted that having a clear picture of whether differential achievement occurs along ethnic, class, gender, disability or other lines, monitoring by ethnicity, class etc. is important. In addition therefore to tracking individual performance, such monitoring provides a picture of group factors and allows the school to see what other value-added factors affect pupils. The Pupil Level Annual School Census (PLASC) through which schools collect and update information on their pupils is a useful tool for cross-checking different kinds of information about a pupil. For example, one is able to take attendance information about pupils from different groups and examine it against gender, special educational needs (SEN) and free school meals (as an indicator of social class) in order to provide a more refined picture of truancy in the school.

Free school meals are, however, a crude measure of social class especially as some pupils (especially in secondary school) who qualify may not take up this service for fear of being ridiculed. It might be necessary therefore, to take, for example exclusion information of Caribbean heritage boys, and set that against free school meals but also against knowledge of the pupil's family circumstances (single parent, poverty, housing, street code or address) in order to get a better understanding of which black boys are most affected by exclusion. A similar exercise can be carried out in relation to information about other groups, such as truancy levels among white boys.

Conclusion

Technical competencies in teaching are important but not sufficient in a diverse, class-based, gendered, multi-ethnic, multi-faith, multilingual society. Teachers now need to think in more complex multi-dimensional ways in order to promote a culture of inclusiveness in the classroom and in the school as a whole. This is necessary if one is to fulfil the requirements of QTS set out above. A 'colour blind' approach, that is, an approach that assumes that all pupils are the same and require the same treatment or provision, overlooks the needs and learning requirements of many pupils. On the other hand, an approach which overemphasises differences between pupils is in danger of creating fixed ethnic or other enclaves, which construct groups as 'other' and in the process, marginalises or excludes them. How is the teacher to achieve the balance of perspective that promotes social justice and fairness for all pupils?

This chapter has sought to underline the importance of taking time to think and reflect upon the demands brought about by this diversity. Pupils are not 'the same' because the dynamics of class, gender, sexuality, disability, ethnicity/culture, to name but a few, position people differently and lead to different experiences. The promotion of justice and fairness for all pupils requires an understanding of history, namely Britain's relationship with former colonial subjects (Cole and Blair 2005). The processes of globalisation and their general impact with respect to ethnicity, class and gender on different groups around the world, extends the need for a *global* as well as a local awareness of policies and politics, if justice and fairness are to prevail.

The classroom is often a good starting place for this kind of personal growth and development for the teacher. Faced with pupils from diverse backgrounds, this is a rich source of information and knowledge about the world, provided one is open and willing to let go of strongly held beliefs and opinions. It is the inward focus, the examination of one's own world view that is the starting point for high expectations, respect for others and commitment to one's pupils. It can be a challenging place to be, but is nevertheless essential. Haberman (1995) advises that one examines the source of one's beliefs and prejudices, understands how one came to see the world in this way and then finds ways of moving forward in a direction which is always reflective and seeks to take responsibility, rather than blames others for problems.

The ability to do this provides a strong foundation for fulfilling one's duties towards pupils from all backgrounds. It might help to strengthen one's feelings for social justice and one's ability to be fair to all pupils in one's care. It also provides a firm basis for thinking imaginatively about teaching and learning and about creative ways of providing a curriculum that is inclusive of all pupils and that promotes social justice in the wider society.

References

Abbott, D. (2002) 'Teachers are failing black boys', *Observer*, 6 January.

Bhattacharyya, G., Gabriel, J. and Small, S. (2001) *Race and Power: global racism in the twenty-first century*. London: Routledge.

Bhavnani, R. (2002) *Rethinking Interventions in Racism*. London: CRE with Trentham Books.

Blair, M. (2001) *Why Pick on Me? School Exclusion and Black Youth*. Stoke-on-Trent: Trentham Books.

Blair, M. and Bourne, J. (1998) *Making the Difference: teaching and learning in successful multi-ethnic schools*. London: DfEE.

Bowles, S. and Gintis, H. (1976) *Schooling in Capitalist America: educational reform and the contradictions of economic life*. London: Routledge and Kegan Paul.

Campbell, E. (2000) 'Professional ethics in teaching: towards the development of a code of practice', *Cambridge Journal of Education*, 30 (2), 203–21.

Cline, T. and Shamsi, T. (2000) *Language Needs or Special Needs?* London HMSO: DfEE.

Cole, M. (1989) 'Monocultural, multicultural and anti-racist education', in Cole, M. (ed.) *The Social Contexts of Schooling*. Lewes: Falmer Press.

Cole, M. (1998) 'Racism, reconstructed multiculturalism and anti-racist education', *Cambridge Journal of Education*, 28 (1), 37–48.

Cole, M. (ed.) (2005) *Education, Equality and Human Rights: issues of gender, 'race', sexuality, disability and social class*, 2nd edn. London: Routledge/Falmer.

Cole, M. and Blair, M. (2005) 'Racism and education: from Empire to New Labour', in Cole, M. (ed.) *Education, Equality and Human Rights: issues of gender, 'race', sexuality, disability and social class,* 2nd edn. London: Routledge/Falmer.

Commission on British Muslims and Islamophobia (2002) *Changing Race Relations: race equality schemes and policies.* London: CBMI with Runnymede Trust.

Connolly, P. (1995) 'Boys will be boys? Racism, sexuality and the construction of masculine identities amongst infant boys', in Holland, J. and Blair, M. (eds) *Debates and Issues in Feminist Research and Pedagogy.* Clevedon: Multilingual Matters.

Cullingford, C. and Morrison, J. (1997) 'Peer group pressure within and without school', *British Educational Research Journal,* 23 (1), 61–80.

Cummins, J. (1991) 'Inter-dependence of first and second language proficiency in bilingual children', in Bialystock, E. (ed.) *Language Processing of Bilingual Children.* Cambridge: Cambridge University Press.

DfES (2004a) *Every Child Matters.* London: The Stationery Office.

DfES (2004b) *Pupil Characteristics and Class Sizes in Maintained Schools in England.* London: The Stationery Office.

DfES (2004c) *More Advanced Learners of English as an Additional Language at Key Stage 2.* London: The Stationery Office.

Fine, M. (1991) *Framing Dropouts: notes on the politics of an urban public high school.* New York: Suny Press.

Gillborn, D. (1990) *'Race' Ethnicity and Education.* London: Unwin Hyman.

Gillborn, D. (1995) *Racism and Anti-racism in Real Schools.* Buckingham: Open University Press.

Gillborn, D. and Gipps, C. (1996) *Recent Research on the Achievement of Ethnic Minority Pupils.* London: Ofsted.

Gillborn, D. and Mirza, H. (2000) *Educational Inequality: mapping race, class and gender.* London: Ofsted.

Haberman, M. (1995) *Star Teachers of Children in Poverty.* West Lafayette, Indiana: Kappa, Delta, Pi.

Hall, D. (2001) *Assessing the Needs of Bilingual Pupils: living in two languages.* London: David Fulton.

Halpin, D. (2000) 'Hope, utopianism and educational management', *Cambridge Journal of Education,* 31 (1), 103–18.

Hargreaves, A., Earl, L. and Ryan, J. (1996) *Schooling for Change: re-inventing education for early adolescents.* London: Falmer.

Hatcher, R. (2005) 'Social class and school: relations to knowledge', in Cole, M. (ed.) *Education, Equality and Human Rights: issues of gender, 'race', sexuality, disability and social class,* 2nd edn. London: Routledge/Falmer.

Hill, D. and Cole, M. (2001) 'Social class', in Hill, D. and Cole, M. (eds) *Schooling and Equality: fact, concept and policy.* London: Kogan Page.

Ison, L. (2005) *Ethnicity and Education: the evidence on minority ethnic pupils.* London: DfES.

Ladson-Billings, G. (1994) *The Dreamkeepers: successful teachers of African American children.* San Francisco: Jossey-Bass Publishers.

Macdonald, I., Bhavnani, R., Khan, L. and John, G. (1989) *Murder in the Playground: the Burnage Report.* London: Longsight Press.

Maylor, U. (1996) 'The experiences of African, Caribbean and South Asian women in initial teacher education'. PhD thesis, Open University.

Myers, K. and Grosvenor, I. (2001) 'Policy, equality and inequality: from the past to the future', in Hill, D. and Cole, M. (eds) *Schooling and Equality: fact, concept and policy.* London: Kogan Page.

Office for Standards in Education (Ofsted) (2002) *The Achievement of Black Caribbean Pupils: good practice in secondary schools.* London: Ofsted.

Office for Standards in Education (Ofsted) (2003a) *More Advanced Learners of English as an Additional Language in Secondary Schools and Colleges*. London: Ofsted.

Office for Standards in Education (Ofsted) (2003b) *The Education of Asylum-seeker Pupils*. London: Ofsted.

Peters, M. (2002) Paper presented to DfES conference on the collection of ethnic background data and ethnic monitoring, 6 February.

Petitto, L. A., Katerelos, M., Levy, B., Gauna, K., Tétrault, K. and Ferraro, V. (2001) 'Bilingual signed and spoken language acquisition from birth: implications for mechanisms underlying bilingual language acquisition', *Journal of Child Language*, 28 (2), 1–44.

Rampton, A. (1981) *West Indian Children in our Schools*. London: HMSO.

Sewell, T. (1997) *Black Masculinity and Schooling*. Stoke-on-Trent: Trentham Books.

Sharp, R. and Green, A. (1984) 'Social stratification in the classroom', in Hargreaves, A. and Woods, P. (eds) *Classrooms and Staffrooms: the sociology of teachers and teaching*. Milton Keynes: Open University Press.

Sivanandan, A. (1985) 'RAT and the degradation of the black struggle', *Race and Class*, 22, 1–33.

Sleeter, C. (1993) 'How white teachers construct race', in McCarthy, C. and Crichlow, W. (eds) *Race, Identity and Representation in Education*. New York: Routledge.

Soltis, J. F. (1986) 'Teaching professional ethics', *Journal of Teacher Education*, 37 (3), 2–4.

Stenhouse, L. (1983) *Authority, Education and Emancipation: a collection of papers*. London: Heinemann.

Swann Report (1985) *Education for All: report of the Committee of Inquiry into the Education of Children from Minority Ethnic Groups*. London: HMSO.

Teacher Training Agency (TTA) (2004) *Qualifying to Teach: professional standards for Qualified Teacher Status and requirements for initial teacher training*. London: TTA.

Virani, Z. (2002) *Listening to Somali Pupils and Parents: a research project*. London Borough of Harrow.

Wright, C., Weekes, D., McGlaughlin, A. and Webb, D. (2000) *Race, Class and Gender in Exclusions from School*. London: Falmer.

Consideration for pupils as learners

Joanna Oldham

Those awarded Qualified Teacher Status must understand and uphold the professional code of the General Teaching Council for England by demonstrating . . . [that] they treat pupils consistently, with respect and consideration, and are concerned for their development as learners.

(TTA 2004: 7 Section 1.2)

Learning objectives

To understand and become familiar with:

- trends in learning pedagogy
- the research context for considering individual pupils
- the concept and practice of formative assessment in learning
- the use of assessment in a cycle of planning, teaching and assessment.

Introduction

THIS CHAPTER DEALS WITH TEACHERS' concern for learning and how this affects their treatment of pupils. In the first of three sections, I discuss the TTA's description of the behaviours, attitudes and understanding that entrants to the teaching profession must be able to demonstrate in relation to consideration of pupils as learners. Having done so, in the second section, I discuss the implications of this standard for teachers' pedagogical knowledge. In the third and final section, I consider the assessment of beginning teachers against this standard.

Section 1: professionalism regarding concern for learning and treatment of pupils

It is impossible to reduce a concept like 'professionalism' to atomised components. Consequently, the TTA's elaboration of professionalism regarding consideration for pupils as learners taken from the TTA's *Qualifying to Teach: handbook of guidance* (TTA 2003)(below) should be regarded, not as a checklist but rather, as exemplifications of behaviours from which wider inferences about your appropriate relationships with pupils can be reliably made. Such an approach prevents expectations regarding professional relationships and professionalism from being reduced to a handful of (disputed) principles.

Scope of professionalism of those to be awarded QTS

Pupils are more likely to learn if they recognise that their teachers value them as individuals and respond to them consistently. Pupils are more likely to treat others with respect and consideration if their teachers demonstrate such behaviour towards them. Pupils have a range of interests, preferences and attitudes and these will affect how they respond to specific topics or particular ways of communicating. [Beginning] teachers are expected to take this into account in their planning, teaching and assessment, and to know how they can help pupils to take an active and developing role in their own learning.

(TTA 2003: 7)

The content of this quotation can be broadly divided between how teachers should treat pupils and how teachers should manage pupils' learning and in this section I deal with both issues. The second issue, managing pupils' learning, requires explicit pedagogical knowledge and so I also return to it in the second section of the chapter. I begin by considering the significance of individual pupils in teaching.

The significance of individual pupils in teaching

To some extent, the TTA's clear acknowledgement that pupils' interests, preferences and attitudes are different is undermined by the existence of a National Curriculum (DfEE 1999) which obliges all pupils to study the same elements during their schooling. While the curriculum is the same, the pupils who must study it are different. As a result, the artistry of the teacher is perhaps most in evidence in the ways in which teachers mediate between what is being taught and how and to whom. In requiring teachers to acknowledge pupils as individuals in its guidance accompanying the standards, the TTA is making reference to the complex dynamic of the classroom in which teachers with responsibility for whole groups of pupils also address the range of individual learning needs present in any group.

These learning needs of individual pupils inform teachers' planning and teaching. What is being taught cannot be considered independently of the pupils to whom it is being taught. Teachers identify the learning needs of the pupils in their class by assessing them. The three elements (planning, teaching and assessing) form a cyclical process which is crucial for learning and I discuss this in depth later in the chapter. For now, suffice to say that teachers show their concern for pupils' development as learners when they use information derived from assessment in order to decide what to teach and how. This explains why the scope of the standard relating to concern for learning links pupils' interests, preferences and attitudes on the one hand with teachers' planning, teaching and assessing on the other. The emphasis the guidance places on pupil individuality is an issue I turn to later. In the meantime, I wish to focus on the implicit reference made to relationships and classroom management.

Relationships and classroom management

Teachers should recognise that pupils regard them as adults on whom they can depend and rely. As such, they may consciously wish to confide in you or, since children may be less able to conceal things than adults, they may inadvertently reveal personal and sensitive information about themselves to you. The teacher–pupil relationship is not the same as a pupil–parent/carer relationship and it also differs substantially from a relationship between peers because of the inherent power relations which, acknowledged or otherwise, exist between teacher and pupil. Research conducted into how classrooms operate suggests that boundaries and relationships are in a constant state of negotiation between teachers and pupils. This means that no one pattern of behaviour or set of preconceived responses can be unproblematically applied to every situation. This is a potential source of worry for beginning teachers who could be forgiven for wanting to know everything they need to know before they set foot in a classroom!

A paramount concern for teachers at the beginning of their practice is often classroom management and pupil behaviour, anxieties about which sometimes threaten to undermine the teacher's resolve to be courteous and polite. As a general principle, teachers should model the sorts of courteous and polite conduct they expect from their pupils. An orderly classroom is required but you cannot afford to obtain one at the expense of mutually respectful relationships with pupils. Experienced teachers use a range of techniques for managing behaviour. Some of these techniques can be very subtle. Techniques which do not rely on punitive measures, for example use of good humour, can be the most effective.

Relationships with pupils are influenced by the teacher's implicit and explicit expectations. Pupils receive messages about what the teacher's expectations about behaviour are not only from what they say, but also from more subtle clues including the tone of voice the teacher uses, facial expressions and body language. Teachers learn that in order for their expectations to be met by pupils, their expectations need to be consistent. Consistency results in pupils being clear about what is expected of them. Some teachers' classroom procedures follow established routines which pupils are expected to learn.

Teachers should form relationships with each pupil by learning about them and being interested in trying to understand them. The guidance is clear that teachers should respond to pupils as individuals. Moreover, it links the teacher's relationship with the individual pupil to the likelihood of that pupil learning. In showing concern for learning then, the guidance suggests that the quality of relationships between pupil and teacher is an important aspect of professionalism.

Making school subjects appealing to pupils

The guidance implies that pupils' interests, preferences and attitudes will influence how they respond to specific topics or ways of communicating. It is axiomatic that learners are better at learning that which they perceive to be useful or interesting to them. One significant aspect of the teacher's role, therefore, is the ability to explore the particular curriculum subject's relevance and interest for the particular pupils in the class. Teaching is a social activity (social in the sense of being concerned with people). As such, it is partly shaped by the individuals who make up a class and their personal qualities and interests.

Part of the teacher's artistry is in making school subjects appeal to a range of different pupil interests, such that there are always elements of any lesson in which all pupils can engage enthusiastically. Bruner's (1986, 1990) concept of scaffolding gives us a useful rationale for harnessing pupils' particular interests for learning, since he suggests that familiarity and competence in one domain could be used in the acquisition and development of competence in another.

Multiple intelligences and learning styles

Pupils' individual interests aside, the significance of what have been termed 'multiple intelligences'(Gardner 1983) has implications for the ways in which schools teach individuals. Gardner created a typology for distinguishing between different types of (unhierarchical) intelligences: linguistic intelligence, logical-mathematical intelligence, spatial intelligence, bodily-kinesthetic intelligence, musical intelligence, interpersonal intelligence, and intrapersonal intelligence (*ibid*.) Gardner's work presupposes that any individual can be characterised by one of these types. According to Gardner, people with each different intelligence type will possess different knowledge, skills and understandings about different aspects of the world.

While it may be possible to match aspects of Gardner's multiple intelligences to the content of the National Curriculum, Gardner himself recognises that schools as institutions value the linguistic and logical-mathematical above other intelligence types. In spite of this, the theory of multiple intelligences (*ibid*.) has influenced recent thinking about pupils as learners and has, arguably, resulted in a shift of focus in education from issues of teaching to those of learning.

The theory of multiple intelligences implies that people corresponding to a particular multiple intelligence type have different knowledge, skills and understandings about different aspects of the world. As such, the different types of people might learn about the world in different ways. Education is particularly concerned with three different learning styles: the visual (concerned with sight), the auditory (concerned with hearing) and the kinesthetic (concerned with physicality). Advocates of a learning styles approach encourage teaching the (same) curriculum using means appropriate for different learning styles.

While Gardner identified seven different intelligence types, three learning styles (visual, auditory and kinesthetic) have been presumed sufficient to saturate them. Recognition that learning styles may be more individualistic has led to the advocation of 'personalised learning' by David Miliband (2004) which seeks to tailor education to individual need, interest and aptitude.

Personalising the teaching of the curriculum is not the only way to approach learning however. In their work on cognitive acceleration, Shayer and Adey (2002) have shown that the incorporation of specific elements into lessons taught to whole classes of pupils (concrete preparation, cognitive conflict, construction, metacognition and bridging) has benefits for the learning of all students.

Assessment

In addition to thinking about teaching, concern for learners also involves assessment. Teachers' responses to pupils' work is an important issue not least because teacher expectation and pupil success are correlated. The teacher's response to a pupil's work gives the pupil an impression of how successful the teacher thinks the work is. In terms of learning, the teacher needs to ensure that responses to work do not to undermine pupils' confidence. Pupils' own perceptions about their levels of success in school in the past and the present influence the likelihood of their success in school in the future. If pupils perceive themselves to be unlikely to succeed at school, this could be dangerous given that human beings tend to decide how much effort to put in on the basis of how likely they think they are to succeed. Equally, when responding to high quality work, teachers should not imply that there is nothing more for the pupil to learn. Maximum expectations could set a limiting ceiling on pupils' attainment.

What we know about human achievement is that it is possible for an individual to be good at one thing and not at another. Valuing individuals therefore manifests itself in the practice of a teacher who does not rigidly predict which pupils will be able to engage with particular tasks, nor how successfully. A fair teacher also expects equal effort from all pupils and gives them equality of opportunity. In practical terms, this means identifying what pupils need to learn such that their attainment is raised (how this can be done is the topic of section 2 of this chapter). Your preconceptions and prejudices about which pupils are likely to produce good work might appear to be justified by pupil performance. Preconceptions and prejudices, however, they remain. Teachers must also have sufficiently flexible expectations of different pupils and not overly prescribe the allocation of pupils to differentiated tasks in order to avoid pupil performance becoming a teacher-fulfilled prophecy.

There are minimum expectations for pupils' attainment set by the Government. However, valuing all individuals equally involves understanding that some pupils (in fact, half of them) will always perform beneath any norm. It would be therefore catastrophic to concern oneself only with the education of pupils who are above average: such pupils will constitute only 50 per cent of the school population.

It would appear clear that all human achievement, if plotted on a graph, would result in a normal distribution curve (sometimes called a bell-shaped curve) which shows that a small minority of performance falls at the extremes. Very few people will perform at the lowest levels and, similarly, very few will perform at the highest levels; the vast majority of performance will fall in the mid-range, though there will be differences between individuals here too. This variation demonstrates what we already know from the application of common sense: that, while genuine extremes are rare, we are all different from each other. With regard to classes of pupils, variation in their performance will still occur (even in setted classes, demonstrably, pupils are not the same).

Age-related trends in attainment have some bearing on how teachers rate and respond to a piece of work. For example the same piece of work could be regarded as high quality if it were produced by a nine-year-old pupil, but low quality if produced by a 14-year-old pupil. But since teachers are expected to develop and extend all pupils, they should also develop and extend even pupils who are producing work of a quality normally associated with much older pupils.

As you become more experienced, you will learn what is expected in terms of the levels of attainment for different age groups and your understanding of these expectations might influence the way you respond to a pupil's work. Remember, however, that these expectations are based on norms of large populations and that any individual pupil might have much greater or lesser ability than the notional average pupil.

Factors that can affect attainment

It might seem paradoxical to try to understand the needs of an individual pupil by looking at data which gives information about groups of pupils. However, educational research provides important insights into factors apart from chronological age which can affect attainment. I have argued above that any given pupil may perform above or below what is regarded as average performance for pupils of the same age and that this is a statistical inevitability. However, if we sort the pupils who perform above and below average into sociological groupings, pupil-performance data continues to indicate overwhelming trends in underattainment across certain social groups. This suggests that social groupings may also be a factor which influences attainment.

There are many factors (possibly an infinite number) which affect educational outcome: education is a complex social phenomenon and so it is unlikely to be determined by only a handful of variables. Some variables might appear to be key (gender for example), but the ubiquity of such variables might be better explained in terms of research investigating what is measurable. Some of the variables which form the focus of research may be regarded as more significant than they actually are; some significant variables may not have been researched at all.

Certainly a wealth of educational research attests to the complexity and variety of factors which influence what happens to pupils during their education. Of all of the factors which have been shown to have an impact on education, the closest correlate between educational performance and any other factor is home background. This finding, derived from studies of groups, has implications for the way in which we understand an individual pupil.

If a given pupil is attaining above the norm of a given age group, are we to understand this in terms of the statistical inevitability of the normal distribution curve or are other factors relevant? If so, which? There are various explanations for pupil attainment. While some of the explanations imply that teachers have little bearing on pupil attainment, others attest to the teacher's responsibility for how pupils fare. In my discussion, I examine in greater depth those findings with implications for teachers' practices.

Previously, there were theories that some social groups are inherently more intelligent than others. These theories are now not only unpopular, they have also been discredited. Pollard explains that both 'race' and class have been 'wrongly understood' (2002: 347) as determining factors in intelligence and behaviour. Such theories misunderstood data which indicates that certain socio-ethnic and racial groups were over-represented in the highest levels of pupil attainment (in the UK, they include the white middle class) and other socio-ethnic and racial groups were over-represented in the lowest levels of performance (African-Caribbean pupils for example). Pollard describes deterministic interpretations of this data as a 'confusion' (*ibid*.) and more pointedly as a 'distortion' (*ibid*).

More recently, research (PISA 2002) has attested to the clear advantages of attending schools with pupils from more advantaged family backgrounds since these pupils are three times more likely to attain five or more GCSEs. It would, however, be a mistake to infer from this that wealth is a causal factor in attainment. The data is much more likely to signify the 'cultural capital' (Bourdieu 1977) of individual pupils (where 'capital' becomes a metaphor for different social groups' values and ways of doing things, only some of which are credited by schools). This extrapolation regarding cultural as opposed to monetary capital is likely to mean that white middle-class pupils for example have what schools recognise as cultural capital, but that other groups do not.

In spite of the close relationship between educational outcome and socio-cultural and socio-economic factors including ethnicity and wealth, neither ethnicity nor wealth nor social class determines what happens to an individual pupil. This means that in spite of the close correlation between educational outcome and certain factors, teachers cannot predict the attainment of individual pupils. I discuss the implications for practice of this point in the second section of this chapter. While individual preferences are likely to influence a pupil's response to school, to what is learned there and how, it is also likely that socio-cultural factors are relevant to how pupils receive particular topics and respond to schools' ways of communicating. I explore this idea next.

School practices and socio-cultural background

Education in the broadest terms is different from schooling. Many schools' procedures are self-referential in that what schools teach is, to some extent, about the business of schools themselves. The single most important lesson that successful pupils learn in school is how to 'do' school. Thus, successful pupils have learned how to behave for school: they learn what to read, what to write, what to say and how, for the purposes of school. Unsuccessful pupils have not learned how to 'do' school. It has recently been recognised that schools have 'come to be such a particular, specialized institution, with (their) own particular brand of learning' (Hull and Schultz 2002: 12).

The significance of home background in terms of educational failure is now understood in terms of a clash of 'practices'. Drawing on the work of Brian Street (in particular Street 1984), Baynham and Baker (2002: 2) explain the concept of 'practices' as incorporating 'the ideas, attitudes, ideologies and values that inform what people do'. Research into differences between ways of doing and knowing in school on the one hand and ways of knowing and doing at home on the other (e.g. Heath 1983; Pahl 2003) indicates that practices in school exclude some children.

Literacy has been acknowledged as the key medium of education and schools: so much so that 'virtually all schooling after the first year or two assumes pupil literacy' (Hannon 2000: 8). Literacy and language uses have also been conceptualised as 'practices' meaning that language and literacy at home may well be different from language and literacy at school for some children (Barton *et al*. 2000). Moreover, schools have been shown to rely on language and literacy practices which are alien to children from other socio-cultural groups (Street and Street 1991). Perhaps the unequal attainment of different social groups in schools can be explained in terms of differences in literacy practices. In school, pupils whose literacy practices used at home match those of school may well be advantaged over those pupils whose home practices are different.

The practices of schools then accord with the ways of doing things of only certain socio-cultural groups. Studies have shown that the home practices of some children give them an advantage when they go to school (Street 2005). Other children are disadvantaged by the fact that schools do not reflect the values which underpin the consciousness of wide sections of cohorts of pupils (Dyson 2002).

While some have interpreted the social practices argument in terms of a deficit model of the pupil, others have argued that schools should widen what they count as knowledge (Gregory and Williams 2000). In addition, some make the educational case for incorporating a wider range of social practices into schools in order that they be more reflective of the home context (Pahl 2003). Such research has led to arguments about whether schools are right to impose their practices, knowledge, values and ideologies onto children. No social practice is neutral nor are they all equal: society accords them different values. It is vital for teachers to be aware of the hegemonic or dominant practices (likely to be those promoted in schools) at the same time as being sensitive to the existence of others. Sensitivity, however, may not be enough. To succeed in schools, all pupils also need access to the dominant practices.

Other explanations for unequal pupil attainment with implications for teachers' practice suggest that schools rely on only a limited range of teaching techniques which favour only particular learning styles. Pupils whose favoured learning style relates to the linguistic and to written language are surely advantaged in the context of schools where language and literacy are the medium of education. The needs of pupils who favour other learning styles such as those depicted by Gardner (1983) may be less well met. The extent to which a print-centric curriculum and assessment framework can be successfully delivered to for example, kinaesthetic learners, is likely to be limited.

Section 2: pedagogical knowledge required for consideration of pupils as learners

Learning to teach in a way which displays consideration for pupils as learners does not only require exposure to the sorts of ideas of the previous section. It also requires specialist pedagogical knowledge. Elaborating pedagogy is the purpose of this section. I begin with a distinction between teaching and learning.

Teaching and learning

If the learner hasn't learnt anything, what the teacher is doing cannot accurately be described as teaching. A teacher can be operating the procedures of teaching, for example, talking to the pupils, but if learning has not occurred, there is an argument for saying that no teaching has taken place. Teaching and learning then are mutually dependent but the latter is not necessarily the result of the former. As I explained in section 1, assessment combines with planning and teaching to form a cyclical learning process and I continue here by explaining how.

Learning is conspicuously different from the demonstration of *prior* learning. If, for example, a teacher asks a pupil in a music classroom to sit at the piano and play, the pupil will be demonstrating that which he or she could already do before entrance into the classroom. This is a demonstration of prior learning and not learning *per se*. Teachers, because they are obliged to assess pupils' learning, do provide occasions for pupils to demonstrate what they can already do, but this is an activity separate from learning and an issue I return to later.

In the first instance, it is vital for beginning teachers to know how learning occurs. Returning to my example of the pupil playing the piano in class, if the teacher listens to the pupil's demonstration of *prior* learning and forms an opinion about how well the pupil is playing, then learning is what happens *after* this point. Let me explain how. If the teacher identifies the next step for the pupil's development in piano playing and gives advice to the pupil about how to make that next step, and if the pupil uses the teacher's advice and plays the piano better the next time, then the teacher has taught and the pupil has learned.

Learning and assessment

Learning then is intimately linked to a certain type of assessment sometimes called formative assessment (Black *et al.* 2002) or assessment for learning. This type of assessment is different from the sort (called summative assessment) that simply allows the teacher to find out what the pupils can already do. Summative assessment has no effect on learning. If our piano-playing student plays the piano for the teacher who evaluates the performance and that is the end result, then this assessment is summative and has not, in itself, had an effect on the pupil's level of performance. Formative assessment's intention, however, is to *improve* performance. It is defined as the teacher's adaptation of teaching for pupils' learning needs (*ibid.*). A crucial factor in this process is the teacher's communication to the pupil known as 'feedback'.

Learning does not automatically result from all feedback: it is the *quality* of the feedback which is significant in determining whether learning will occur. Feedback which tells a pupil to 'be more analytical' is only useful if the pupil knows what being more analytical means and understands *precisely* what steps to take to make the piece of work on which feedback is being given more analytical. It has been suggested (Wiliam and Black 1996), that if a pupil knew what being more analytical looked like, he or she would probably have been analytical in the first place. The feedback has to be understandable by the pupil.

For learning to occur, when the teacher sets the task, he or she needs to explain clearly what is expected from the work. As an example, take the task to be an essay and the expectation to be pupils' use of quotations from sources in the essay. In addition to experience and clear expectations about the task, pupils also need an opportunity to redraft their work in the light of the teacher's feedback. The feedback should be in response to a first draft and directed towards improving the pupil's second draft.

At the point of feedback, the teacher might want to discuss with the pupil *how well* he or she has used quotations in the first draft of the essay, or, if the pupil's quotations are already very good, the teacher might direct the pupil to improve a different aspect of the work. To develop my example of how teachers facilitate learning, assume that the teacher wants the pupil to improve the way in which quotations were used in the first draft of the essay. It is not enough for the teacher to say 'your use of quotations needs to be better': this does not tell the pupil what aspects of quotation use needs to be better, nor how this can be done. *It is your job to show the pupils how.* It is not enough either to present examples of work to the whole class and inform the pupils which example was excellent and which merely satisfactory. Teachers must also explain the criteria by which they deem one pupil's essay 'excellent' and another's 'satisfactory'. Thus teachers need to be able to explain precisely what work which is excellent contains. This involves not only giving the information that 'quotations are used very skilfully in this essay', but also an explanation of exactly what makes the example skilful and how a skilful example differs in nature from a weaker example.

How do teachers make these formative assessments which, as I have indicated above, are crucial to the learning process? Teachers' assessments (and subsequently, their feedback) come not from criteria relating to the task pupils are engaged in (e.g. use of quotations in a literary essay) in a verbal description (e.g. 'skilfully used') but by reference to their wide understanding of quality.

Teachers have an understanding of quality because of the wealth of knowledge and experience they have of their subjects. They know what a good translation in languages looks like; they know what a good mathematical proof looks like; they can recognise an effective poem etc. Teachers' own subject knowledge proficiency is so well developed that they know the full (unwritten) criteria of their subject: the task is to share this information with the learner.

Formative assessment which by definition intends to improve performance has to take place prior to an opportunity for the pupil to make use of the teacher's feedback. This is not to suggest that the timing of formative assessment is the only significant factor. On the contrary, successful formative assessment is reliant on a teacher's ability to respond to a pupil in a way that is helpful for that particular pupil. For this reason, formative assessments cannot follow a set procedure.

If pupils are asked to answer the question 'What matter produces a chemical that causes bubbles to be formed in hydrogen peroxide solution?' (answer: living cells), and a pupil asks for assistance, informing the pupil that a leaf will cause bubbles but a stone will not, only gives the pupil an example. It will not help the pupil to answer another question about whether matter of a different type is likely to have the same bubbling effect, unless the pupil already knows that the teacher's example of a leaf is offered *as an example of a living cell*. The teacher can accept the credit for a pupil's improvement in performance only if the pupil has used the teacher's feedback. Feedback, then, has to be tailored to the individual pupil's capabilities, existing knowledge and understanding. This is where a teacher's knowledge of the pupil's performance through summative assessment is useful in assisting learning: it helps the teacher know what kind of feedback is appropriate for the pupil.

Assessment also helps teachers to decide how and what to plan in subsequent lessons. This is because assessing pupils reveals to teachers what pupils do not yet know and need to be taught. Teachers develop their knowledge of individual pupils and assess what they do and do not know by listening to them and observing them. Such assessments are not undertaken simply to be recorded (summatively) in a mark book: instead they inform planning. Planning, then, should take account of what assessment (in the form of listening to and observing pupils) suggests pupils need to be taught in the next lesson. In that next lesson the assessment process continues, which leads, in turn, to another lesson planned with respect to assessment information. This forms a cycle of planning, teaching and assessment.

Facilitating pupil's control over their learning

In order that pupils can take an active role in their own learning, (the remaining aspect of the guidance for the professional standard concerning learning), teachers need to be able to share assessment criteria with pupils. This is also crucial for formative assessment. To facilitate pupils' control over their own learning, the teacher needs to ensure the learner has the following: first, an understanding of the full criteria against which work is assessed; secondly, some sense of the aspired level of performance; and thirdly, an ability to *compare* their actual levels of performance to the higher, aspired level of performance. Without these things, 'students' efforts in production are likely to contain elements of random trial and error' (Sadler 1987).

So taking those three things in turn, first, teachers can share criteria with learners by showing pupils how the criteria apply to specific examples of pupils' work in concrete terms. Secondly, pupils can learn about the level of aspired performance by seeing examples and having the teacher explain precisely how and in what ways higher performance is different. Thirdly, teachers can enable pupils to compare their own performance to the higher level by involving pupils in the evaluation of their own work. Once pupils have this knowledge and understanding, they are also able to evaluate each other's work. Looking at other pupils' work *in the light of* the teacher's feedback raises achievement (Wiliam 1998).

The ability of teachers to give feedback comes from their notions of quality. For pupils to be able to appraise their own work, they too must acquire a sense of quality. Understanding the quality of, for example, a piece of art comes most importantly from a wealth of experience of and exposure to art and to making art.

> Knowledge of the criteria is 'caught' through experience, not defined. It is developed through an inductive process which involves prolonged engagement in evaluative activity shared with and under the tutelage of a person who is already something of a connoisseur.
>
> (Sadler 1989)

Experiential learning is fundamental. The knowledge of the expert (in this instance, the teacher) comes about through experience, apprenticeship and tutelage. The novice's knowledge (the pupil's) is acquired in the same way.

Section 3: demonstrating meeting the standards

If the standards the TTA has proposed are intended to have a gatekeeping function whereby only those beginning teachers who can demonstrate professional competence will be granted admission to the profession, then your professionalism in regard to consideration for pupils as learners must be assessed. This final section of the chapter considers what will be assessed, when and by whom and it aims to clarify the nature of evidence that will suggest you have met the standards.

Professionalism in teaching is an underpinning concept and, as such, quantitatively and qualitatively different from a person's ability to behave professionally for a given occasion. That being the case, your professionalism will be observable at all times, and by all of the people (including the pupils) with whom your school practice brings you into contact. The evidence of your professionalism will be also reflected in the documentation that initial teacher education (ITE) generates.

Evidence of your developing professionalism will thus be observable during the lessons in which you participate (either as observer or teacher) and in your general conduct in the school. The people who will assess your professionalism on this evidence will be staff with responsibility for your school practice and your university tutors. Your professional concern for pupils as learners will be particularly evident in your lesson planning as well as the actual lessons you teach. It will be evident in the use you make of assessment information in the cycle of planning, teaching and assessing.

Conclusion

Although there are different ideas about the purpose of schools, all of them place fundamental significance on the value of learning. In the present context, schools are increasingly entrenched in the education culture of league tables, parental choice and Ofsted inspections with the power to close schools. One ironic result of this is that attention is sometimes forced away from the issue of learning and focused on results. In classrooms, one potential consequence of the results-oriented pressure on teachers is that assessment of pupils (of the summative variety) happens more often in order that pupils' development can be shown. Measurement must not become the end rather than the means in education. Consideration for pupils as learners manifests itself in teachers prioritising learning not assessment.

References

Barton, D., Hamilton M. and Ivanic, R. (eds) (2000) *Situated Literacies: reading and writing in context*. London: Routledge.

Baynham, M. and Baker, D. (2002) 'Editorial', in Baynham, M. and Baker, D. (eds) *Ways of Knowing*, 2 (1), 10–22.

Black, P., Harrison, C., Lee, C., Marshall, B. and Wiliam, D. (2002) *Working Inside the Black Box: assessment for learning in the classroom*. London: NFER Nelson.

Bourdieu, P. (1977) *Outline of a Theory of Practice*. Cambridge: Cambridge University Press.

Bruner, J. (1986) *Actual Minds, Possible Worlds*. Cambridge, MA: Harvard University Press.

Bruner, J. (1990) *Acts of Meaning*. Cambridge, MA: Harvard University Press.

DfEE (1999) *The National Curriculum for England*. London: HMSO.

Dyson, A. H. (2002) 'The Drinking God Factor: a writing development remix for "all" children'. Keynote talk given for United Kingdom Literacy Association. Chester, July 2002.

Gardner, H. (1983) *Frames of Mind: the theory of multiple intelligences*. New York: Basic.

Gregory, E. and Williams, A. (2000) *City Literacies: learning to read across generations and cultures*. London: Routledge.

Hannon, P. (2000) *Reflecting on Literacy in Education*. London: Routledge/Falmer.

Heath, S. B. (1983) *Ways with Words: language, life and work in communities and classrooms*. Cambridge. Cambridge University Press.

Hull, G. and Schultz, K. (2002) *School's Out: bridging out-of-school literacies with classroom practice*. New York: Teachers College Press.

Miliband, D. (2004) Speech to the North of England Conference http://www.standards.dfes. gov.uk/personalisedlearning/about/ (accessed January 2005).

Pahl, K. (2003) 'Children's text making at home: transforming meaning across modes', in Jewitt, C. and Kress, G. (eds) *Multimodal Literacy*, 139–54. New York: Peter Lang Publishers.

Pollard, A. (2002) *Reflective Teaching: effective and evidence-informed professional practice*. London/New York: Continuum Books.

Programme for International Student Assessment (PISA) (2002) *Reading for Change: performance and engagement across countries; results from PISA 2000*. Organisation for Economic Co-operation and Development (OECD).

Sadler, D. R. (1987) 'Specifying and promulgating achievement standards', *Oxford Review of Education*, 13 (2), 191–209.

Sadler, D. R. (1989) 'Formative assessment and the design of instructional systems', *Institutional Science*, 18 (2), 199–244.

Shayer, M. and Adey, P. S. (eds) (2002) *Learning Intelligence*. Maidenhead: Open University Press.

Street, B. (1984) *Literacy in Theory and Practice*. Cambridge: Cambridge University Press.

Street, B. (ed.) (2005) *Literacies Across Educational Contexts: mediating teaching and learning*. Philadelphia: Carlson Press.

Street, B. and Street, J. (1991) 'The schooling of literacy', in Barton, D. and Ivanic, R. (eds) *Literacy in the Community*, 143–66. London: Sage.

Teacher Training Agency (TTA) (2003) *Qualifying to Teach: handbook of guidance*. London: TTA. http://www.tta.gov.uk/php/read.php?sectionid=160&articleid=1741 (accessed February 2005).

Teacher Training Agency (TTA) (2004) *Qualifying to Teach: professional standards for Qualified Teacher Status and requirements for initial teacher training*. London: TTA.

Wiliam, D. (1998) 'Enculturating learners into communities of practice: raising achievement through classroom assessment'. Paper to European Conference on Educational Research, Ljubljana, Slovenia, September.

Wiliam, D. and Black, P. J. (1996) 'Meanings and consequences; a basis for distinguishing formative and summative functions of assessment?', *British Educational Research Journal*, 22 (5), 537–48.

3

Promoting positive values

Linda Rice

Those awarded Qualified Teacher Status must understand and uphold the professional code of the General Teaching Council for England by demonstrating . . . [that] they demonstrate and promote the positive values, attitudes and behaviour that they expect from their pupils.

(TTA 2004: 7 Section 1.3)

Learning objectives

To encourage teachers to:

- develop an awareness of the dynamic and complex nature of values and beliefs
- routinely reflect upon their own values in the light of their practice
- develop a critically reflective attitude to the links between culture, policy and practices that challenges hitherto unquestioned stereotypes and assumptions
- begin to identify examples of practice that support inclusive education.

Introduction

EXAMPLES OF THE VALUES THAT teachers can expect from their pupils include 'respect for other people; a positive attitude towards learning; respect for cultural diversity; care for the environment; and social responsibility' (TTA 2002: 4). Values have been defined in many and varying ways, and this chapter uses Halstead and Taylor's (1996) definition of values as simply the principles and fundamental beliefs, which act as general guides to behaviour and as points of reference in decision making.

Principally I set out here to raise awareness of some of the formidable and controversial issues that arise in considering professional values and the role of the teacher and also to signpost some of the resources which may be of interest. There are two inherent assumptions in the standards. First, that teachers see it as their role to influence the development of pupils' values and secondly that 'children's values will be influenced, consciously or otherwise by the example set by their teachers in their relationships, attitudes and teaching styles' (Halstead and Taylor 2000: 177). I would also wish to stress the importance of teachers and pupils developing critical thinking and an understanding of a variety of ways of interpreting the world. This allows a conception of values as relative and changing over time, rather than absolute.[1] This is a significant consideration given that the standards are stated in broad, somewhat unspecific statements, which offer little in the way of guidance to teachers.

There are thus three issues that inform this chapter. First, that the values as expressed in the standards, which Blair and Daly, in Chapter 2, state are a necessary set of guiding principles for teachers, are in fact a 'work in progress'. By this I mean that the standards have to be turned into something workable and that there is no easy or straightforward answer as to how this might be accomplished. It is not my intention to be pessimistic, but rather to be realistic in acknowledging the complexity and ongoing nature of the task of turning aspirations into observable behaviours. Secondly, and central to this discussion, teachers need to consider where values come from. This will better enable them to think about how they impact upon teaching and learning and how they are then negotiated on a day-to-day basis by both pupils and teachers alike. This will necessarily involve teachers reflecting upon their own values and, most importantly, as part of an honest and objective self-evaluation, is likely to necessitate change. Thirdly, I consider some of the ways that teachers might express these values in every aspect of their work. How might teachers make explicit and clear to parents, pupils and colleagues, the values that underpin their practices? For this standard to be fulfilled I suggest that teachers must not just hold particular values, but they are required to make planned and explicit decisions, visibly reflected in their daily work. Darder (2002) refers to this as to 'walk our talk'. It requires that we struggle to become critically conscious about our practices. In this way teachers are more likely to uncover unexamined assumptions and beliefs about the world that can creep unwittingly into one's practice.

The question of coherence between what teachers think and say they believe and do and what they actually do in practice (Freire 2000) is central to this discussion. However, much of the influence that teachers have upon pupils might best be described as indirect, that is to say, without pupils or teachers being consciously aware of it. 'The indirect moral influence on children is deeply embedded in the daily life of the school, either within normal teaching activities or within the contingent interactions at classroom level' (Halstead and Taylor 2000: 177). In the classroom, this could be, for example, verbal and subtle non-verbal behaviours, more obvious behaviours such as prompt arrival to lessons, careful differentiation of lessons and sensitive marking of work and more easily observed differences in teaching styles. This picture is complicated by the fact that these teacher behaviours will be interpreted differently by different pupils.

Teachers also have a responsibility to clarify their own values and attitudes, and to articulate them, in order to be able to enter into reasoned debate when confronted with opposing views. Teachers often have difficult professional choices to make and understanding their own values may provide them with some rationale for judgements and decisions. Reflecting on their practices may also give them some indication or insight into what it is they value. This is particularly important when challenging the dominant cultural beliefs, such as concepts of 'special educational needs'. Values need to be examined in terms of the experiences of pupils, of teachers' expectations of pupils, and wider economic and political factors that influence the 'what' and the 'why' of our values. The role of the teacher as critical transformative intellectual should not only resonate with all members of the school community, but should extend beyond, in the local community, in teacher unions and other associations, and in the world at large. Learning to teach is a complex and lifelong process. It is much more than the ticking of boxes that demonstrates achievement of competencies. It is also more than a set of technical skills.

The development of professional values is dynamic and complex. It is ongoing and deeply influenced by one's personal history long before one's initial professional teacher education even begins. It is for this reason that this chapter considers raising awareness in three key dimensions. The first section looks at pupils' prior experiences and their influence upon the values pupils bring with them to school and while attending school. The second section considers teacher values and their associated expectations and practices in an inclusive classroom. The final section focuses on the influence of economic and political factors, with particular emphasis on the role of teachers in scrutinising policy and practice in relation to their own beliefs and values.

Clearly all of the chapters in this volume attend to the ways teachers promote positive values. The emphasis in this chapter is on how this operates in the context of inclusive classrooms.

Pupil experiences

Pupils experience school differently, depending on, for example, their age, gender, ability, social class, ethnicity, and how they interact with their teachers and their peers. We know that an individual's values change over time and that their development is a lifelong process (Cairns 2000). Our values are thus constructed in a particular social and political context and climate. Crucially, they are forged in the struggle between conflicting social forces in any given society. Out of these conflicting social forces, collective values and identities may be formed. 'Gender, "race", ability, class, "academic" or "non-academic", anti-school or pro-school may be the salient characteristics of one's identity, but only when school structures and the nature of the school's social mix push that feature into social prominence' (MacBeath and Mortimore 2001: 13).

Social influences on values

Values are thus socially constructed, adopted and adapted in the contexts in which we grow up. The influences of home and community and peer group are clearly significant as are the influences of pop culture and the media. Pupils may be involved in activities out of school, e.g. leisure and religious groups. Guy Claxton (2002) refers to these different groups as nested cultures or clubs, and they can 'vary dramatically in the beliefs and values that underpin the ways of speaking, acting and interrelating which they deem "normal" or proper' (Wells and Claxton 2002: 22). These culture clubs may also value differentially, learning styles and achievements, such as placing a higher value on empathy or co-operation rather than individual effort or academic achievement, preferring a didactic teaching style over discovery learning or 'learning how to learn'. Values encountered in taking part in a range of clubs or activities will be both explicitly and implicitly articulated. 'Some of these interests serve to promote not only personal and social development, but also a growing awareness of being a member of several communities with differing values' (Taylor 1996: 134). For all pupils community language and beliefs are central to their identity and the way they live. Their awareness of the differences that exist between themselves and their peers, though part of the development of self, may give cause for concern or even conflict. Clearly, this has relevance for teachers. Schools and teachers have a significant role in empowering pupils to understand and manage conflict and difference not least by acknowledging that differences are just that, different, and not in any way inferior. In terms of context, school plays a significant part in most children's formative years, and will inevitably have an impact upon the individual's developing value set.

The influence of school on values

Schools vary enormously. They may be rural, urban, inner city, Faith, fee-paying, state, Beacon, selective or comprehensive. They may serve predominantly mono-cultural or multicultural communities. Schools are increasingly requested to articulate in their policies, their underlying values more explicitly and to reflect on the way that the life of the school may contribute to the development of the pupils' values and attitudes (Halstead and Taylor 2000: 176). All will have values enshrined within policies that are likely to differ in a minor or major way from each other and which may in fact not reflect practice. In this context of pupil experience, the type of school one goes to can profoundly effect one's values and indeed life chances. For example, where selection still exists, pupils going to primary school experience selection at age 11, through a narrowly defined examination process known as the 11-plus exam. This system segregates pupils into secondary modern school or grammar school, each with its own particular curriculum, expectations and set of values.

Selection

In the 1950s and 1960s, selection was the norm and pupils who had experience of this segregated education bear the scars even as adults. Writing in the *Times Educational Supplement*, Andrew Granath (2002) cites examples of permanent feelings of inferiority and the creation of family rifts caused by pupils being selected at age 11. Adults reporting back on the experience talk about bearing the weight of parental disappointment, being shamed for lack of academic ability, family tensions caused by one sibling passing the 11-plus and the other failing, chances of going to university denied due to inferior school facilities and low teacher expectations. Alongside this gloomy picture there are, naturally, exceptions: pupils who achieved in spite of discrimination, often citing the support of individual teachers who valued individual difference. None the less, this is an example of values that conspired to devalue individuals and create low expectations of large groups of pupils. We must consider carefully the significant effects on pupils of groupings in classroom organisation, in the light of this experience, and this is discussed further in the next section.

While selection in the form of the 11-plus examination is still apparent in some LEAs, such as Kent and Birmingham, selection is still exercised in schools in England. Standard Assessment Tests (SATs) could be said to perform the current selection process in all schools in England. This is apparent in the form of within-school selection, which sees pupils assigned to particular groups or sets based upon expected or actual performance in National Curriculum tests and between-school selection, in the form of parental choice based upon league tables. SATs exercise a powerful pressure upon teachers, pupils and parents. For pupils, research suggests (Reay and Wiliam 1999; Benjamin *et al.* 2003) that the expected level of performance, as anticipated by teachers' SATs levels, contributes significantly to the way pupils see themselves as learners. Pupils in Year 6 are well aware of the levels they are expected to achieve and it is hard to imagine that this does not have an effect upon their self-esteem. Indeed the research cited above gives real examples of how SATs contributes to the way pupils identify themselves as learners.

For teachers, SATs exerts a powerful and overriding influence upon pedagogy. This is well illustrated not only by random school observations that might be made by any teacher in the school term prior to SATs, but by the research carried out by Kathy Hall and colleagues (Hall *et al.* 2002). They found that teachers spend significant amounts of time teaching to the tests. Group working and discussion is largely abandoned in favour of individual work focusing teaching upon earlier SATs test papers and how to get the 'right answer'. The author's research into group working (ESRC SPRinG project) further supports this change in pedagogical approach. Teachers in the project who were apparently committed to using talk in group working as a means of learning, subjugated this approach in response to the imperative to reach higher levels of achievement in the SATs. One might describe this as SATs shaping the pedagogy. This does not give meaning to the variety of pupil achievements and is thus exclusionary rather than inclusive in its approach. Selection becomes excluding when it values pupils differently, reflected in the ranking of pupils and schools through the mechanism of SATs. In the context of this chapter, teachers will experience dilemmas in reconciling their choices and identifying their values, since compliance with one government policy, such as compliance with summative testing, may mean non-compliance with another such as valuing diversity (Booth 2003). The competitive school market places pressures on schools to exclude some pupils who are unlikely to enhance their status in the league tables. This is the current status and tension of selection in schools.

Importance of teachers listening to pupils

Schools both reflect the values of society and interpret them according to their own local context. In so doing, schools can also provide a forum in which dominant values can be challenged. In recent years schools have increasingly acknowledged the importance of teachers actively listening to their pupils on a variety of issues. Recent research into finding positive alternatives to school exclusion for pupils, has shown that there is a significant link between teachers and schools who actively listen to their pupils and a decrease in the number of pupils excluded. Teachers who enter into a dialogue and who empathise with their pupils 'made a crucial difference to the quality of the students' lives and their commitment to school' (Cooper *et al.* 2000: 188). In terms of how pupils experience school and their perception of themselves as learners then, teachers must give this research serious consideration.

In terms of whole-school approaches, school councils have been developed to 'promote a practical understanding of democratic procedures and the rights and responsibilities of citizenship' (Halstead and Taylor 2000: 178). School councils provide pupils with the opportunities for increased understanding of management issues, enhancing problem-solving abilities by taking into account the perspectives of others, and improving behaviour through an increased consideration of the rights of others and commensurate responsibilities. In their summary of research findings, Halstead and Taylor (2000) cite John and Osborn (1992), who suggested that:

> Schools with more participation and freedom of expression had a stronger influence on pupils' values than the traditional school; in the former, pupils were more supportive of race and gender equality but also more sceptical about the democratic operation of government.

Such research indicates that where schools have a more democratic ethos, where teachers listen and genuinely consult with pupils, school councils operate more effectively and have a significant role in the formation of inclusive values.

'Circle time' is a well used method, particularly in primary schools and increasingly in secondary schools, as a means of promoting confidence, self-esteem and social responsibility and cohesion within the class.

> Circle time may also help pupils to learn to talk about their feelings, to gain a sense of belonging to a group or community, to develop qualities such as trust, responsibility, empathy, co-operation, caring behaviour and respect for the feelings of others and to engage in personal reflection and clarify their own values.
>
> (Halsted and Taylor 2000: 185)

For this method to be effective, it requires teachers to have a clear understanding of the rationale and ways of facilitating the process that empowers the pupils. Not surprisingly, 'Circle time' is most effective if its underlying values are consistent with those of the teacher, the classroom and the school. Jenny Mosely has published several invaluable handbooks explaining the rationale and ethos of Circle time, lesson plans for teachers and ideas for whole-school implementation (Mosely 1993, 1996).

Careful use of language to avoid labelling pupils

Pupils learn a great deal about values from the feedback they receive from their teachers and this is discussed further in Chapter 1. It is suggested that this may be overt or implicit. Furthermore, the language and jargon used by teachers and experienced by pupils, to describe individuals, will not only impact upon pupil performance but on their concepts of self-esteem. There is currently a culture in schools that encourages teachers, through the Government's emphasis on performativity, to consider pupils in terms of 'ability'. It is rare to find a class in England where pupils are not routinely grouped according to so-called 'ability' or what Benjamin calls 'perceived academic ability' that is, performance in tests (Benjamin *et al.* 2003: 548). What is the impact on pupils who are categorised in this way? This was put into sharp focus when I recently worked with a group of 'high ability' seven-year-olds who described one of the 'lower ability' groups as 'they are the weakest link', a reference to the television programme where contestants are eliminated or excluded, as the weakest. What is a child's experience of being pigeon holed in either group and what are the consequences? The expectations that teachers have of their pupils, the way they demonstrate respect and how they value individuals is explored in more detail in the next section.

The labelling of pupils by teachers can lead to self-fulfilling prophecies and negative associations and this is explored more fully in the third and final section of this chapter in the context of government guidelines and policy. In acting with integrity, teachers must be mindful of the language they use to describe pupils both publicly in talking with other professionals, parents/carers and in writing reports or assessments, as well as in discussions with colleagues within the confines of the staff room. The quality of teachers' comments can influence the expectations of pupils, parents/carers and other colleagues.

Valuing pupils' opinions

Do pupils have a sense that their opinions are valued? As reflective teachers, we should also allow our thinking to be challenged and changed by feedback from pupils. This will demonstrate and model the value we put on our own learning through reflective interaction. Pupils' sense of self is shaped by their experiences, and how they construct understanding through experiences has, in turn, significant implications for teachers. How do schools respond to and validate the social and cultural environment in which their pupils live? As has been discussed earlier, actively listening to what pupils have to say about their experiences of school, is one of the most significant values a teacher can both model and encourage. Research shows (Cooper *et al.* 2000; Corbett 2001; O'Brien and Guiney 2001; Hargreaves and Fullan 1998) that teachers who view problems as opportunities for reflection, who are ready to consider that the feedback they receive from their pupils is information upon which they can act in order to better develop their practice, in short, teachers who listen and learn from their pupils, are teachers who value pupils. The processes of inclusive education requires teachers to negotiate and re-negotiate a wide range of pedagogic choices and the intended or unintended outcomes in terms of pupils experiences. This leads us to the second section, teachers' values and expectations, which considers some of these issues and others, in different contexts.

Teachers' values and expectations

Qualifying to Teach states that teachers must have high expectations for all pupils (TTA 2004: 2; see also Chapter 1 in this volume). This is echoed within numerous government documents and guidelines (e.g. *National Curriculum 2000*; *Special Education Needs Code of Practice* (DfES 2001a); *Inclusive Schooling* (DfES 2001b); *Key Stage 3 National Strategy* (DfES 2003a); *Excellence and Enjoyment* (DfES 2003b); *Primary National Strategy* (DfES 2004a); *Removing Barriers to Achievement* (DfES 2004b); *Every Child Matters* (DfES 2004c)). But what does 'having high expectations' mean or look like in our classrooms? According to the standards it means that teachers will have an understanding that 'all their pupils are capable of significant progress and that their potential for learning is unlimited' (TTA 2004: 2). Raising attainment for all through inclusive educational practices is central.

Fostering inclusion and the motivation to learn

The National Curriculum has set out three key principles that are essential to developing inclusive education:

1. Setting suitable learning challenges;

2. Responding to pupils' diverse learning;

3. Overcoming potential barriers to learning and assessment for individuals and groups of pupils.

These are accompanied by examples of good practice and are to be welcomed. Teachers are able to find a growing body of exemplification materials that support inclusive teaching practices for all key stages that are produced by the Qualifications and Curriculum Authority (QCA).

I would like to take this opportunity to clarify the term inclusion. There is much written and debated about inclusive education, featuring as it does in numerous government documents and guidelines. Inclusion in education is about the processes that schools, local education authorities and others undertake in order to develop their culture, policy and practices that removes barriers to learning and participation for all. Inclusion is not about location nor is it narrowly confined to children with special educational needs (SEN), but it is about processes and change. It necessarily involves a critique of the discriminatory and exclusionary social practices that exist, including a close scrutiny of notions of what is mean by 'normal'. It is a journey undertaken by teachers that has no end, as we seek to understand the issues of human rights, equal opportunities and social justice.

To be an inclusive teacher requires imagination and no doubt a certain amount of risk taking. If teachers see inclusion as processes of growth and change then it becomes less threatening. Inclusive approaches to education require teachers to hold inclusive values. Inclusive values are about education for diversity, the political act of placing value on all, and are articulated through the choice of pedagogy, curriculum, organisation, ethos and relationships. Jenny Corbett (2001) suggests that a connective pedagogy is at the heart of inclusive practices. A connective pedagogy addresses individual needs without isolating or stigmatising individuals, engages institutional resources and relates to community values. It is, most importantly, about linking individuals into the curriculum so that it has relevance and is meaningful to them. Important aspects of pedagogy will include encouraging pupils to think about how they learn, to evaluate their learning and the effectiveness of their current strategies (Moore 2000). Motivation to learn was cited as long ago as the Elton Report as a key factor in managing behaviour – 'Good behaviour has a lot to do with pupils' motivation to learn' (DES 1989: para. 4.70).

An essential element of this connective pedagogy is the requirement of teachers to develop emotional literacy (Hanko 2003; Sharp 2001; Bennathan and Boxall 2000) for themselves and their pupils. Teachers who provide emotional support for their pupils understand the vital links between feelings and motivation to learn. The use of 'Circle time' has already been mentioned as one approach, where pupils are 'encouraged to share solutions to situations that all of them would have experienced at some time, and would experience again as part of the human condition, such as feeling sad, lost, angry or disappointed' (Hanko 2003: 127). The strategy know as 'Circle of Friends' (Newton and Wilson 1999), is organised so that the pupils most at risk of exclusion or bullying, are supported by their peers. Nurture groups, most often found in primary schools, are 'designed to bridge the divide between emotional, social and cognitive development for children who had missed out on such crucial pre-school experiences as care and trust' (Hanko 2003: 127). These are but a few approaches to meeting the emotional dimensions of learning.

At the time of writing the Government has acknowledged the importance of the affective curriculum and is in the process of piloting materials within the context of The *Primary National Strategy* (DFES 2004a) 'promoting social, emotional and behavioural skills in the primary school'. There is guidance on the way so that teachers can model appropriate behaviour as well as guidance on teaching and learning strategies, language, relationships, class routines, understanding the often complex reasons for the way pupils behave and beliefs with regard to equal opportunity and inclusion. Clearly these factors will contribute to pupils' motivation to learn and many of these factors are addressed in this volume.

A connective pedagogy also requires of teachers a readiness to use different styles in their teaching (see Chapter 2 in this volume) and, most importantly, to take account of cultural factors. Moore suggests that while teachers cannot have an intimate knowledge of all the cultures of their pupils, 'they can avoid making easy assumptions about those cultures or refusing to acknowledge that they exist at-all' (Moore 2000: 114). Teachers must critically question occasions of inclusion and exclusion and the reproduction of inequalities.

It has been suggested that the National Curriculum supports a largely monocultural approach to education (Runnymede Trust 2000), and it marginalises and excludes through its curriculum and assessment procedures, large numbers of pupils in multicultural Britain (Gillborn and Mirza 2000). This is dramatically illustrated through quotes taken from Focus Group Research from pupils who find it difficult to relate to curriculum content. One pupil commented, 'at school . . . you read books about white people . . . you never see anyone in a book like a black hero,' while another remarked 'when I was at school, they weren' teaching me history and geography that was relevant to me and my experiences' (Runnymede Trust 2000: 4).

Are teachers aware of the cultural bias that exists in the National Curriculum? While the National Curriculum and TTA standards for teachers make statements that refer explicitly to respecting cultural diversity, 'their mere inclusion does not amount to a curriculum with cultural diversity at its very core' (Runnymede Trust 2000). Teachers should consider how they incorporate pupils existing experiences and cultural preferences into all curriculum areas. The valuing of cultural diversity and the combating of racism and antiracism needs to permeate the teaching and learning materials of all curriculum subjects. Welcome developments are being made by QCA to provide teachers with examples of resources and opportunities that enrich the curriculum to embrace diversity and combat racism. An example is *Respect for all* (QCA materials available on their website) which sets out the principles of valuing all pupils cultures and diversity and of challenging racism through the curriculum. As a teacher it is of vital importance that we take advantage of such resources and ideas, making them relevant to local context. To look at the ways the formal curriculum is planned and taught, so that it 'helps children acquire appropriate positive attitudes and values and a healthy self-esteem' (Macpherson 2000: 99).

Bourdieu's (1977) ideas about 'cultural capital' suggests that learners are advantaged or disadvantaged by the value systems they encounter at school (see also Chapters 2 and 4 in this volume). How do teachers acknowledge, respect and value the 'cultural capital' that learners bring to school? Schools and teachers must be sensitive to and value the identities of students and make efforts to reinforce the confidence, motivation and self-esteem of pupils by including in the curriculum their histories, languages, religions and cultures (Blair *et al.* (1999)

cited in Moore 2000). Teachers can ensure that antiracist and multicultural issues and perspectives are integral in resources they use.

There is no doubt that pupils are influenced by the quality of relationships which they experience in school. It is important for pupils, to feel that their teacher knows and is interested in them as an individual and not just a member of a group. Teachers can do this formally through records that are kept of pupils, but also through informal chats where they get to know more about individual pupils including their language, likes and interests. The way that teachers relate to their pupils will significantly contribute to a pupil's own sense of developing values and self-esteem. In order to learn effectively pupils need to feel secure, be involved in the formation of class rules and routines that guide behaviour, understand the consequence of their choices and have a sense that the adults can be trusted to create a safe environment where pupils have a right to learn and teachers the right to teach (Docking 2002).

The way teachers communicate feedback about engagement with tasks to their pupils, can foster what Claxton refers to as resilience (Claxton 2002). This is the ability of a pupil to stick with a task when it starts to get difficult, which is clearly a useful quality for learners. The kind of feedback teachers give to pupils can give subtle or not so subtle messages about their 'ability'. Put simply, there appears to be two views of 'ability'. One view sees ability as fixed, somewhat akin to intelligence, and something that determines performance and success. The other sees it as something that is changeable and related to learning resources. Pupils who encounter discourse that is associated with the fixed view of ability (as reflected in many of our classrooms where grouping is by fixed ability, for example), are more likely to encourage less resilient learners, having the attitude that they 'can't do it' because of some innate deficit. Whereas a culture that values effort as much as achievement is more likely to foster robust attitudes to learning. If teachers value perseverance as much as achievement this is likely to teach pupils that effort is valued, can lead to success and in this way is more likely to lead to pupils valuing themselves as learners.

The beliefs a teacher has about attitudes to learning are reflected in comments they make to pupils during the learning process. Are reassuring comments made when a teacher notices a pupil battling against difficulty? Are positive comments made only when success is achieved? A teacher who says, 'Let's think about how we can do this' gives the pupil the idea that success is possible, given persistence and of course tasks that are within the grasp of pupil. Teachers can also model being learners themselves through, for example, admitting if they don't know the answer to a problem and discussing how they might go about finding out something new. In this way they demonstrate to their pupils that learning is something we all do and it never stops.

Promoting intellectual curiosity – interactive approaches

I have already identified the way that the personal beliefs of teachers are reflected in many and subtle ways which impact upon the pupils they teach. If it is the role of teachers to meet the needs of all learners in their classes, then it is incumbent upon teachers to 'reflect on their pedagogical repertoire, their assumptions about curriculum and classroom and school organisation, along with the ideologies that inform these components of schooling' (Cole 1997: 64). A teacher's pedagogical approach will influence the learning opportunities offered to pupils. Teachers who value and encourage spirited and enquiring minds will do so in a way that complements and supports a broad and balanced educational experience, which includes diverse cultural and linguistic dimensions. The promotion of attitudes that foster enquiry and investigation rather than the right answer will be an integral part of a culture that promotes intellectual curiosity. So, how do teachers model and promote intellectual curiosity working as they do within a well-defined, some might say, overly prescribed curriculum? Observations in classrooms reveal that teachers who foster interactive approaches to teaching and learning, where pupils explore, experience and investigate, are better able to maintain that intellectual curiosity characteristic of young children. The principles of an interactive approach according to Collis and Lacey (1996: 13) are:

- Learning is contingent upon good interpersonal relationships.
- There is sensitivity to feedback from the learner.
- Focus on understanding rather than skill acquisition.
- Emphasis is on respect, negotiation and participation. The pupil's contribution is valued and positively built upon.

Within classrooms this is represented by a range of organisational choices, such as co-operative group working, the use of talk to co-construct knowledge, pupils making choices and thus having more responsibility for their own learning, evaluating and monitoring their own learning and progress. This kind of interactive learning is usually fun and motivating. The use of games is often observed in interactive teaching since they provide opportunities to practise skills in a modelled way, where it is safe to make mistakes. Creative thinking and behaviour can be promoted in all National Curriculum subjects and allows pupils the opportunity to discover and pursue their own particular interests and talents (DfEE 1999; QCA 2004a).

Research over the last 30 years has shown that collaborative group working has the potential to be highly beneficial to all pupils in terms of raising attainment and increased motivation to learn (*International Journal of Educational Research* 39, Issues 1–2, 2003). However, for group working to be successful, teachers are required to have an understanding of the social pedagogy that is involved; put simply this is the integration of the social as well as task components. For group working to be successful, as with any teaching strategy, it must be carefully planned by the teacher so that it is fit for purpose and the pupils themselves will require the skills necessary to be able to operate as a member of a group. This will involve taking into account:

- group size (e.g. twos, threes or fours)
- the membership of the group (e.g. based on, friendship, mixed attainment, mixed or single sex, interest or random)
- the task (does it lend itself to group working?)
- the level of skills of the pupils that enables them to work constructively in a group.

The Government has recognised the value of collaborative group work and of the benefits of talk to co-construct meaning and has produced a useful INSET package (QCA 2004b).

The *Index for Inclusion*

An important aspect of having high expectations, is concerned with the language teachers use. Language is a powerful medium with great potential. It can, among other things, raise self-esteem through the use of specific praise; or it can lead to a negative, self-fulfilling prophecy, reinforcing stereotypes based on characteristics that are traditionally attached to a label, for example the stereotype of the child with Down's Syndrome child as being happy and loving. The *Index for Inclusion* (CSIE 2000) makes a point of not using the label of 'special educational needs' (SEN) unless it is referring to its embodiment in legislation or policy framework. The reasons for this are comprehensive and reflect certain values. The label 'SEN' can lead to lowered expectations and can encourage teachers to think that pupils who are categorised as having SEN are primarily the responsibility of a specialist teacher or school. An approach that focuses on individual difficulties 'has limitations as a way or resolving educational difficulties and can be a barrier to the development of inclusive practices in schools' (CSIE 2000: 13).

Teachers are concerned with reducing barriers to learning for a broad range of pupils, including, for example, those from minority ethnic communities and those disadvantaged for reasons of gender, disability, sexuality and social class (Cole 2005a; Hill and Cole 2001). They have a responsibility to cater for the needs of travellers, looked-after children, refugees, children who move schools frequently, pupils for whom English is an additional language and pupils living in poverty.

Peter Mittler suggests that 'although we use the language of diversity, social justice and equal opportunities, the society in which we live is still riddled with inequalities, which are in turn reflected in the education system' (Mittler 2000: 12; see also Cole 2005a; Hill and Cole 2001). Teachers thus have a significant role to play in shifting the interests of disadvantaged groups, from the margins of society and school to centre stage, in part through a close examination of their own attitudes and beliefs. How a teacher's values chime with local, national and global directions on equality issues, how far they are prepared to enter into a reflective debate at both a conceptual and a real-life classroom level, will determine how successful change might be (Mittler 2000). Research (e.g. Sebba and Sachdev 1997) and personal experience indicates that the greatest barriers to inclusion are the attitudes and values that teachers possess. How hearts and minds are won over will remain to be seen, but certainly the use, by schools, of the *Index for Inclusion* (CSIE 2000) is a step in the right direction for a close scrutiny of values in policy, practice and culture.

While it is not in itself a curriculum, The *Index for Inclusion* does encourage schools to take an approach that celebrates diversity in all forms. It is a tool that can assist teachers and schools in 'a detailed examination of the possibilities for increasing learning and participation in all aspects of their school for all students' (CSIE 2000: 7). In attempting to make the curriculum accessible and relevant, teachers will be required to differentiate what they teach and how they teach it, in ways that do not lead to further segregation (Mittler 2000).

The importance of reflection

To summarise this section, our values contribute to the kind of teacher we are or hope to be. The things we believe in underpin our professional identity. We teach in certain ways because we have certain beliefs that guide our teaching methods. Reflecting on our practices as a teacher may give some insight or indication into what we value and why. It is important, therefore, for teachers to have a thorough understanding of how pupils learn as well as knowledge of the way ethnicity, gender, class, religion, poverty and disability impact upon teaching and learning and educational achievement.

> A key implication of all this is that teachers need to review on a regular basis their beliefs and attitudes about learners and learning and challenge constantly the expectations they have of their pupils, as well as seeking to understand and enhance the motivation of those they are teaching.
>
> (Gipps and MacGilchrist 1999: 59)

In order to enter into this spirit of reflection, teachers will need the time, support and the inclination to think and discuss, both with colleagues who are likely to share a greater degree of consensus and with others that may have very different values (Ghaye and Ghaye 1998).

Perhaps one of the most significant issues for teachers is to realise that education is a political act. Teaching and learning in all aspects within schools constitutes 'a political act tied to the ideological forces of the dominant class' (Darder 2002: 56). For a simple example of this we need to look no further than the introduction of the National Curriculum in 1988. It emanated during a period in the 1970s when there was government concern about declining manufacturing industries, mounting unemployment and a skill shortage in vocational occupations. Social policy, particularly education policy was seen as a way of addressing these issues. The Government saw education as a way of 'servicing the needs of industry and the economy – as opposed to addressing social inequalities by providing equality of opportunity' (Runnymede Trust 2000: 1). As teachers develop their understanding of the politics of class, ethnicity, religion, sexuality, gender and disability they will be better placed to bring about the changes required of inclusive practitioners. The hidden values and practices of an educational system that perpetuate inequalities, such as labelling pupils according to test performance and school league tables that officially classify schools and pupils as failing and produce large numbers of excluded pupils, will be exposed through critical thinking.

In this way teachers will be 'thoughtful, questioning, perceptive as well as skilled in the pursuit of a democratic, anti-authoritarian, socially responsible, socially just and equal society' (Hill *et al.* 1997: 108).

Economic and political factors

It is almost impossible to separate out the personal development of one's values from wider economic and political influences. As we have seen through the previous two sections, we do not grow up and go to school in a political or cultural vacuum. Our experience of life and of school is inevitably controlled by the economic and political agenda of the day. This is evident from the discussion so far, which has made reference to a number of government policy initiatives that have had a profound impact upon what happens in schools. As teachers are required to have regard to government guidance, I should like to consider the influence of political policy on values and practice.

Teachers are responsible for the education of all the pupils in their class. It is vital, therefore that they adopt an inclusive attitude to teaching and learning. This value is not negotiable. '*Removing Barriers to Achievement* sets out the Government's vision for giving children with special educational needs and disabilities the opportunity to succeed' (DfES 2004b). It is disappointing that the opportunity to include all pupils who experience barriers to learning and participation, is missed. Focusing on SEN and disability continues to perpetuate the narrow view of inclusion. Even within this volume there is an assumption that we all know what 'SEN' means, that it is child-deficit centred, clearly observable and measurable and is often the domain of the specialist teacher. It is, I suggest, not this fixed state, but a social construct that changes over time and place. An excellent overview of this is provided by the video *Altogether Better* (Mason and Rieser 1995).

This is not to deny that there are many pupils who experience barriers to learning, but to highlight the limitations of this way of categorising people. One of the dangers is that it encourages teachers to believe that pupils who experience barriers to learning and participation are the responsibility of other professionals, such as speech and language therapists or the behaviour support service, for example. It is pertinent to flag up the contradiction here between the revised *SEN Code of Practice* (DfES 2001a) and the *Index for Inclusion* (CSIE 2000), both of which are endorsed by the Government, but which convey very different, and one might suggest, contradictory values. Inspite of a brief acknowledgement in the *SEN Code of Practice* that schools may exacerbate or even cause children to have difficulties in learning (and behaviour for that matter) (DfES 2001a 18: para. 5) the Code still focuses essentially upon within-child deficits, with its emphasis on Individual Education Plans (IEPs). The Index, however, not only embraces the learning of all pupils, but more importantly, encourages us to consider factors beyond the individual pupil, to the impact of the culture, policy and practice of schools. As teachers, we can only reconcile these two pieces of guidance through critical reflection not blind acceptance.

Such initiatives are in turn affected by global economic processes. For example, Cole (1998, 2005b) has argued that the Blair Government's mantra of 'Education, Education, Education' needs to be seen in the light of New Labour's commitment to global capitalism. In order for Britain to produce a flexible workforce, a requirement of contemporary capitalism, it is important for education to be reformed (for business to have a greater influence both within schools and as the recipient of contracted out education services). Globalisation is used ideologically as the *raison d'être* of New Labour's education policy, and modernisation (a final break with Old Labour and socialist values) is the conduit through which the policy is introduced (Cole 2005b; see also Allen *et al.* 1999). As I have suggested above, however, education does not only reflect social and economic processes, it can also challenge them. An understanding of this dynamic will certainly be part of any discussion that is related to values, including a consideration of the consequences of policy on teaching and learning. It is clear that there are negative effects of government policy on how schools and teachers take on board the concept of inclusion as an equal rights issue. Legislation and guidance has seen an emphasis on standards and league tables, and competition that exerts exclusionary forces for example, while at the same time encouraging the inclusion of pupils with complex learning and social and emotional needs.

Legislation and the value systems enshrined therein have always heavily influenced education. Currently there appears to be, at best, a somewhat fragmented and contradictory number of government policies contributing to an education system where there are conflicts of values and thus incompatible demands. We are now living in an enterprise culture, driven by the market forces of competition, consumer choice, targets, league tables, a national system of normative assessment with the results used to measure school effectiveness, yet at the same time, a tenuous encouragement towards inclusive education. What is the potential impact of consumer-type policy upon teachers' and pupils' values? To return to a view expressed earlier in this chapter, it is incumbent upon teachers to scrutinise their values and practices to analyse and reflect on economic and political realities and to enable and encourage their pupils to do likewise in order to ensure the promotion of equality, to challenge stereotyping and to counter discrimination.

Conclusion

It is not possible to discuss professional values without being clear about our own values. Changes imposed by government legislation impacts upon the culture and values of the school we work in. In this situation, how can a teacher shape what kind of teacher they are or aspire to be and what goes on in their classrooms? Susan Hart reminds us that,

> while the pressures of classroom teaching clearly impose major constraints on what is possible, the extent to which teaching is reflective is also a function of teachers' values and aspirations for children's learning and the extent to which classroom practices have been developed and adjusted reflect these
>
> (Hart 2000: 41)

What is taught, how it is taught, how long a topic is given and how it is given prominence, what materials are used, how pupils are allowed to interact with each or not are just a few examples of the power given to teachers. Teachers must therefore accept that they have this power and make thoughtful and informed decisions in the pursuit of social justice (Darder 2002). This is why teachers must be clear which values underpin their decision making.

Whatever their background, teachers have to respond to the diversity of values of the pupils, parents/carers and community they work with. Teachers must be able to support their pupils so they appreciate that differences between and among people are usual and at the same time develop the skills necessary to cope with any conflicts this might cause.

Teachers will need to have opportunities to discuss values, to reflect on their values and scrutinise their practices in honest and transparent ways. This is a challenging task, but in this way we might ensure a community in which everyone is valued, in order to secure the highest social, emotional and academic achievements of all students.

Note

1   While pupils need to understand that values are relative, they also need to consider the possibility of a core of absolute values – social justice being one.

References

Allen, M., Benn, C., Chitty, C. *et al.* (1999) *Business, Business, Business: New Labour's education policy*. London: Tufnell Press.

Benjamin, S., Nind, M., Hall, K., Collins, J. and Sheehy, K. (2003) 'Moments of inclusion and exclusion: pupils negotiating classroom contexts', *British Journal of Sociology of Education*, 24 (5), 547–58.

Bennathan, M. and Boxall, M. (2000) *Effective Intervention in Primary Schools – Nurture Groups*, 2nd edn. London: David Fulton.

Blair, M. and Bourne, J. with Coffin, C., Creese, A. and Kenner, C. (1999) *Making the Difference: teaching and learning strategies in successful multi-ethnic schools*. DfEE Research Briefs, Research No. 59. London: Department for Education and Employment.

Booth, T. (2003) 'Inclusion and exclusion in the city: concepts and contexts', in Potts, P. (ed.) *Inclusion in The City*. London: Routledge/Falmer.

Bourdieu, P. (1977) *Outline of a Theory of Practice*. Cambridge: Cambridge University Press.

Cairns, J. (2000) 'Schools, community and the developing values of young adults: towards an ecology of education in values', in Cairns, J., Gardner, R. and Lawton, D. (eds) (2000) *Values and the Curriculum*. London: Woburn Press.

Centre for Studies on Inclusive Education (CSIE) (2000) *Index for Inclusion*. CSIE in collaboration with Centre for Educational Needs, University of Manchester; Centre for Education Research, Canterbury Christ Church College.

Claxton, G. (2002) *Building Learning Power*. Bristol: TLO Limited.

Cole, M. (1997) 'Equality and primary education: what are the conceptual issues?', in Cole, M., Hill, D. and Shan, S. (eds) *Promoting Equality in Primary Schools*. London: Cassell.

Cole, M. (1998) 'Globalization, modernization and competitiveness: a critique of the New Labour Project in education', *International Studies in Sociology of Education*, 8 (3), 315–32.

Cole, M. (ed.) (2005a) *Education, Equality and Human Rights: issues of gender, 'race', sexuality, disability and social class*, 2nd edn. London: Routledge/Falmer.

Cole, M. (2005b) 'New Labour, globalization and social justice: the role of education', in Fischman, G., McLaren, P., Sunker, H. and Lankshear, C. (eds) *Critical Theories, Radical Pedagogies and Global Conflicts*. Lanham, Maryland: Rowman and Littlefield.

Collis, M. and Lacey, P. (1996) *Interactive Approaches to Teaching*. London: David Fulton Publishers.

Cooper, P., Drummond, M. J., Hart, S., Lovey, J. and McLaughlin, C. (2000) *Positive Alternatives to Exclusion*. London: Routledge/Falmer.

Corbett, J. (2001) *Supporting Inclusive Education*. London: Routledge/Falmer.

Darder, A. (2002) *Reinventing Paulo Freire: a pedagogy of love*. Boulder, Co: Westview.

DES (1989) *Discipline in Schools Report of the Committee of Inquiry chaired by Lord Elton*. London: The Stationery Office.

DfEE (1999) *All Our Futures: creativity, culture and education*. London: The Stationery Office.

DfES (2001a) *Special Educational Needs Code of Practice*. Annesley, Nottinghamshire: DfES.

DfES (2001b) *Inclusive Schooling: children with special educational needs*. Annesley, Nottinghamshire: DfES.

DfES (2003a) *Key Stage 3 National Strategy: key messages pedagogy and practice*. London: The Stationery Office.

DfES (2003b) *Excellence and Enjoyment: a strategy for primary schools*. London: The Stationery Office.

DfES (2004a) *Primary National Strategy*. London: The Stationery Office.

DfES (2004b) *Removing Barriers to Achievement*. London: The Stationery Office.

DfES (2004c) *Every Child Matters*. London: The Stationery Office.

Docking, J. (2002) *Managing Behaviour in the Primary Classroom*, 3rd edn. London: David Fulton.

Freire, P. (2000) *Pedagogy of the Oppressed*. London: Continuum.

Ghaye, A. and Ghaye, K. (1998) *Teaching and Learning through Critical Reflective Practice*. London: David Fulton Publishers.

Gillborn, D. and Mirza, H. (2000) *Educational Inequality: mapping race, class and gender*. London: Institute of Education, University of London.

Gipps, C. and MacGilchrist, B. (1999) 'Primary school learners', in Mortimore, P. (ed.) *Understanding Pedagogy and its Impact on Learning*. London: Paul Chapman.

Granath, A. (2002) 'Rift at 11-plus still smarts after 40 years', *Times Educational Supplement*, 'Talkback', 3 May 2002.

Hall, K., Collins, J., Nind, M., Sheehy, K. and Benjamin, S. (2002) 'Assessment and Inclusion/Exclusion: SATurated models of pupildom'. Presented at the BERA Conference, Exeter.

Halstead, J. M. and Taylor, M. J. (eds) (1996) *Values in Education and Education in Values*. London: Falmer Press.

Halstead, J. M. and Taylor, M. J. (2000) 'Learning and teaching about values: a review of recent research', *Cambridge Journal of Education*, 3 (2), 169–202.

Hanko, G. (2003) 'Towards an inclusive school culture – but what happened to Elton's affective curriculum?', *British Journal of Special Education*, 30, 3.

Hargreaves, A. and Fullan, M. (1998) *What's Worth Fighting for in Education?* Buckingham: Open University Press.

Hart, S. (2000) *Thinking Through Teaching: a framework for enhancing participation and learning*. London: David Fulton Publishers.

Hill, D. and Cole, M. (eds) (2001) *Schooling and Equality*. London: Kogan Page.

Hill, D., Cole, M. and Williams, C. (1997) 'Equality and primary teacher education', in Cole, M., Hill, D. and Shan, S (eds) *Promoting Equality in Primary Schools*. London: Cassell.

John, P. D. and Osborn, A. (1992) 'The influence of school ethos on pupils' citizenship attitudes', *Educational Review*, 44, 153–65.

MacBeath, J. and Mortimore, P. (2001) 'School effectiveness and improvement: the story so far', in MacBeath, J. and Mortimore, P. (eds) *Improving School Effectiveness*. Buckingham: Open University Press.

Macpherson, P. (2000) 'Creating a positive classroom climate', in Jacques, K. and Hyland, R. (eds) *Professional Studies*. Exeter: Learning Matters Ltd.

Mason, M. and Rieser, R. (1995) *Altogether Better: from 'special needs' to equality in education* (video). London: Charity Projects.

Mittler, P. (2000) *Working Towards Inclusive Education*. London: David Fulton Publishers.

Moore, A. (2000) *Teaching and Learning: pedagogy, curriculum and culture*. London: Routledge/Falmer.

Moseley, J. (1993) *Turn Your School Around*. Wisbech: LDA.

Moseley, J. (1996) *Quality Circle Time*. Wisbech: LDA.

National Curriculum 2000 http://www.lsda.org.uk/curriculum2000/ (accessed January 2005).

Newton, C. and Wilson, D. (1999) *Circle of Friends*. Dunstable: Folens.

O'Brien, T. and Guiney, D. (2001) *Differentiation in Teaching and Learning*. London: Continuum.

QCA (2000) *Curriculum 2000. Appendix on General Inclusion Statement*. London: QCA.

QCA *Respect for All: valuing diversity and challenging racism through the curriculum* www.qca.org.uk/301.html (accessed January 2005).

QCA (2004a) *Creativity: find it, promote it*. London: QCA.

QCA (2004b) *Developing Speaking and Listening*. London: QCA.

Reay, D. and Wiliam, D. (1999) ' "I'll be a nothing": structure, agency and the construction of identity through assessment', *British Educational Research Journal*, 25 (3), 343–54.

Runnymede Trust (2000) 'Curriculum 2000 – monocultural or multicultural?', Briefing paper, September. http://www.runnymedetrust.org/publications/pdfs/curriculum2000. pdf (accessed February 2005).

Sebba, J. and Sachdev, D. (1997) *What Works in Inclusive Education*. Ilford, Essex: Barnardo's.

Sharp, P. (2001) *Nurturing Emotional Literacy*. London: David Fulton.

Taylor, M. J. (1996) 'Voicing their values: pupils' moral and cultural experience', in Halstead, J. M. and Taylor, M. J. (eds) *Values in Education and Education in Values*. London: Falmer Press.

Teacher Training Agency (TTA) (2002) *Handbook on Guidance on QTS Standards and ITT Requirements*. London: DfES.

Teacher Training Agency (TTA) (2004) *Qualifying to Teach: professional standards for Qualified Teacher Status and requirements for initial teacher training*. London: TTA.

Wells, G. and Claxton, G. (2002) *Learning for Life in the 21st Century*. London: Blackwell.

Communication with parents and carers

Linda Hurley

Those awarded Qualified Teacher Status must understand and uphold the professional code of the General Teaching Council for England by demonstrating . . . [that] they can communicate sensitively and effectively with parents and carers, recognising their roles in pupils' learning, and their rights, responsibilities and interests in this.

(TTA 2004: 7 Section 1.4)

Learning objectives

To encourage teachers to:

- be aware of the importance of including all parents and carers in their children's education
- understand some of the challenges, the reasons for them and to reflect on some possible solutions
- identify opportunities for parental/carer involvement
- reflect on their own attitudes and behaviours towards parents and carers in order to develop sensitive and professional working relationships.

Introduction

'We have one mother we're definitely not encouraging to come in. The child's got a statement and we feel it's in their best interests – she's very awkward. We haven't encouraged it.'

Susan, head teacher

'When she spoke to me I didn't like it. There was a lot of us who felt like that . . . She looked down on all of us – you're not good enough. If you carried a brief case you were all right.'

Norma, parent

PARENTAL SUPPORT FOR SCHOOLS IS widely recognised as a crucial determinant of children's educational performance. Since the Plowden Report of 1967 (DES 1967), which highlighted the importance of schools and parents working together, the relationship between the two is regularly pulled back into focus (Bastiani 1989; Epstein 1995; Sammons *et al.* 1995). For some time, despite universal recommendations for schools and parents to work together, implementation of this as a practice was patchy and arbitrary. There is now much current, practical advice for schools on how to engage parents (DfES website http://www.dfes.gov.uk/; CSIE 2000). There are also clear criteria for the effectiveness of this from Ofsted (Ofsted 2003).

However, parent/carers are often seen as a homogenous group, devoid of class, culture, sexuality and diversity, and whose willingness to engage in their children's education is whimsical. There is extensive research which has investigated the nature of parent response and the factors affecting it (Lareau 1989; Brown 1993; Pollard and Filer 1996; Vincent 1996, 2000; Reay 1999; Hughes and Macnaughton 2000). This research concludes that some parents are more easily included by schools than others and links this fact with features such as ethnicity and social class, as above. However, literature which advises schools on strategies to include parents and carers rarely takes into account excluded groups and if it does, social class is ignored.

This chapter attempts to address inclusion for *all* parent/carers. It builds on a body of research and extends the issue to one of teacher identity. It attempts to identify problematic areas, the reasons for them and the challenges they present to teachers. It draws on the work of Epstein (1995) and research cited above, and sets parental involvement against the backdrop of inclusion. It includes data from my own research on parental involvement in areas of social exclusion.

Inclusion

In 2000, the Centre for Studies on Inclusive Education (CSIE) published an *Index for Inclusion*, a document giving guidance to schools and promoting the Government's agenda on providing inclusive education for all children.

The *Index* challenges schools to reflect the communities they serve, to celebrate differences, and become places where 'diversity is not seen as a problem to be overcome but a rich resource to support the learning of all' (CSIE 2000: 12).

It includes a recognition that parents and families are members of communities which have a right and a responsibility to be included in the education of children, that they have valuable contributions to make and are an essential part of the community of the school. It takes for granted that a truly inclusive school welcomes *all* parents and regards them as *'partners'* in a child's education. Even in schools with a strong commitment to home–school partnerships, a dialogue with *all* parents is difficult to achieve. In all schools some parent/carers are highly active while others are rarely seen. Why is this? What makes communication with some so easy while with others it is laboured, misunderstood and fraught with tensions? Parents can be seen as uncaring, difficult, obstructive, to be 'dealt with' rather than included. All this results in a 'them and us' situation where a 'legitimate discourse' (Habermas 1973) is seen by the school as impossible. How does this happen and what can teachers do about it?

Parents as partners

The document 'Effective schools and home–school partnership roles: a framework for parental involvement' provides a model for parents as 'co-communicators, co-supporters, co-learners and co-decision makers' (Chrispeels 1996).

In school policy documents, including Ofsted data (Ofsted 2003), parent/carers are often referred to as 'partners'. However, the term 'partners' assumes a balance of equality in the relationship. The literature points to relationships between lay people and professionals, which are often imbalanced in terms of knowledge and, therefore, power (Merttens *et al.* 1996; Vincent 1996; Reay 1999). While this is true, even parent/carers who are familiar with the world of education can feel inadequate to deal with their own children's schooling (Bastiani 1989). (How many teachers do you know who dread attending their own children's open evenings?)

Ofsted (1999: 24) reports that 'the link between low attainment and disadvantage remains strong and persistent'. The growing gap between the rich and the poor has become accepted as 'the way things are' for many, us as well as them. This acceptance feeds into a culture where those without are seen in some way as responsible for their own situation. What's more, 'Life makes some people drop out of school and for some reason they tend to blame themselves' (Ball *et al.* in Reay 2004).

In recent years, schools have recognised a responsibility to meet the needs of an increasingly multicultural society and begun to address this by, for example, introducing multicultural literature and recognising a variety of faiths and practices. This is the beginning of a dialogue between home and school for those from minority ethnic communities. However, ethnicity is not the only reason for parental exclusion. Social class is a factor largely unrecognised by teachers as being responsible for parents' exclusion from their children's schools.[1] The overwhelming reason for this is not a lack of interest or commitment, but:

- their own experience at school, which was one of alienation leading to poor attendance and leading to . . .
- lack of skills and knowledge, leading to . . .
- low self-esteem and fear of school, sometimes compounded by teachers' lack of awareness of the significance of the above.

(Hurley 2000a)

Reay notes that although working-class parents are anxious to support their children's schooling, this support is characterised by 'lack of knowledge, of inappropriate educational standards and an uncertainty about their competence as educators' (Reay 1999: 78).

In fact, however confident and successful parents are as members of their community, this success is often not transferrable to school (Vincent 2000; Hurley 2000b). Often parent/carer skills are not known about or recognised by the school as being important (e.g. parent/carers who are able to fix electrical equipment, mend clothes, look after one another's children). This lack of recognition for a different kind of cultural capital make working-class parents the most acceptable to ignore and can make them the most difficult to include. These findings reaffirm the critical importance of sensitive teacher–parent relationships. They are issues which we, as teachers committed to the notion of inclusion, need to consider by examining our own perceptions and attitudes and the ethos of our schools.

What follows is an analysis of the different types of parental involvement as defined by Epstein (1995), the challenges they pose to us as professionals, and some practical suggestions for meeting these challenges. All teacher and parent quotes are from recent research (Hurley 2000a, b, 2002)[2] unless otherwise stated.

Six ways to involve parent/carers in schools

Epstein (1995) identified six types of parental involvement. These are:

1. Parenting
2. Communicating
3. Volunteering
4. Learning at home
5. Decision making
6. Collaborating with the community.

These six types are followed by an explanation of the school's role and suggestions of opportunities in practice.

1. Parenting

This section discusses ways to help all parent/carers establish home environments to support children as students.

Effective parenting skills have a significant impact on a child's development and progress at school. In most cases parents feel their role is paramount and demonstrate an impressive list of skills which reflect devotion to their children:

'The kids are my job.'

Bunty, a mum

Jane, a learning support teacher helping children and parents with their literacy skills, was working with Carol and her daughter. Carol had been banned from school premises for aggressive behaviour but always turned up for the literacy session, which took place in an annexe:

'Carol came every single week, even though she'd just been banned from the school. She always had her folder with her games in it, brought all the books back.'

Jane, learning support teacher

Research has shown conclusively that *all* parents are interested in their child's education (Tizard *et al.* 1981; Lareau 1989; Reay 1999). However, some schools have their own ideas about what makes a 'good' parent:

'The home I went in was clean, very organised, but there were no books . . . which was quite shocking because it was one of the better homes and I did expect to see things around.'

Susan, teacher

'She's worn those clothes every day for two years. Goodness knows when she washes them.'

Catherine, teacher

These comments summarise a school's notion of a deficit in some homes. Susan had been 'shocked' because of a predetermined idea of what she would see in a 'better home'. She recognised cleanliness and order and how these might be significant in a child's application to school, but she didn't see books. Books are an obvious link between home and school. They represent cultural resources common to both contexts, and children who come from literate families where books are part of their lives will bring that experience to school. Different cultural practices and financial priorities are embedded in homes and their material resources and do not necessarily replicate the classroom. There are also many styles of parenting, linked with social class, financial resources and culture. Both quotations fail to make the connection between poverty and resources. Catherine expresses a value judgement on the quality of mothering. It is based on her own experience of being a mother and what she thinks is 'normal' while ignoring the inequality, oppression and exploitation of poverty. This ideal is one which 'the reality of most women's lives makes impossible for them to achieve' (Reay 1999: 12) and where children's lack of educational success is seen as the failure of an unstable home life. It is dangerous because mothers, responding to unobtainable popular images of motherhood in the media, and endorsed by the school through expectations of cleanliness and prudence, are being judged, and will come to judge themselves, as inadequate (Bourdieu 1984).

The comments are those of teachers who see themselves as 'natural guardians of democracy' (Walkerdine and Lucey 1989: 40) commenting on what they see as 'inappropriate' parenting skills. It is about teachers having fixed ideas about what homes should look like, based on their own homes, and what parents should do, but has nothing to do with partnership or 'co-communication'. Sound relationships are built on respect and many children from disadvantaged families are happy and secure, which is a good basis for education. Parents need to know how teachers value the contribution they have made so far and teachers need to be sensitive to parents whose financial resources are limited.

Home visiting is common practice for early years teachers. It is an opportunity to share information about culture, background, children's talents and needs, and the challenge for teachers is to listen as well as lead. It is an opportunity to learn of different cultural attitudes to education and schools, for example, different cultural practices in learning, and acquire vital information about, for example, religious beliefs, languages spoken at home etc. Some parents are bemused by western educational informality and teaching methods such as the use of play. It is also the case that some parents feel vulnerable with a professional visiting their home. These parents need to know that no value judgements are being made and that teachers visiting are genuinely interested in what they have to say about their children and in them as people. This requires a disposition which accepts diverse life-styles without making judgements, and a sensitivity which reflects that disposition. What needs to be communicated is a desire to help schools understand families and families to understand schools. I once asked Brenda, a parent, whether she felt she could challenge the school about a decision the school had made about her son with a special educational need. Her response was:

'Oh no! There's them up there and there's me down here. I could never do that!'

Working-class parents consistently defer to teachers and are afraid to ask questions (Vincent 2000). One can only imagine Brenda's concern in wanting the very best for her child, but not feeling she could make a contribution to the dialogue. How much would it take for Brenda to feel included in decisions taken about her son? It would mean a teacher's recognition that Brenda is an essential part of that process, and someone values what she has to say.

Some schools advise parents on providing a home environment supportive to school. They run meetings about school issues to inform families and provide a forum for debate. Where these are successful the school will respond to parents' requests for topics or information. These might begin as queries about practical issues like school lunches, but have the potential to develop into parents' concerns, such as anxieties about behaviour. There may be projects in the community which support parents, particularly of very young children (e.g. Sure Start). Schools should be aware of these so groups can work together. They should also beware of 'taking a moral high ground' on styles of parenting, as it is invariably working-class parents who are seen to need this tutelage (Vincent 2000).

The challenge for schools regarding meetings is how to include *all* parents, so the agenda must be something relevant and important. While crèche provision is useful for some, it is essential to others and a selection of rotated times including evenings might enable more people to attend. It might also be useful to remember that meetings do not have to be held at school, and some schools take advantage of community facilities such as health centres, family centres, community centres and churches. Finally, teachers should recognise that not everyone belongs in a conventional family setting. For those with disabilities, access must be considered and a home visit organised if this is not possible. The message here is flexibility. For parents whose own school experience was less than satisfactory, these initial meetings will set the scene for future involvement and mutual support.

2. Communicating

This section discusses ways to design effective forms of school-to-home and home-to-school communications about school programmes and children's progress.

Schools are obliged to inform parents of school policies and procedures. Communication can be written, as in the school prospectus, newsletters and end-of-term reports, or can be verbal, as in curriculum meetings or meetings on open evenings.

Teachers are, evidently, communicators. They share expertise and experience with one another and with professionals from other agencies. They share vital information about policies, practice and individual children. We accept that good teachers share messages.

Parents are statutorily entitled to information about their children's progress according to national assessment tests and also according to teacher assessments (Ofsted 2003). Teachers regularly report to them on pupils' attainment and progress in face-to-face meetings and in writing. For younger children parents are involved in sharing and providing information which is included in *The Foundation Stage Profile* (DfES 2003).

Needless to say, if reports are to mean anything at all, parents will be aware of children's targets, of progress made, of assessment procedures, and how their child compares with other children of the same age. If children have special educational needs, parents will need to be informed of those needs, know what the school is doing and how they themselves can give support. Parents, legally, must be regularly consulted about a child's Individual Education Plan (IEP) and be informed in order to support learning at home (e.g. *exactly* what strategy is the school using to improve the child's playground behaviour? Can this process be continued at home and how?). Written information must be clear, concise and readable but always be based on what the child *can* do as well as what she or he is working towards. In this way, parents are enabled to be 'co-communicators, co-supporters, co-learners and co decision makers'. Establishing this will depend on a real dialogue between home and school. Parents need to know about how schools work, but to be effective, schools and teachers need to listen to parents. What do children like to do when they are at home? Which TV programmes do they watch? Is there anything happening at home which might have an effect on behaviour and learning? The school ethos will influence the success of this.

> 'At my last school parents had access to school quite freely. If wet, parents would come in and wait – here they are kept outside . . . I don't think it helps.'
>
> Pat, teacher

> 'The school has an "open door" policy. If I'm worried I can just pop in.'
>
> Alice, parent

The quotes above are about two very different schools. In one, parents were kept outside even in the rain, while in the other they could 'pop in' when there was a concern. It is obvious in which school relationships were more successful. Parents who are less confident about their role in their children's education are quite likely to think that what they have to say isn't important enough to warrant teacher time, and the same parents can be reluctant to make appointments to see a teacher (Reay 1999), but may grab an opportunity to relate significant information. Vital information can be shared at any time, particularly incidentally, first thing in the morning. Many beginning teachers form and sustain valuable relationships with parent/carers in this way. Similarly, information about learning can be communicated not only in end-of-term reports but also in memos, reading diaries and behaviour logs and can provide a regular, sometimes daily dialogue between home and school. These methods of communication are accessible for all practising teachers and provide opportunities for beginning teachers in school to develop important skills.

Communication with parents always has the potential to be challenging and will depend on sensitivity and tact while delivering clear messages. For anyone whose children are having problems at school it is a worrying time. It is for this reason that teachers need to understand parents' perceptions in order not to make assumptions, generalisations and stereotypical judgements. So listening is important.

Open evenings can be nerve-racking for young teachers, who feel that most parents are more knowledgeable than they themselves are. Teachers notoriously use these meetings as a forum to give information rather than receive it (Bastiani 1989), when this is an ideal time to do the reverse. In the present educational climate, where parents are seen more as clients and consumers than they were, some expect to play a more active role and can be demanding (Vincent 2000). Concerned parents can be seen as 'interfering' or 'too involved'. The challenge for teachers is how to work alongside parents who are anxious about their children, providing useful guidance and reassurance.

Schools produce written material for parent/carers and should review the readability of notices. Are they also produced with non-English readers in mind? Are they clear and simple and are teachers aware of parents whose literacy skills are poor? Is there support for these parents in the form of informal and verbal information? If other agencies such as the Educational Welfare Officer or the Speech Therapist are involved, whose responsibility is it to make sure everyone is informed regularly? Simple posters can be effective, perhaps because these are likely to be more striking than a paragraph in a newsletter. In addition, terminology is important – 'workshop' sounds more interesting than 'meeting' and might be less prohibitive to parents who are more comfortable with an informal setting. Some schools have found it useful to draw on friendly and established parents to look out for those who need support, particularly if those parents can act as interpreters or mentors.

3. Volunteering

This section discusses ways to recruit parent/carer help and support.

Increasingly, teachers depend on voluntary help from parents. Classroom helpers are a common feature of primary schools and many teachers would say they could not meet the demands of the children and the curriculum without them. Parents are often seen in school offices helping with administration, and seasonally, staff rooms are taken over by groups of parents making decorations and counting money. These parents are 'co-supporters'. In some schools they are easy to find but in others they are hard to come by. It is often the schools in affluent areas where parents are most commonly seen, where even though parents lead hectic lives, sometimes juggling work and family, with access to resources (such as a car) they are able to fit classroom sessions into busy schedules. These parents recognise the importance of a child's success at school. They know their own education gave them opportunities and are determined that their own children should have the same advantages (Ball 2003). In other less affluent areas, parents can be elusive. Though some adults may be unemployed and therefore may have more time, helping in their child's classroom is the last thing they would choose to do. Requests from school for help are often ignored and schools are left with the false impression that parent/carers don't care.

'I listen to the children read, sharpen pencils. I didn't care what I did.'

Anna, parent

'I come in to help sort out the library and that kind of stuff, not actually doing anything with the children . . . it's just that with reading, if there's a word they don't know and I don't know it, that's when I'm going to have trouble.'

Alice, parent

These quotations are from parents with very different experiences. Anna is a confident woman with professional qualifications who took time out from her job in a bank to bring up her children. She has just gone back to work part time but goes into her children's school regularly. She is so confident in school that she could be mistaken for one of the teachers, and teachers saw her as,

'one of us. Not like our normal parents.'

Susan, head teacher

She will 'do anything'. In fact, she sees it as part of her role as a mother to find out what is going on:

'to make sure that what we're doing at home doesn't contradict what they're doing at school'.

Anna, parent

However, for Alice, volunteering to help in the classroom is a different matter. Alice's reading skills are poor. Alice could not be mistaken for one of the teachers. It would be easy to exclude Alice because she is not 'one of us'. She frequently worries that someone will ask her to do something she can't manage and under-stands why some parents are reluctant to get involved:

> 'I manage to come to school and not be frightened but I've heard lots of people say because of what happened to them at school when they were children, they've found it difficult to get involved in stuff at their children's school.'
>
> Alice, parent

In the same school another parent had been approached personally by a teacher looking for a volunteer. On arrival, she admitted:

> 'I've been dreading this all day.'
>
> Chloe, parent

To teachers this might seem strange, but for some parents, fear of school is very real.

We know that some parent/carers are more in tune with schools than others. They 'fit in' more easily, they know what to do more or less without being told. They will 'do anything'. We are also aware that there are significant benefits for children and parent/carers as well as schools when they are included. Involvement in the classroom can give knowledge about what's being taught and how, which clearly benefits the child, but parents and children who are part of the school also acquire 'institutional habitus' (Reay 1999), a sense of belonging which demystifies what might otherwise be an unfamiliar environment. Habitus is knowledge and acceptance of 'the way things are', the 'social game embodied and turned into second nature' (Bourdieu 1991: 63). Research has shown that children with institutional habitus are more likely to succeed at school than those without (Pollard and Filer 1996; Reay 1999; Hurley 2000b). Alice had poor literacy skills, so was nervous about helping in the classroom, but her mum had been the caretaker in her primary school and with her institutional habitus she had the confidence to get involved. She helped in the library, she made cakes for the school fair and she broke up tiles for the mosaic artist during Art Week. Both of Alice's children were doing well at school and the teachers valued Alice's support. Alice was included.

Even confident parents can be reticent about coming in to help. They are often aware of the dynamics between the professional and the lay person and feel unsure of their competence. For these parents some schools provide training and find work which will reflect their interests. In Alice's school parents regularly make props for school plays. Another group of parents is currently making 'story sacks' to go with books they themselves have chosen from the local bookshop. These parents feel valued.

Challenges for schools are how to involve *all* parents. Teachers will not know of interests and skills unless they listen and ask, which means setting time for a dialogue with parents and giving the message that all skills are valued – particularly those which give the children experience of the community, of its culture and diversity. Some parents are puzzled by requests by schools for volunteers. They expect school matters to be handled by teachers. For some families from minority ethnic communities, participation in children's education may be an unfamiliar experience and the informal atmosphere of the primary classroom very different from their own schooling. Opportunity for classroom observation, along with parent–teacher dialogue, will help dispel misunderstandings and give insight into teachers' aims and methods.

Very often, classroom intervention is left to the discretion of individual teachers. These teachers should consider excluded parents. It is easy for teachers to give reasons why certain parents are 'of little use' (teacher quote, Hurley 2000a) in the classroom but these are the parents who, along with their children, will benefit the most.

Men are rarely seen in some primary schools, but can give credence to activities normally seen to be undertaken by women, such as sewing and reading, and all adults can validate non-academic skills which might reflect the interests of the community, for example preparing food, growing things, playing music and sport. Both male and female parent/carers need to know that their skills are recognised and valued even if they did not 'do well' at school themselves and teachers need to remember that schools do not have the monopoly on learning. Parents will teach their children a variety of important skills which, with a little imagination, can be linked with the curriculum and make vital links between education at home and at school.

Schedules for volunteers need to be flexible. Working parents might be able to 'pop in' on an *ad hoc* basis rather than make a regular commitment, or come regularly for half an hour in the morning. Those who are less confident may find it prohibitive to have to sign up on a regular basis, but will respond to individual requests for giving up a short time the following day. Some teachers have found that parents will sign up on a blank weekly timetable to commit themselves that week, or that they are willing to come with a friend. Other teachers will welcome parents with toddlers (having done this myself, it is not for the faint-hearted but the benefits outweighed the drawbacks). Some teachers are more successful than others at including parents (Lareau 1989), and other teachers and beginning teachers can learn useful strategies from them. Parents in classrooms are usually mesmerised by what goes on and the experience increases their respect for the teacher role. Their needs are simple. They want to see that their children are happy and they want to see what they can do. For any teacher feeling anxious about including parents in the classroom, they need to remember that most of them are already on their side.

4. Learning at home

This section discusses ways to provide information to parent/carers about how to help pupils at home with homework and other curriculum-related activities, decisions and planning.

Schools often have a homework policy explaining to parents how often homework is set and how it should be monitored, but knowledge of the current curriculum and how it is taught in school today is, at best, out of date for non-teachers who are not aware of recent educational changes. To counteract this, schools give information explaining current initiatives, and hold meetings and workshops for new parents on how they teach core subjects and how parents can help. There have also been innovative projects like the *Impact* [maths] *Project* (Merttens and Vass 1993) encouraging parents to become involved in their children's learning. Schools tend to believe that parents will be able to support learning at home but McNamara notes that 'even parents who have excellent contact with school still know little of what their children learn or how to help them' (McNamara *et al.* 2000). For parents whose own experience of school was less than satisfactory, we are asking the impossible:

'It's changed a lot since I went to school. It's like with maths – times and long division, no worries. But then you go on to areas. I never really understood that myself. I say "Tell your teacher your mum can't even do this".'

Chelsea, parent

Chelsea's comment shows a recognition of educational changes and a feeling of inadequacy with her own level of curricular knowledge, but, as a parent, the school's expectation is that she will support her child's learning. This places her in the position of a teacher, for which she is ill-equipped, it compounds her feelings of inferiority and confirms her idea of the school as an academic institution in which she has no place.

In my own research, homework was one of the areas which caused parents most concern. Those who are least equipped to deal with homework are those from cultures where their school experience has been very different, and those whose own school experiences and attendance were poor. It is also those who live in poor housing:

'Brian's a bit more *au fait* with computers and stuff so he'll help set up the computer if they need it . . . J had to make a mask the other day . . . so he helped him do that.'

Bella, parent

Bella's comment shows how both she and her partner have developed a *modus vivendi* for homework support. Bella and Brian live in a two-bedroom flat with their four children. They have had to become highly organised and have developed a homework routine which involves finding a quiet space, providing a computer and rotating their time so all the children get attention and someone can look after the toddler. Bella and Brian have each other for support, but for single parents or those, for example, without access to a computer, this would be impossible. It is sometimes for reasons like these that homework can present a problem. It can also create added stress.

> 'I say "What have you got to do?" and he says,
> "I don't know! My teacher never explained it properly," and I say
> "No! You weren't listening!" – in one ear and out the other.
> He starts crying like your boy does.'
>
> Amelia, parent

While there has been much literature on the effects families have on schools there has been little discussion on the effects school has on family life or parent–child relationships (Reay 1999).

Challenges for schools are, therefore, complex. If parents are to support learning effectively they need to know about the curriculum, teaching methods used and targets for their children which means closer communication with schools.

Homework clubs, with a teacher to give support, work well for some schools. Could the nature of homework also be reviewed? What is homework supposed to do and how? If children are not motivated and parents feel de-skilled, what can schools do? Homework activities do not have to be set, written or recorded but can be based on a tea-time discussion or a game. Homework can also be activity-based, and linking school work to real life. Looking for information on a cereal packet, going to the cinema or feeding the ducks in the park are educational experiences which can be recognised by schools as such. Schools need to see 'helping at home' as not just about teaching the school curriculum but about 'encouraging, listening, reacting, praising, guiding, monitoring, and discussing' (Epstein 1995).

5. Decision making

This section discusses ways to include parent/carers in school decisions and how to develop parent/carer leaders and representatives.

> 'Parental involvement is a good idea as long as parents are vetted.'
>
> Rita, teacher

If parents are true partners they will be involved in school decision making. However, teachers rarely see this as part of their role (Vincent 2000).

The process of making decisions in schools operates at two levels. For practical day-to-day matters the head teacher will make decisions, probably in consultation with the staff and perhaps taking into account views of parents. Decisions regarding policy changes or their implementation will be made by the governing body of the school which will include parent/carer representation. However, the opportunity for willing parents to be members of a governing body are necessarily limited by numbers, and those likely to be accepted as 'suitable' representatives both by the school and by other parents are likely to be those whose lives reflect the institution. This will exclude many working-class parents. In addition, opportunities for parents to meet and discuss important issues are limited. There is no forum for them like the staff room for teachers, and minority voices can easily be lost.

Schools may have an active parent–teacher association or the equivalent, supporting practical activities like fund raising. But even where parents are actively involved, their role is often seen by the school as supportive, not constructively critical. Whether parents have a voice in any decision-making process will depend on the willingness of the school to give them such an opportunity.

The Parents' Charter (DfES 1991), updated in 1994, claims to have made an attempt to accommodate the opinions of parent/carers in the running of their children's schools, but, as previously noted, not all are included. It is white, middle-class, heterosexual parent/carers who remain those most likely to take advantage of the avenues cited above. Although there are, theoretically, opportunities for all parents to participate, the likelihood of this is remote, resulting in a lack of diversity in those having an active voice. Social class, culture, sexuality, gender and disability are all important factors in determining opportunities and willingness to be involved. Initiatives set up by schools to include more families are 'primarily designed to legitimate the more general action of the institution concerned. Thus they may result in bringing a few, previously excluded individuals into the decision-making process but do little to affect the position of excluded groups' (Vincent 1996). Therefore, parent groups tend to validate established practices rather than challenge them. Only too often, head teachers manage the process so parents included are those, from the quotation of the teacher above, 'vetted by the school'. This is how some remain 'one of them' rather than 'one of us'.

Some parents have always 'got on' with schools better than others, though most work hard to co-operate with their children's teachers. Where these relationships work, families and teachers are mutually supportive, but for others, conflict will make an honest dialogue difficult. Their 'assertiveness, aggression or timidity' (Reay 1999) often a result of marginalisation by society, promotes a feeling of inadequacy and is reinforced inadvertently by relationships with teachers

(Hurley 2000b). Nevertheless, the individual parent–teacher relationship remains the primary mechanism through which parents can gain access to the workings of the school and the opportunity for parents to be 'co-decision makers' is remote.

A challenge to schools would be to encourage active discussion among parents and to provide a forum for this to happen, perhaps in the form of regular workshops. Schools can be pro-active in creating an environment where parents can see diversity of experiences and opinions are celebrated and respected. Parents who have had very different experiences of education will need a more detailed explanation of the way the school works, and its philosophies. Parents on the governing body should be representative of all ethnic and socio-economic groups and members of the governing body should be given training to demystify the processes of making decisions. Schools should also be prepared to consider that parents have a right to be part of the decision-making process in schools, and this might instigate challenge and change. The Plowden Report (DES 1967) embodied a consensus of home–school relationships which included those parents who were co-operative and supportive. Now schools should consider those who are not and ask themselves why and what they can do about it. Sharing decision making is not the handing over of power as a quantifiable property where the giver is the loser, but a democratic process where goals are explored and achieved.

6. Collaborating with the community

This section discusses ways to identify and integrate resources and services from the community to strengthen school programmes, family practices, and student learning and development.

> Whilst complaining that minority group parents do not come to the school, very few teachers visit them at home, spend time in the neighbourhood, for instance in local shops and cafés, or visit the temples, churches or social centres which play an important part in the lives of the families.
>
> (Tizard et al. 1981: 224)

The word 'community' has recently figured large in government attempts to promote a regeneration of moral responsibility. Concepts of 'community care' and, more generally, 'community spirit' have positive associations of shared values and life-style while assuming a homogenity which supersedes diverse groups (Vincent 1996). However, present-day communities are increasingly heterogeneous in terms of ethnicity, religion, sexuality and social class, and it could be argued that to ignore differences suppresses an opportunity for learning and understanding.

Schools serve communities, and links are essential if children are to be valuable community members. In this way a community can validate what a school does.

There are many examples of practices currently existing in schools which link schools and communities. An Ofsted inspection will evaluate 'the extent to which a school provides a resource for and draws from the community' (Ofsted 2003). Good practice would be demonstrated in schools which give information about cultural, recreational, health and social support for parent/carers and pupils, maintain links with churches and other religious centres, have links with local newspapers, participate in recycling schemes, perform drama productions in centres for the elderly, link with local businesses for work experience or school visits, and maintain links with feeder nurseries. Schools provide literacy schemes for adult learners, weekend workshops for family learning (e.g. to develop computer skills) and community reading projects where retired community members come into school to support children with reading. These schemes support the school while at the same time value and develop the skills of adults taking part. However, those volunteering will be those with the time, motivation and inclination to be involved in a school-based project.

The challenge to schools might be how to involve more members of the community who might not see themselves as participants in such schemes or as learners. Places on adult literacy schemes are generally taken up by those adults who want to improve their existing skills to enhance their employability rather than those who are semi-literate or have few literacy skills at all (Finlay 1999). Parents embarrassed about their skills may be reluctant to volunteer for an opportunity to publicise this need and may reject opportunities to revisit an experience which has previously resulted in failure and humiliation (Hurley 2000b). However, learning is not confined to school. It is about the broadening of experiences and enjoyment. In one school, parent/carers accompanied their children to an opera. Chelsea, although living a short distance away from the theatre, had never been:

> 'I went to G . . . with them last week. It was brilliant . . . It did open my eyes to the other side, sort of thing, to music.'
>
> Chelsea, parent

Social class and culture, not to mention financial resources, affect exposure to community and cultural experiences. Schools are in an ideal position to provide experiences for children and include families and carers in those experiences. Good community links will be drawn in schools where 'classroom and extra-curricular activities encourage the participation of all students and draw on their knowledge and experience outside school', and where 'staff mobilise resources within the school and local communities to sustain active learning for all' (CSIE 2000: 45).

For parents from minority ethnic communities, there may be a suspicion of school bred by fears of racism. Here, teachers may have to work hard to become more than just an official figure. Home visiting alongside an interpreter, and spending time in the community may be a way of teachers acquiring essential information about families and their lives in order to be pro-active in creating an environment where racism is unacceptable. It will provide teachers with important, basic information about languages, religions, customs and any possible manifestations of racism, and the acquisition of that information will enhance the status of the teacher.

Conclusion

Relationships between teachers and parent/carers are not just between members of a community and an institution, but between individuals. However, 'interpersonal relations are never, except in appearance, individual to individual relations . . . the truth of the interaction is never entirely contained in the interaction' (Reay 1995). Teachers are agents of the school and their relationships are 'constrained by the hegemony embedded, not just within the practices and understandings of institutions but also within a whole range of social relations and regularities' (Vincent 1996: 6). Thus teachers behave as 'teachers' and think as 'teachers', and their interaction with parents reproduces the social phenomenon that exists outside the individual. It is the way teachers are; not consciously, but because of an unequivocal understanding of their position within the institutional structure which insists on their place in the social structure.

Think about parents collecting outside classrooms at the end of the day to pick up their children. Which of them do we look forward to seeing? That's easy – those who are like us. Are there any we would rather avoid? Now think about why. Just as some children are easier to teach than others, some parent/carers are easier to communicate with than others. This is about diversity.

Teachers are different, too, with a range of backgrounds and circumstances, and though much of the literature points to teachers, particularly primary teachers, as middle class, white and female, some would argue this is no longer the case. However, teachers have a collectivity. When teachers become teachers they undergo a 'socialisation' (Lacey 1977). They 'become' teachers. As Waller says, 'teaching does something to those who teach' (Waller 1984). This doesn't mean we all get bossy, which of course, we may, but it does mean we have a tendency to see ourselves as 'social and cultural missionaries' (Grace 1978). We feel that 'being' a teacher transcends all previously owned locations such as class (Lee 1987; Sharp and Green 1975). If we ignore social class issues in school we are in danger of rendering 'well-intentioned practice ineffective and tokenistic' (Sharp and Green 1975: 133). Teachers assume the 'orienting practices' of their identity and translate these into 'normal values' – the values of common sense (Bourdieu 1984). However, 'some people's common sense becomes formally recognised when other peoples' does not' (Gramsci, cited by Young 1971: 28). The result is that some families, both children and parent/carers, those who are co-operative and compliant, who share our cultural capital, are approved, while others, whose lives are different, whose cultural capital is different, are seen as unco-operative and unreasonable and responsible for their children's educational failure (Reay 1999). They are 'undeserving', they have only themselves to blame for their exclusion.

This ideology results in power differentials where, only too often, it is teachers who have the power and parents the anxiety (Bernstein 1990). To blame teachers for a lack of participation when that responsibility has always been laid firmly at the feet of parents themselves, would be to replace one fiction with another (Reay 1999). However, to ignore a situation which is unjust is unacceptable. 'Nothing is less innocent than non-interference' (Bourdieu 1999: 629) and 'educational change depends on what teachers do and think – it's as simple as that' (Fullan 1991: 91).

The vague, consensual terms of 'partnership', 'involvement' and 'dialogue' obscure uncertainties in interpretation and, while consistent with parent/carers as 'co-supporters', do little to address *all* parents in their roles as 'co-communicators', 'co-learners' and 'co-decision makers'. Parents, on the whole, respect and admire teachers but often this is not reciprocated. Teachers need to reflect on why some parents are so easy to work with and why others are not. Does this in itself justify exclusion? They need to acknowledge that parental involvement for some parents is easy while for others it has to be worked for extremely hard (Hurley 2002). Today, most schools include some parents. What about the rest?

Notes

1   'Social class' as used here is based on the classification of the Office for Population Census Studies (OPCS), first used in the census of 2001, which updated that of the Registrar General, previously used since 1911. Based on occupation, life-style and status, it is useful here in that it accords with popular understandings of social class differentiation; in particular, the distinctions between white-collar workers, on the one hand, and blue-collar workers and those classified as long-term unemployed, on the other. While for the purposes of this chapter, and for sociological analyses in general, it has its uses, its limitations are recognised (Hill and Cole 2001).

2   All names have been changed to protect identity.

References

Ball, S. (2003) *Class Strategies in the Educational Market. The middle class and social advantage*. London: Routledge/Falmer.

Bastiani, J. (1989) *Working with Parents. A whole-school approach*. Windsor: NFER-Nelson.

Bernstein, B. (1990) *Class, Codes and Control*. Vol. 4. London: Routledge.

Bourdieu, P. (1984) *Distinction*. London: Routledge Kegan Paul.

Bourdieu, P. (1991) *Language and Symbolic Power*. Oxford: Polity Press.

Bourdieu, P. (1999) *The Weight of the World*. Oxford: Polity Press.

Brown, A. (1993) 'Participation, dialogue and the reproduction of social inequalities', in Merttens, R. and Vass, J. (eds) *Partnerships in Maths: parents and schools. The Impact Project*. London: Falmer Press.

Centre for Studies on Inclusive Education (CSIE) (2000) *Index for Inclusion*. CSIE in collaboration with Centre of Educational Needs, University of Manchester; Centre for Educational Research, Canterbury Christ Church College.

Chrispeels, J. (1996) 'Effective schools and home–school partnership roles: a framework for parental involvement', *School Effectiveness and School Improvement*, 7, 297–323.

Department of Education (DES) (1967) *Children and their Primary Schools. A report of the Central Advisory Council for Education.* London: HMSO.

Department of Education and Science (DES) (1991) *The Parent's Charter. You and your child's education.* London: HMSO.

Department for Education and Skills (DfES) (2003) *The Foundation Stage Profile.* London: HMSO.

Epstein, J. (1995) 'School/family/community partnerships', *Phi Delta Kappan*, 76 (9) May, 701–11.

Finlay, A. (1999) 'Exploring an alternative literacy curriculum for socially and economically disadvantaged parents in the UK', *Journal of Adolescent and Adult Literacy*, 43 (1) September, 18–26.

Fullan, M. (1991) *The New Meaning of Educational Change.* London: Cassell.

Grace, G. (1978) *Teachers, Ideology and Control. A study in urban education.* London: Routledge Kegan Paul.

Habermas, J. (1973) *Legitimation Crisis.* Oxford: Polity Press.

Hill, D. and Cole, M. (2001) 'Social class', in Hill, D. and Cole, M. (eds) *Schooling and Equality: fact, concept and policy.* London: Kogan Page.

Hughes, P. and Macnaughton, G. (2000) 'Consensus, dissensus or community: the politics of parental involvement in early childhood education', *Contemporary Issues in Early Childhood*, 1 (3), 241–58.

Hurley, L. (2000a) 'Education and equality. Where are we now?' Unpublished MA degree, University of Sussex.

Hurley, L. (2000b) 'School and parents. The school perspective.' Unpublished MA degree, University of Sussex.

Hurley, L. (2002) 'Being and doing. Involving parents in school. Teachers, social class and the role of habitus in the process of change.' Unpublished MA degree, University of Sussex.

Lacey, C. (1977) *The Socialisation of Teachers.* London: Methuen.

Lareau, A. (1989) *Home Advantage; social class and parental intervention in elementary education.* Lewes: Falmer Press.

Lee, J. (1987) 'Pride and prejudice: teachers and class in an inner city infant's school', in Lawn, M. and Grace, G. (eds) *Teachers, the Culture and Politics of Work.* Lewes: Falmer Press.

McNamara, O., Hustler, D., Stronach, I. and Rodrigo, M. (2000) 'Room to manoevre: mobilising the "Active partner" in home–school relations', *British Educational Research Journal*, 26 (4), 473–89.

Merttens, R. and Vass, J. (eds) (1993) *Partnerships in Maths: parents and schools. The Impact Project.* London: Falmer Press.

Merttens, R., Newland, A. and Webb, S. (1996) *Learning in Tandem. Involving parents in their children's education.* Warwickshire: Scholastic.

Ofsted (1999) *Primary Education. A review of primary schools in England 1994–98.* London: Ofsted.

Ofsted (2003) http://www.ofsted.gov.uk/publications/docs/hb2003/frame03/hmi1525-06.html (accessed February 2005).

Pollard, A. and Filer, A. (1996) *The Social World of Children's Learning.* London: Cassell.

Reay, D. (1995) 'They employ cleaners to do that. Habitus in the primary school', *British Journal of the Sociology of Education*, 16 (3), 353–71.

Reay, D. (1999) *Class Work: mothers' involvement in their children's primary schooling.* London: University College Press.

Reay, D. (2004) 'Finding or losing yourself', in Ball, S. (ed.) *Reader in the Sociology of Education.* London: Routledge/Falmer.

Sammons, P., Hillman, J. and Mortimore, P. (1995) *Key Characteristics of Effective Schools*. London: Ofsted.

Sharp, R. and Green, A. (1975) *Education and Social Control*. London: Routledge and Kegan Paul.

Teacher Training Agency (TTA) (2004) *Qualifying to Teach: professional Standards for Qualified Teacher Status and requirements for initial teacher training*. London: TTA.

Tizard, B., Mortimore, J. and Burchell, B. (1981) *Involving Parents in Nursery and Infant Schools*. London: High Scope Press.

Vincent, C. (1996) *Parents and Teachers. Power and participation*. London: Falmer Press.

Vincent, C. (2000) *Including Parents? Education, citizenship and parental agency*. Maidenhead: Open University Press.

Walkerdine, V. and Lucey, H. (1989) *Democracy in the Kitchen*. London: Virago.

Waller, W. (1984) 'What teaching does to teachers, determinants of the occupational type', in Hargreaves, A. and Woods, P. (eds) *Classrooms and Staffrooms: the sociology of teachers and teaching*. Maidenhead: Open University Press.

Young, M. (1971) *Knowledge and Control*. London: Collier Macmillan.

Contributing to school life

Krishan Sood

Those awarded Qualified Teacher Status must understand and uphold the professional code of the General Teaching Council for England by demonstrating . . . [that] they can contribute to, and share responsibly in, the corporate life of schools.

(TTA 2004: 7 Section 1.5)

Learning objectives

To encourage teachers to:

■ have a clear understanding of what it means to contribute to wider participation in the school community

■ be able to conceptualise clearly what the term 'community' means and its consequences for individuals and schools

■ have an ability to contribute to the life of the school beyond their own classroom and know how to do this.

Introduction

THE USE OF THE TERM, 'corporate' in the above quotation reflects the present Government's preoccupation with the 'businessification' of education, with respect to both the business agenda *for* schools (meeting the needs of industry) and the business agenda *in* schools (controlling aspects of education and using schooling to make profits) (e.g. Hatcher and Hirrt 1999; Rikowski 2002; Cole forthcoming). This chapter takes the position that schools should properly be thought of as communities rather than corporations. It aims, therefore, to fulfil the TTA requirements, but in a critical way. The chapter develops a critical review of some of the issues involved with how beginning teachers can contribute to, and share responsibility in a wider participation in the school community and later in the chapter, I will review some of the issues involved around community education. It is directed at beginning teachers, but it is also relevant to teachers generally.

Strategies for contributing to the life of the school

The guiding principle behind the contribution that the beginning teachers can make in their school and beyond is to *become involved* in as many activities as practicable to support pupils' learning. Schools are part of and an extension of the local community, therefore every effort should be made to develop networks, partnerships and collaborations to enrich both the school and the community. However, given the complexity of schools and the huge range of social goods the community may expect from schools to deliver, beginning teachers need to tread carefully when balancing which opportunities and challenges to undertake. Thus working with others and through others may be a better strategy than working in isolation. That does not exclude beginning teachers undertaking, developing and nurturing individual initiatives with their pupils and learners.

Beginning teachers may want to share in a department meeting an assessment technique which establishes targets for pupil improvement or a strategy that develops partnership with parents and the community. How can beginning teachers lead on a policy of pupil-centred approach where enjoyment, interest and achievements are stressed? How can beginning teachers develop an awareness within the community about ensuring appropriate models of learning (see Joyce *et al.* 1997) in a repertoire for specific learning outcomes? In the latter example, the process involves working together or being guided by a subject leader or head of department to collect information, observe lessons, analyse assessments and discuss strategies for improvement.

Beginning teachers may want to take a lead in identifying opportunities for the use of ICT across the school, but within their own phase, department, key stage initially. For example, in one humanities department in a comprehensive school, the main process taken to identify and integrate ICT opportunities involved whole-faculty participation and was given priority in time allocated for training and development. An initial meeting with all staff asserted the expectation that everyone had a responsibility to contribute to this collective aim and to further develop the use of ICT across the department. Beginning teachers may want to share their expertise in using multimedia in preparing resources, for example see British Education and Training Technology (BETT) 2002 Creative Media Project at

Colbayns School, Essex found at http:/improbability.ultralab.net.bett-2002 or see www.learn.co.uk a site provided by the *Guardian* offering online lessons and other materials (not all ICT).

The development of ICT in learning therefore can be an excellent focus for beginning teachers to work individually, in teams or in cross-curricular ways to enhance the school and/or community relationships. Theory suggests that delegating resource management to individuals within their school close to the point of resource use should result in greater responsiveness. So beginning teachers may want to investigate this further by undertaking an audit of the resources available to their department or in the science area for example. They will need to consult with colleagues to find out what resources they would ideally like to have in order to improve teaching and learning. They will need to cost these additional resources and attempt to draw up a strategic plan while still working within budget constraints.

Any involvement by beginning teachers in out-of-school learning, extra-curricular or enrichment activities can offer excellent ways of reaching out to and involving the community. The main advantages being that it *generates ownership* and *commitment*, it focuses on what the school and community may think is important and it can be timed to fit in with the work of the school. The disadvantages include requirement of staff time, skills which may not be available to the beginning teachers or key issues that may be missed because they were not thought of or seemed not to be important. All these strategies are not exclusive. An external perspective, through **networking** with other schools, businesses, and others can add to the way in which beginning teachers can contribute to the life of the school and community. The idea about forming partnerships is central to the Government's thinking to get schools to work even closer together and is considered next.

New partnerships

School improvement researchers like Teddlie and Reynolds (2000) argue that schools can improve by changing, developing and establishing new ways of educational partnerships with various groups or stakeholoders. So strategies like the development of home–school relations advocated by Sammons *et al.* (1994) are accepted as sound practice, but they feel that schools could do much more to harness skills and expertise, knowledge and experience of parents and carers that go beyond the capacities of beginning and experienced teachers. By **auditing** what a school does in forging partnerships with parents and carers, community representatives and agencies, LEAs, businesses, industry, higher education institutions, government agencies and educational consultants, among others, beginning teachers can begin to identify where the strengths, weaknesses, opportunities and threats are in further strengthening such a provision. It should be noted, however, that much of the literature on partnership acknowledges that the relationships on which they are based are characterised by an imbalance of power in favour of the teachers (Vincent 1993).

Contributing to and sharing responsibility in the community life of a school requires enhancing beginning teachers' knowledge about what the term 'community' means and how communities work, in addition to enhancing beginning teachers' abilities and interpersonal skills of working with a range of people and organisations. It is assumed that home–school partnerships, among others, may well facilitate improvement in for example, pupil attainment and school improvement, as long as there is a common understanding between the school and community of the concept of **'shared' power**.

Organisational and resources issues

In this section, beginning teachers are introduced to the idea of resource and environment management as this is one way by which beginning teachers can contribute to the community life of a school. Burton (2004) argues that all resources used in educational activity depend heavily on availability of financial resources. These resources may be buildings or equipment or human. Beginning teachers will be well aware of any differences in the way in which different subjects or key stages deploy resources. It is important therefore to get involved with experienced teachers in understanding how the policies, systems and structures in a school have a 'controlling and unifying approach' (Burton 2004: 183) to the management of overall resourcing.

Schools are having to be accountable to different agencies much more than before. The devolved financial management in schools has brought decision making on how resources are used closer to the point of delivery of the education experience. This means that systems must be operating in schools to ensure that finances are managed honestly and reliably. This requires beginning teachers to understand how schools maintain **probity** (i.e. that all parties are dealt with on a fair and equitable basis), **accountability** (the school is publicly accountable for its expenditure and the conduct of its affairs) and **value for money** (to demonstrate economy, efficiency and effectiveness in the use of public funds) (NCSL 2002).

In this spirit then, beginning teachers have a crucial input within the school to improve educational practice. Beginning teachers may also have the knowledge to acquire 'new' resources which enhance the quality of the learning environment for pupils and staff alike. Beginning teachers may already be involved in a host of activities that increase staff and pupil morale. An example here is where a beginning teacher was involved in finding the resources to furnish a departmental staff office with quality furniture, workspaces for staff and attractive pictures to hang on the walls. But given the current debate on workforce reform, getting value for money may well be undermined if it leads to an excessive use of valuable staff time. It may be more efficient to delegate such tasks, once the required resources are identified, to an experienced 'buyer' in the administrative team.

Making useful contributions to wider school policies

Good communication between staff is an important feature of effective schools and colleges. Equally significant is the art of negotiation in communication where the message has to be fully received, accepted by the recipients concerned and acted upon. Tensions arise when the communication is not seen as a two-way exchange, but as a directive from above, without seeking an individual person's views. Staff meetings can be vital arenas for a two-way exchange of ideas and information, but much is dependent on whether a bureaucratic or collegial mode (Bush 1994) of management characterises the organisation. What this means is that beginning teachers may find a hierarchical authority structure with formal chains of command between the different positions in the hierarchy. This suggests that power resides at the apex of the pyramid with head teachers by virtue of their position. This top-down view of educational management may be appropriate at certain times, and for certain reasons, but it remains an ambiguous notion where a collegial approach is the dominant management style. Beginning teachers will have to be aware of the need to assess the tension between professionalism and hierarchy. Bush (1994) contests that teachers have the subject expertise which may come into conflict with the positional authority of the head teacher.

Staff meetings in primary and secondary schools then remain an open arena where teachers and beginning teachers can undertake such activities as to:

- briefly discuss behavioural issues in each class (where problem pupils are targeted)
- allow each subject co-ordinator/head of department to offer feedback on any progress or initiatives which are forthcoming so that all staff are aware
- allocate or delegate responsibilities for forthcoming events to staff, thus requiring an input and support of all staff.

Beginning teachers will have to engage with others in curriculum planning and development meetings in such ways as:

- being given responsibility for planning a particular area of the curriculum for the following week, or to share ideas for festivities such as harvest time
- clarifying the activities that support staff/parent helpers will be doing the following week, and communicating appropriately to them

- liaising with outside agencies, for example the vicar or other people that the children are learning about at the time

- visiting teachers in other schools to share ideas of good practice.

Effective teamwork is an ideal to aim for, but it may not be a readily attainable norm in many schools. Coleman and Bush (1994) explore how teamwork might be developed and highlight the notion of interdependence between managing with teams and development for those teams. Some of the ways in encouraging collaborative work and learning associated with effective teamwork could be through the use of quality circles (FEU 1989) for staff development, experiences of learning networks (Goddard and Clinton 1994) and the role of an institution itself perhaps through peer mediation. Beginning teachers will have to sharpen their interpersonal skills, leadership and ability to communicate to make the teamwork process successful through knowledge of the 'curriculum players and pressure groups' (Lofthouse 1994: 143). Indeed, teaching staff are not the only stakeholders in a school; there are other individuals like the support staff and governors who carry the reputation of the school through the local community and are good allies as team members. Curriculum planning is based on the premise of a culture of collaboration (Nias *et al.* 1989) and a culture of support where openness and valuing of group work can be seen to lead to self-confidence within the school. Within such an environment, beginning teachers can flourish, but being mindful of the constraints and opportunities of being in a team.

Involvement in school activities

Beginning teachers within early years settings, primary/secondary schools, or further education and sixth form colleges will be expected to contribute to a whole range of internal and external activities connected with the institution. To enhance the teaching and learning process, schools must find new allies and build new connections to the community of which they are a part. Developing an effective home and community curriculum based on learning partnerships, with parents and carers as co-educators of children in parallel with teachers/lecturers, is advocated by Brighouse and Woods (1999).

Beginning teachers can be a catalyst in such partnerships, strengthening the capacity of a school to provide effective learning through holding open weeks for parents covering topics such as the teaching of reading and numeracy. As a result parents can understand and participate in the learning process involved and support their children appropriately. Beginning teachers may be able to foster links with other important agencies of community involvement which support teaching and learning, for example service and business providers to develop in pupils a greater economic understanding, an awareness of the world of work and of the nature of citizenship. Some business volunteers help secondary schools/colleges with their Young Enterprise programmes and work through Education Business Partnerships. Links with local public libraries are a further boost to teaching and learning through homework and independent study. The provision of curriculum enrichment and extension opportunities provide a real opportunity to prepare for lifelong learning.

Extra-curricular provision is defined in a DfEE (1997) report:

- curriculum enrichment: traditional extra-curricular activities such as sport, drama, chess, photography and other clubs and societies.
- curriculum extension: study opportunities provided before or after school or during the breaks in the school day, such as homework clubs, extra revision classes and extra after-school tuition, whether undertaken voluntarily or as the result of teacher direction.
- homework: work set in lessons, integral to the curriculum, to be done either at home or in curriculum extension time at school.

(DfEE 1997)

A further DfEE publication in 1998, entitled *Extending Opportunity: a national framework for study support*, defines study support as 'learning activity outside normal lessons which young people take part in voluntarily' (p. 3). What is very important for schools and colleges is that the good practices of curriculum enrichment and extension are carefully monitored by age, gender and ethnicity and to ensure that there is a large proportion of staff involvement, including beginning teachers, which will encourage participation by as many pupils as possible.

A number of secondary schools have homework clubs, breakfast clubs, subject surgeries, study weeks, Easter revision programmes for Year 11 students, summer literacy schools and help with key skills (Brighouse and Woods 1999). Similarly, primary schools have developed 'Early Bird' (Brighouse and Woods 1999: 101) schemes for children who want to be in school early.

Looking through the annual calendar of events, one can see a whole host of school functions which may make demands on your time. The main theme of community education is that education is a partnership between home and school. Home visiting is one way to establish a strong bond between pupils, parents and the school community. Home visiting recognises, values and builds on the principle that parents/carers are the **first educators** of their child. For example, in the early years setting, beginning teachers may be asked to make home visits prior to admissions, to explain procedures and allay any parental/carer's fears. It is important that a programme of home visits starts with discussions with all staff to agree principles and procedures and to be aware of the various needs, attitudes, and values of a pluralist community. Beginning teachers will need to consult and involve other colleagues, such as multilingual assistants, in their preparation, and ensure that they are giving sensitive and jargon-free messages. One good example of how to carry out a home visit is a paired visit, where one person talks with parents/carers while the colleague plays and talks with the children, all the time, being *sensitive* to parents'/carers' feelings so the presence of two 'professionals' is not threatening.

Home visiting is always going to be a sensitive arena for all of us working in this field. This means that we must be culturally aware of the needs of the family being visited, especially where there may be issues regarding talking to men/women, for example, in a Muslim family. There may be an issue of dialect/accent which may make communication between both parties difficult sometimes, but it ought not to be the key concern of establishing relationships. Effective communication necessitates both parties to listen actively. Most schools have a good home–school policy where such issues have already been identified and a code of practice established. The important message is that the content of the policy needs to be spelt out explicitly to avoid any potential misunderstandings between the school and home. (See the website http://www.standards.dfes.gov.uk/parentalinvolvement/ for further information about working with parents.)

Beginning teachers' expertise and experience, in addition to enthusiasm and energy, might have to be channelled through involvement in areas such as: parents' evenings, school councils, sporting events, parent–teacher association, school trips, prize-giving events and school plays and rehearsals. In a primary school, each class usually has to contribute towards the school assembly, to share the ongoing work of the classes and to celebrate the learning across the school. Parents are invited to class assemblies or end-of-term concerts so beginning teachers may have an opportunity to join in. Beginning teachers may find themselves involving parents, governors and community leaders to help in fund raising or the school sports day. If the school is actively involved in arranging field trips, school visits or a residential experience, then beginning teachers' expertise or just providing extra adult support may prove to be very welcome. Parents' evenings are a very important element of the home–school partnership. Creating displays that show work from all areas of the curriculum, including photographs and diaries of visits, adds to the experience of the parents' evening and best shows off the institution to the community. In one infant school, each governor was assigned to a teacher as a partner, for example a governor keen in ICT was assigned to the ICT Co-ordinator, thus building partnerships in different ways.

Some of the negative aspects of getting involved with so many activities can be attributed to such factors as:

- lack of time to liaise with outside agencies and arrange events due to full teaching timetables, and lack of non-contact time (in the early years and primary school setting specifically)

- lack of money for supply cover for when you want to go and see teachers in other schools

- constraints of the curriculum and timetable which limit flexibility

- perceived lack of support and advice from the senior management team (SMT) regarding liaising with particular outside agencies.

Whatever the expertise of a beginning teacher, it is important to demonstrate that some kind of contribution is being made to the welfare of the school and its community.

Roles and responsibilities of governors

The roles and responsibilities of governors is constantly under review brought about by many changes to do with legislation and practice. Beginning teachers need to be well aware of the challenges and difficulties faced by many school governors. Sometimes, perhaps mistakingly, there is a common perception that governors have little knowledge about education and there is the danger of the misconception that governors also perform the job of school inspectors. These are sensitive issues which need tactful handling based on sound information.

The roles and responsibilities of governors in maintained schools in England are wide and varied (see Drayton 1999 and the DfES 2002 governors' website). Inspection evidence shows that where there is an active involvement by governing bodies in their school's planning, then they are better informed and more effective in assisting the school to progress (Ofsted 1994). The Education Reform Act of 1988 (DES 1988) gave governors responsibility for the school's budget once financial delegation had occurred. It also added to governors' power and duties with regards to the appointment and dismissal of staff. *School Governors: a guide to the law* (DfE 1994) defines the responsibilities of school governing bodies in 'helping to establish [with the head] the aims and policies of the school, and how the standards of education can be improved' (DfE 1994: 15), with the emphasis on a strategic view, monitoring and evaluation of school's effectiveness being made in the paper on *Governing Bodies and Effective Schools* (BIS/DfE/Ofsted 1995: 2).

The duties of governing bodies also encapsulate accountability. Governors are themselves accountable to parents through their annual report and meeting with parents, with Ofsted commenting on the work of the governing body in their reports of school inspections. Giving time to the school and sharing tasks among the governors are some of the important features of an effective governing body. But as Corrick (1996) notes, there is often notable passivity about the debate on school improvement or strategy to improve standards of education. Instead, there is a tendency for governors to become involved in matters with which they feel familiar and comfortable. It could be that some head teachers may be reluctant to allow governors to get involved in the day-to-day running of the school.

Governors need support and guidance to work collaboratively with all those who make contact with a school. They need to feel self-assured that they are asking the right questions. These questions and how they are asked are important indicators of good school–governor relationships. Sometimes tensions arise with teachers and governors when each other's roles are unclear or there is an assumption that one party has more 'power' than the other. This is an opportunity for governors not to feel inhibited about questioning the judgements of teachers or to be blinded by educational jargon; each (the governor and a beginning teacher) has a crucial role to play in shaping the future direction of a school. Corrick (1996) argues that taking ownership of the vision of the future of a school demands a high level of skills, knowledge and confidence on the part of governors. A kind of detachment is required at times from immediate concerns, to look at all the options from a different viewpoint, a situation likely to be faced by many beginning teachers.

As a governor in a comprehensive school, the author chaired a marketing committee composed of two teacher representatives, a parent governor and an executive from a large motor company. The teachers offered invaluable data about the current school practices related to 'marketing' and the brief of this committee was to develop other links which would enhance the quality of provision of the school and which would best target greater pupil attainment. So for example, a strategic **marketing plan** was developed after assessing what the needs of the school were and how this would make a difference to the pupils' learning and attainment. The committee prepared a briefing paper for staff consultation and analysed the feedback. The contributions from everyone were crucial. This committee could not claim to make a direct impact on the details of teacher practice, but could attempt to influence the whole strategy of the school.

Beginning teachers can contribute to the development of improvement within a school by working alongside governors, sharing their vision with them, sharing and reflecting on good practice to raise awareness and collaborating on planning activities. Creese (1998) adds caution that where there are weaknesses to be addressed within a school, then there has to be 'a high level of mutual trust between governors and staff' (p. 123), so that they can be dealt with frankness and openness.

As a past advisory teacher, the author was privileged to be involved in supporting clusters of primary schools in curriculum development, in service education and training (INSET) and policy development. In one cluster, made up of three infant and junior schools' governing bodies, a presentation on the development of a multicultural policy was made. Good practice within the classroom was the starting point for discussion and debate, to understand the need for such a policy and how to develop it further, how to support staff in resourcing, what to monitor, how to reach out to the parents and how to measure the success of the impact on learning and attainment. Success of this training lay in knowing the schools well, enjoying a good relationship with the staff and pupils, collaboration and teamwork and helping to target a specific need and training requirements of the staff. The important message for beginning teachers here is that they should continue to form close and frequent contacts with all those who are in touch with the school – parents, governors, advisors, learning support staff, health visitors and others. This requires development of good channels of communication, openness, trust and mutual respect for institutional improvement. Creese (1998), in his research notes that, in one secondary school a retired head teacher was brought in to lead team-building sessions for the governing body, which then turned, into a viable and regular induction programme for its new governors.

Community life of schools

In understanding how beginning teachers can contribute to the community life of a school, I have used the term 'community' rather than 'corporate life of the school' as it encompasses a much wider notion of schools acting as a catalyst in bringing the community together. Beginning teachers may find that this notion of community does not at first glance address this standard, but in the next section an attempt is made to explain 'community education' and its potential benefits. It explains how communities work and how interdependent individuals are. It presents a policy framework, and covers some of the organisational and resources issues. The chapter goes on to consider some practical approaches by which beginning teachers can make a useful contribution to wider school practices.

What do we mean by community education?

Community education is much wider than the range of statutory provision which education services generally provide. Community education is certainly about access to educational opportunities for individuals or groups. It is about the concept of *building the confidence* of communities so they may thrive. The central notion of confidence is crucial to the successful development of the individual and to the social cohesiveness of communities. All manner of good things flow from communities that are secure and confident.

Within the education service the youth worker, the adult educator, and the college lecturer surely have as much to contribute to community education as the teacher in early years settings. The important contributions made by the many bodies in the voluntary sector must also not be overlooked.

There are many initiatives and partnerships taking place in the UK between primary and secondary schools, and community education providers in local authorities and the voluntary sector. Tett *et al.* (2001) carried out research on community education based on ten case-study schools and found that relatively few schools had strong links with their communities in terms of provision, collaboration and participation in decision making. They found that the differences in community education partnerships were explained not only in terms of people's perceptions of the purposes of the collaboration, the values inherent in such perceptions, the conditions under which collaboration took place and the practices in operation, but also in more analytical terms of institutional boundaries and pedagogic purpose. A corollary is that analysis of various models of collaborative practice may provide a useful way of interrogating different practices, especially the agenda of social inclusion policy.

According to Clegg and McNulty (2002), partnership has become the preeminent mechanism for furthering the Government's social inclusion agenda and they focus on the dynamics of partnership itself at management level. Community education lies at the heart of meeting community needs and aspirations, but schools and their governors have given little attention on how best to provide a holistic provision which goes some way in fostering community cohesiveness.

Benefits of community education

Some of the community education activities might include the following:

- shared use of school facilities (e.g. swimming pools)
- adult education classes
- youth clubs and activities
- provision of meals for the elderly on school or college sites
- summer play schemes.

Those local authorities with substantial experience in the development of community education have noted several benefits. Community education:

- helps people to improve their educational skills, knowledge and qualifications
- acts as a generating force in community life

- improves the relationships between schools/colleges and their communities
- presents the public with a wider range of specialist educational services and
- increases pride in community resources and reduces vandalism.

While government educational initiatives have come and gone, the underlying problems of most (inner) cities (mass unemployment, poverty, a mismatch between local skills and new jobs, a declining infrastructure and a low quality of life for many citizens) have appeared to have remained, and indeed may have intensified over the last two decades. There has been a changing educational landscape over this time period and many of the recent changes in educational policy had been swift and far reaching. The 1988 Education Reform Act (DES 1988) had revolutionised the education system and led to far-reaching structural changes in all sectors of education from the early years settings, primary and secondary schools, to sixth form colleges and further education. It had added a new vocabulary of targets, SATs, performance management, advanced skills teachers and so on, to the old vocabulary of aims and objectives and educational achievement. It could be argued that the community at large felt inadequate somehow in supporting their children and schools, and had no forum to be engaged in this new debate and fight for their rights and entitlements.

Making the educational service more accessible and more relevant are laudable aims for most LEAs, but in the short term, they are unlikely to be entirely acceptable or relevant to everyone. Examples of good practice by LEAs are those that have systems in place to monitor service provision, access, appropriateness and delivery to people's needs. A supposition here is that individual community members understand how to access such a resource and have the necessary skills and power to negotiate access to key decision makers. Vincent (1993) considers that a 'statist reform' (p. 367) model of community education has at its heart the notion of engendering a community spirit, to make available the school's resources and facilities for local residents and to create a sense of shared values and beliefs. Vincent (1993) fails to say what constitutes this 'community', and that community education is a much more complex concept than access to resources only, also, whose values and beliefs are being considered? If the common glue binding schools and communities is not strong enough, then this could mean that schools and their communities have enormous potential either to exacerbate divisions or to help build a consensus of support among members who, on other issues, may hold widely divergent views. Rizvi (1993) asserts that in a free market, the consensus between clients and producers will remain little more than a rhetoric of 'romantic localism' (p. 380), where there is a resolute effort to make more palatable a system that is increasingly controlled by the centre.

It is important that beginning teachers engage with these issues and further develop an understanding and involvement in a cohesive programme of collaboration, liaison and partnerships. The notion of policy development is explored next.

A policy framework

Every community has a wealth of resources both physical and human, that is, clubs, libraries, teachers, school classrooms, sports facilities, youth workers, public houses, retired people, experts and so on. They all have a role to play in a 'collaborative' approach. The community school is ideally placed to act as a centre piece offering advice, information, resources and expertise. The school should not see the community as a resource to fill empty rooms, rather the school is a resource to support the community. In a community school situated in a multiracial community, in which the author taught, every effort was taken to ensure that the community perspective was reflected in the school's approach to education. With involvement and planning with the community representatives in the curriculum and pastoral areas for example, the school soon offered a range of opportunities with the aim to develop community skills, knowledge and capacities, regardless of age, gender, disability, social status, sexuality or ethnic origin. Beginning teachers too can continue to seek to take advantage of such opportunities as:

- Getting directly involved in the development of provision in the locality through establishing 'friendly groups' that meet regularly, somewhere in the community.
- Influencing decision making through active representation and lobbying LEAs to influence their strategic plan.
- Having a regular, well-distributed and attractive community newspaper as a forum and linchpin to co-ordinate activities and meetings.
- Having regular and well-reported meetings of local committees, councils and others.
- Having regular socials – often it is easier to raise problems and discuss needs in a social situation.
- Breaking down traditional barriers and 'opening up' the school to the community.
- Establishing close co-operation of all providers and community agencies whether voluntary or statutory.
- Monitoring, market researching and local networking to identify un-met needs.
- Seeking support, guidance and information from an informed and trained staff (from author's personal experiences).

Conclusion

This chapter explored what kind of contribution beginning teachers could make to the wider school community. Through engagement and involvement with the community life of the school, beginning teachers would have improved their knowledge and understanding of the concept of community. The crucial point about this chapter is that beginning teachers get involved and share responsibility in supporting the school through liaison with the pupils, governors, parents/carers, support staff, professionals and many others to increase beginning teachers' confidence and standing within the school and community.

References

BIS/DfE/Ofsted (1995) *Governing Bodies and Effective Schools, Standards in Education*. London: DfE.

Brighouse, T. and Woods, D. (1999) *How to Improve your School*. London: Routledge.

Burton, N. (2004) 'Resource and environment management', in Brundrett, M. and Terrell, I. (eds) *Learning to Lead in the Secondary School*. London: Routledge/Falmer.

Bush, T. (1994) 'Theory and practice in educational management', in Bush, T. and West-Burnham, J. (eds) *The Principles of Educational Management*. Harlow: Longman.

Clegg, S. and McNulty, K. (2002) 'Partnership working in delivering social inclusion: organizational and gender dynamics', *Journal of Education Policy*, 17 (5), 587.

Cole, M. (forthcoming) 'Marketization, neo-liberalism and education: a Marxist critique of New Labour's five year strategy', in Green, A. and Rikowski, G. (eds) *Renewing Dialogues in Marxism and Education. Volume 1 – openings*. Basingstoke: Palgrave Macmillan.

Coleman, M. and Bush, T. (1994) 'Managing with teams', in Bush, T. and West-Burnham, J. (eds) *The Principles of Educational Management*. Harlow: Longman.

Corrick, M. (1996) 'Effective governing bodies, effective schools?', in Earley, P., Fidler, B. and Ouston, J. (eds) *Improving through Inspection?* London: David Fulton.

Creese, M. (1998) 'The strategic role of governors in school improvement', in Middlewood, D. and Lumby, J. (eds) *Strategic Management in Schools and Colleges*. London: Paul Chapman Publishing.

Department of Education and Science (DES) (1988) The Education Reform Act. London: DES.

Department for Education (DfE) (1994) *School Governors: a guide to the law*. London: HMSO.

DfEE (1997) *School Performance and Extra Curricular Provision*. London: DfEE.

DfEE (1998) *Extending Opportunity: a national framework for study support*. London: DfEE.

Department for Education and Skills (DfES) (2002) *School Governors' Gateway*. http://www.dfes.gov.uk/schoolgovernors/index.shtml (accessed February 2005).

Drayton, M. (1999) 'The role and purpose of school governing bodies', in Cole, M. (ed.) *Professional Issues for Teachers and Student Teachers*. London: David Fulton Publishers.

FEU (Further Education Unit) (1989) *An Evaluation of Quality Circles in Colleges of FE, Planning Staff Development, number 7*. London: FEU.

Goddard, D. and Clinton, B. (1994) 'Learning networks', in Ransom, S. and Tomlinson, J. (eds) *School Cooperation: new forms of local governance*. Longman: Harlow.

Hatcher, R. and Hirrt, N. (1999) 'The business agenda behind Labour's education policy', in Allen, M., Benn, C., Chitty, C., Cole, M., Hatcher, R., Hirrt, N. and Rikowski, G. (eds) *Business, Business, Business: New Labour's education policy*. London: Tufnell Press.

Joyce, B., Calhoun, E. and Hopkins, D. (1997) *Models of Learning: tools for teaching*. Buckingham: Open University Press.

Lofthouse, M. (1994) 'Managing the curriculum', in Bush, T. and West-Burnham, J. (eds) *The Principles of Educational Management*. Harlow: Longman.

National College for School Leadership (NCSL) (2002) Financial management module finance workbook for bursar development programme, Certificate of School Business Management. Nottingham: NCSL.

Nias, J., Southworth, G. and Yeomans, R. (1989) *Staff Relationships in the Primary School*. London: Cassell.

Ofsted (1994) *Improving Schools*. London: HMSO.

Rikowski, G. (2002) *Schools: building for business*. London: Tufnell Press.

Rizvi, F. (1993) 'Williams on democracy and the governance of education', in Dworkin, D. and Roman, L. (eds) *Views Beyond the Border Country: Raymond Williams and cultural politics*. London: Routledge.

Sammons, P. M., Lewis, A. et al. (1994) 'Teaching and learning processes', in Pollard, A. (ed.) *Look Before You Leap? Research evidence for the curriculum at Key Stage 2*. London: Institute of Education/Tufnell Press.

Teacher Training Agency (TTA) (2004) *Qualifying to Teach: professional standards for Qualified Teacher Status and requirements for initial teacher training*. London: TTA.

Teddlie, C. and Reynolds, D. (2000) *The International Handbook of School Effectiveness Research*. London: Falmer Press.

Tett, L., Munn, P., Blair, A., Kay, H., Martin, I., Martin, J. and Ranson, S. (2001) 'Collaboration between schools and community education agencies in tackling social exclusion', *Research Papers in Education*, 16 (1), 3.

Vincent, C. (1993) 'Education for the community', *British Journal of Educational Studies*, 41 (4), 366–80.

6

Working with other professionals

Krishan Sood

Those awarded Qualified Teacher Status must understand and uphold the professional code of the General Teaching Council for England by demonstrating . . . [that] they understand the contribution that support staff and other professionals make to teaching and learning.

(TTA 2004: 7 Section 1.6)

Learning objectives

To encourage teachers to:

- have a clear understanding of the contribution made by support staff and other professionals
- develop an ability to work co-operatively with a range of people to support them and the learners
- understand the limits of their own expertise and authority and know how to seek help from others.

Introduction

THIS CHAPTER OFFERS AN INSIGHT into some of the issues involved in forming collaborations with different people and organisations and is aimed at the beginning teachers specifically, but it is also relevant to teachers generally. It will also look at the implications of the *Every Child Matters* (DfES 2004a) document briefly as it will have massive impact upon working with other professionals, and an overview of some of the implications of the recent *Workforce Reform* agenda (http://www.cabinetoffice.gov.uk/opsr/workforce_reform/: accessed February 2005) is offered.

All schools differ from one another in very many ways although each can demonstrate a shared sense of collegiality (Bush 1994) as is evident in the way the teachers and other professionals, such as teaching assistants and learning mentors, relate to their pupils. Schools and education departments in universities are continuing to explore ways of deploying these staff so that more effective use is made of their abilities and their curricular and pastoral strengths. The DfEE publication *Teachers: meeting the challenge of change* (1998) states that:

> Teaching and learning can be strengthened by using the full potential of teaching assistants and school support staff . . . teaching assistants are playing an increasingly important role in school on tasks such as literacy support and helping pupils/students with special educational needs . . . we want that contribution to be fully acknowledged for the first time.
>
> (DfEE 1998: 55–6)

Although the DfEE acknowledges the contribution of 'other support staff' they fall short of explaining what their role is, nor is there an analysis of the effectiveness of it.

Beginning teachers will have to learn to establish effective collaborative working relationships with experienced teachers, learning support staff and other professionals such as parents/carers, psychologists, learning mentors, personal advisers and so on. Furthermore, effective relationships in schools are fostered where there is a conducive learning environment and where people feel that they are listened to, are valued and regarded as worthwhile individuals by pupils, parents, governors and staff. Mortimore *et al.* (1994), however, found that the voices of associate staff were seldom heard, an image which tends to distort the balance of relationships that exist in schools. It is therefore important for beginning teachers to understand how the structures, systems and interpersonal relationships operate in schools, how certain groups might be excluded and how, if this is the case, to move towards their inclusion.

Over the past few years there has been an increase in the number of teaching assistants (TAs) that schools employ (Bell 2000). In a study by Noble (2002) of an analysis of the cost effectiveness of the employment of associate staff in a primary school, a high value was placed on the work of TAs by staff, children and parents and they were considered to provide very good value for money.

As beginning teachers it is worth remembering that the work of the TAs is more likely to be effective if their role is made clear. Beginning teachers could do this by making their expectations of TAs and the pupils clearer and more precise. The TAs can be given copies of weekly planning at the beginning of each week and the teacher and the TA should find time, say if released from assembly on Monday, to discuss the planning and where possible, to incorporate lists of resources needed throughout the week so these can be prepared in advance. Ainscow (2000) throws doubt on the benefits of the use of TAs in classrooms, suggesting that there can be tensions and barriers built between children who are and are not supported, thus preventing development of good relations. But further research is needed to establish if TAs do make a difference in classrooms (see McPherson 1997; Crowther *et al.* 1998). Indeed, the Green Paper, *14–19: extending opportunities, raising standards* (DfES 2002a) and Estelle Morris, Secretary of State for Education and Skills, in a speech delivered in 2002, emphasised the need to increase the number of TAs in schools and colleges.

The Association of Teachers and Lecturers (ATL) union research found that schools found it difficult to know who did what on issues of pay, training and guidance in their LEA. Seventy per cent said that their LEA did not provide training for teachers on managing TAs; 63 per cent said their LEA published no guidance on teaching assistant deployment; and 46 per cent said their LEA did not provide an induction scheme for TAs (ATL 2003).

How adults/professionals work in school

There are many professionals and volunteers who help and support in schools. In one secondary school, effective collaboration between a beginning teacher and a mentor is established where both have ensured that their working relationship operates smoothly. In a primary school, a school policy for work with social workers, educational psychologists, education welfare officers, youth justice and health professionals and others, is written and used by all, rather than each member of staff having to devise their own ways to manage their working relationship. All schools are different and practice varies from one school to another in connection with the support offered to beginning teachers. This may be due to schools operating as 'open' organisations, subjected to pressures and influences from the wider environment (Coleman *et al.* 1994). However, they are becoming more pro-active in making links with other agencies, like education welfare officers and health professionals, especially in managing the implications of the Children Act 2004 and the *Workforce Reform* agenda. So what are the implications for *Every Child Matters* and the *Workforce Reform* agenda?

Every Child Matters

In a letter to the Chair of the National College for School Leadership, the Secretary of State for Education, Ruth Kelly, recently (DfES 2004b) announced the need to ensure that schools are 'securing improvements on all the five outcome measures identified' in the *Every Child Matters* document. *Every Child Matters: change for children* (www.everychildmatters.gov.uk) is a shared programme of change to improve outcomes for all children and young people. It takes forward the Government's vision of radical reform for children, young people and families to close the gap in outcomes between the disadvantaged and their peers. The five outcomes in *Every Child Matters* are: being healthy, staying safe, enjoying and achieving, making a positive contribution and achieving economic well-being.

The Green Paper mentions a number of related areas to improve the life chances of children at risk including parenting, fostering, young people's activities and youth justice. It proposes to build on what has already been achieved, including Sure Start, raising school standards and steps to eradicate child poverty, through new Sure Start Children's Centres in the most deprived neighbourhoods, full-service extended schools and more activities for children out-of-school through a new Young People's Fund. Visit www.dfes.gov.uk/everychildmatters for more information and to download a summary of the Green Paper, the Green Paper in full or Consultation Response forms. Visit www.homeoffice.gov.uk/justice/sentencing/youthjustice/index.html to download a companion document produced by the Home Office, *Youth Justice – The Next Steps*.

The National Literacy Trust draft response to the Green Paper *Every Child Matters* (2003) states that they want greater emphasis on language and literacy in the strategy as this would support the long-term outcomes required around achievement and parenting support (see http://www.literacytrust.org.uk/socialinclusion/youngpeople/response.html). For example, many children at risk have fallen behind with their schooling and so it would help if the proposed identification and tracking procedure also investigated children's basic skills levels. This would enable the specific learning targets to be shared between schools and other agencies which are involved with individual children.

According to the National Literacy Trust, young people with poor literacy skills have already experienced failure and therefore it is vital to build literacy into activities that interest them and help them see that they can, through even small steps, improve their reading and writing skills. While there is much teachers can do, sometimes those outside the formal education system, such as volunteers, mentors, or voluntary and community groups, are better at developing relationships with young people and encouraging them to take action to improve their skills. Look at www.literacytrust.org.uk/socialinclusion/ for examples of good practice and overviews of 'what works'.

There is also a new thrust by the Government to ensure that increasingly schools will have to offer pupils learning that is personalised to meet their needs. And children and young people will receive increasingly personalised care from health services in line with the standards of the Department of Health's (2004) *National Service Framework for Children, Young People and Maternity Services.* (See also http://www.everychildmatters.gov.uk/key-documents/ for *Every Child Matters: next steps*, the new Children Act 2004 and *Every Child Matters: change for children.*)

Delivery of this vision will require significant change in culture and working practices at every level, thus impacting on the way in which beginning teachers can play their part. There are therefore many implications for beginning teachers in working through the agenda posed by *Every Child Matters*. Beginning teachers will need to consider issues such as how to:

- make things work better for every child, family and carers
- develop better access to information
- have closer working relationships with the voluntary sector
- develop the skill-mix of teams
- form better links with leisure
- better evaluate through looking at the evidence and reviewing what does and does not work to inform other services
- have better training and development, and
- ensure that all this is done in a co-ordinated manner.

Integration may be the key – integrated front-line delivery, integrated processes, integrated strategy, and inter-agency governance.

Workforce Reform agenda

An historic National Agreement between Government, employers and school workforce unions was signed on 15 January 2003. It promised joint action, designed to help every school across England and Wales to raise standards and tackle workload issues (see the National Remodelling Team website at the end of this paragraph). The way our schools are deploying their workforce, from teachers to technicians, from premises manager to office staff, is changing. Schools are being encouraged to use teachers' time to do what they are qualified to do and focus on teaching and learning of the pupils, while allowing other members of support staff to take on more roles and responsibilities to free up teachers' time. Schools are also being encouraged to look at the way they run in general through the remodelling agenda, which was introduced to support schools working towards implementation of the National Agreement and to enable schools to take it much further (see http://www.remodelling.org/what_na.php).

Remodelling is seen by governors and teachers as a way of using and celebrating community spirit, to bring the needs of the school back to the forefront of their, and their community's, thinking. For beginning teachers this implies the need to share their strengths and their creativity towards re-energising and reinvigorating the workforce.

Another significant benefit of remodelling is a chance for all who teach to have the time and energy to plan and teach lessons that inspire and enthuse. This will benefit children's learning. It could also have a positive effect on the way children view all members of the school staff, especially in schools where the support staff have a teaching role. However, in one LEA there is a natural reluctance to change – an obstacle that governors fear of the remodelling agenda, and one that may be hard to overcome. After many years of change, some feel that their school's workforce needs a period of stability. It may be that not all members of staff will see further change as a positive step towards such a period of stability in the future. With almost 50 per cent of teachers within 15 years of retirement, it is these teachers who may well feel the burden of change most. The implications of a change in management, uncertainty of roles and relationships may be some of the issues that beginning teachers will have to face, and an early awareness of such issues would therefore be appropriate.

The role of higher level teaching assistants (HLTAs)

School support staff make a vital contribution to pupils' learning and achievement. With the introduction of a new programme of training and assessment, support staff who achieve higher level teaching assistant (HLTA) status (see HLTA website http://www.hlta.gov.uk) will be able to offer proven skills to support teachers even more effectively in the future. The Teacher Training Agency (TTA) has developed and published standards for HLTAs, linking to those for Qualified Teacher Status (QTS). HLTA roles have greater complexity and autonomy than other classroom support roles. The HLTA standards reflect the significant contribution HLTAs are expected to play in teaching and learning activities, for example:

contributing to the planning and preparation of lessons; monitoring pupils' participation and progress; providing feedback to teachers; giving constructive support to pupils as they learn; and working with individuals, small groups and whole classes where the assigned teacher is not present.

(http://www.teachernet.gov.uk/wholeschool/teachingassistants/training/HLTAs/ (accessed February 2005))

Beginning teachers will need to keep abreast of such developments. In the following section, issues about accountability are addressed.

Accountability

The links between schools and external advisors and support personnel inevitably needs careful management. In turbulent times for example, a school needs to be 'flexible and adaptive' (Hoyle 1986: 98), whereas in a stable environment, a more formal 'mechanistic' model may be most effective. Additionally, with schools forming a range of relationships with people, they are increasingly called to be accountable.

Accountability, as discussed by Scott (1989) may be multifaceted and could be public accountability, professional accountability or consumerist accountability. Beginning teachers should be able to identify examples of all three types of accountability in their establishments. Within the normative concept of professional accountability for example, stress is upon the accountability of teachers to their profession. It is linked with self-reporting or self-evaluation, but may involve some level of dialogue with interested parties. This type of accountability would not appear totally compatible with responsiveness to the customer in a market environment.

In planning a collaborative partnership with other professionals, the notion of accountability to parents, pupils and other stakeholders is crucial. So the need to understand each other's role and differing responsibilities is vital for beginning teachers. For example, in analysing the needs of an SEN child through observations and notes made, beginning teachers could refer to an experienced staff member first and then with their help and guidance, the Special Educational Needs Coordinator (SENCO) needs to be involved. For anything more serious, for example in cases of suspected abuse, beginning teachers need to consult an identified person, usually the head teacher (see Chapter 8).

An understanding of the roles and responsibilities of different professionals in meeting the needs of pupils is an important element of teaching. Not only do beginning teachers have to know who to call on, like social workers, educational psychologists, education welfare officers, youth justice and health professionals, beginning teachers also need to be aware of the systems which exist to support them. Beginning teachers may also find that the school has a range of communication networks with voluntary agencies as well. It is therefore essential to be pro-active and strategic in collaborating with a range of professionals as this will reduce the likelihood of duplication (Sweeney 1999).

Establishing relationships

The key to collaboration with a range of people within different environments lies in forming lasting relationships. Relationship marketing (Payne *et al*. 1995) seems an especially helpful perspective and approach to be considered for schools in this collaboration. This concept recognises that marketing is about a relationship built over time between individual people inside and outside the organisation, and not a distant, impersonal link between the 'customer' and the 'corporation' (Stokes 1996). It seems that such an approach to external links characterises much of what primary and secondary schools have attempted to do for many years for sound 'educational' purposes, without the word 'marketing' being mentioned. Whether such a view of marketing is accepted or rejected, it seems that most schools are actually rather good at it.

Effective working relationships with others then requires teachers having an overview about the roles and responsibilities of all the partners. In one school, all staff had a list of professionals associated with the school and knew their reasons for being involved. It is necessary therefore for beginning teachers to get involved in the development phase, be it planning, team teaching, evaluating a project or disseminating information, but ensuring it is done in a collegial fashion. Beginning teachers can take the opportunity to involve other adults in this process across all stages of the education phase. For example, as observed by Ms Mistry, a class teacher, being actively engaged in the development phase may well involve some of these approaches:

- liaising with teachers to gain informal reports on the pupils
- discussing with members of staff the simplest way of completing standard assessment sheets, which can be passed throughout the school to maintain continuity and progression
- taking responsibility for a curriculum area requiring liaison with other teachers to ensure the correct delivery of the subject in question
- having team planning or briefing meetings on a regular basis providing the opportunity to discuss any new issues or air any concerns. Furthermore, it indicates that everyone is following the same plan and working together as a team.

Managing the work of generalist teaching assistants, parents, volunteers and/or mentors in the classroom to enhance learning opportunities for pupils requires clear objectives for the adults to work towards. These adults, especially volunteers and parents, also need to work with pupils where they can see progression in these pupils' learning, therefore boosting the adults' self-confidence.

As Ms Mistry, an experienced teacher, noted, 'Beginning teachers need to be aware of the need for co-operative planning and through such meetings develop self-confidence and respect from other members of staff.'

Working collaboratively with specialist teachers requires meticulous written plans and targets that can be shared easily and communicated effectively. Joint planning with the appropriate adults clarifies and defines roles and outcomes and reduces tensions which may impact learning. If the learning support staff are not involved in planning then they do not know the reasons why they are doing a particular activity.

In a busy classroom, the need to manage time effectively is crucial, especially during pupil assessments and record keeping. Encouraging and involving additional adults can ease the task by requesting an adult to help make observations or keep tick lists. Also by talking to them just for a few minutes after the session helps to monitor progress. Such discussions help to foster better working relationships to advance the pupils' learning. In a study of learning support work by Balshaw (1999), it was found that support staff carried out a huge array of tasks, including cataloguing reading books, recording television programmes, liaison and co-ordinating tasks. Beginning teachers should understand and acknowledge the wide range of skills and abilities the support staff have and maximise these to the benefit of pupil learning.

As beginning teachers are used to being observed when undertaking their teaching practice, it should not pose too much of a threat to be observed by different staff and to get feedback. Beginning teachers should be able to handle constructive criticism and suggestions for improving classroom practice with professionalism.

Working collaboratively with colleagues in planning, teaching and assessment, inside and outside the classroom requires professionalism at all times. All members of staff have a key role to play in the education of pupils in a school as well as acting collaboratively with colleagues in pursuance of school or team objectives. Most teachers participate in various types of meetings and take on extra-curricular activities. Beginning teachers can join with an experienced member of staff to run a club if they do not feel confident at doing this independently.

Inclusion

Some of the principles and characteristics of inclusive education are based on viewing inclusion as a human rights issue in which a school has no physical, attitudinal or organisational barriers. Inclusion is seen as a human rights issue because all pupils have the right to learn together, where they are not devalued by exclusion and where pupils do not need to be protected from each other if there is a caring environment. Furthermore, social interaction is likely to reduce fear and build friendship, respect and understanding in preparation for their role as emergent active citizens.

Education should help to make the world less oppressive, less unequal and indeed, help to build greater equality and justice. Through first-hand experiences, pupils should be set challenges which they can argue and reflect upon, and this cannot be limited to a didactic approach by teachers or deferential note-taking by pupils (Richardson 1990). All beginning teachers will have to be aware of the different needs of pupils, based on their individuality. All will belong to a social class, an ethnic group, a religious tradition or none, a gender and a local neighbourhood; some will have special educational needs and, from a certain age, all will have a sexual identity. So for an inclusive education, beginning teachers will have to plan to teach for an inclusive, holistic education where all pupils are encouraged to succeed. What seems an important prerequisite for an inclusive environment is the need for all teachers and learning support staff to foster and nurture this, leading to all pupils playing their part in being educated.

To take the issue of disability as an example, some of the practical steps to achieve inclusion with pupils with disability could be to:

- conduct an access audit of the school/other environment
- ask and involve the pupil in decision making
- discourage negative language
- vary teaching and learning approaches to encourage and celebrate diversity
- consult and collaborate with statutory agencies, health, social services, educational psychologists, specialist teachers, teaching assistants and parent(s)/carer(s) to promote an inclusive ethos
- develop empowerment and self-representation for disabled pupils.

Additionally, beginning teachers will need to be involved in disability equality training for staff and governors and understand how to monitor and evaluate the inclusive process. According to Booth *et al.* (2000), inclusion is about fostering mutually sustaining relationships between schools and communities, suggesting that you should form alliances with various people and go on listening and learning from them. Central to this debate is the need for all schools to be explicit to all what their values and cultures are in developing inclusive practices.

Teachers try to take a pro-active approach to ensure that all pupils are developing a positive sense of identity and self-esteem. As teachers in a classroom learning environment we often try to generate labels which will enable us to group pupils together to make large-sized classes more manageable, for example, 'ability' groups, 'interest' groups and 'friendship' groups. But this strategy carries with it a number of risks. The label may be inappropriate and/or it may not reflect the pupil's perspectives; the label may fit only in certain situations; pupils may be given very few opportunities to demonstrate change and/or development and the pupil may learn to 'fit' the label even though it was not initially an appropriate one. Labelling pupils does not only affect the learning opportunities offered to them and the relationships they are able to develop and sustain, but will also reflect upon their own sense of self-identity and upon their learning behaviours. It is extremely important, therefore, that teachers and other learning support staff use 'labels' sparingly and that the labels they employ are flexible, responsive and regularly up-dated and reviewed.

Staff who are allocated to support a pupil with specific educational needs or those learning English as an additional language need to be clear about their role. They need to be very clear too about which children they are working with and why, as misunderstandings arise when this is not communicated effectively among the staff. Additional support staff may also need to be gently reminded that they are there to help pupils to think for themselves and not to encourage dependence, as noted by a Key Stage 2 class teacher, 'they should not to do the work for them'. It is worth reflecting on recent research and inspection findings that confirm the 'tremendous contribution' made by well-managed and well-trained assistants to the learning process (DfEE 2000).

Some of the strategies to develop a pupil's identity and self-esteem could be through:

- respecting and valuing pupils as individuals and their parent(s)/carer(s) and families

- not doing everything for pupils, but encouraging them to become independent

- providing positive images of a diverse society

- giving pupils opportunities to identify their own needs, abilities and learning in all areas of development

- enabling pupils to build their self-image through the recognition of progress as well as attainment

- accommodating change and development and resisting the use of stereotypical 'labels' for which there is little or no personal 'evidence'.

As beginning teachers may already have come in contact with a range of professionals, they will be aware of who and how these professionals can assist beginning teachers in establishing the practice of inclusion. For example, one LEA has set up an inclusion support unit which works with children, families, schools and other agencies, such as Speech and Language Therapy, Social Inclusion and Health, by negotiation and direct request. They help in schools to improve their practice on inclusion through staff training, project work, monitoring and evaluation and the development of policy and practice. They offer consultation, advice, educational and psychological assessment, through multi-professional working, in line with legislative frameworks and training and advice for parents, carers, children and governors. They undertake monitoring the quality and quantity of provision for pupils with special educational needs; they offer pre-school intervention; and advice and support for children with special educational needs and their families/carers.

Support for schools in providing study opportunities for such pupils can be considered as an aspect of inclusion. Study support is highlighted in the DfES's strategies for both primary and secondary education. Recent DfES publications, *A New Specialist System: transforming secondary education* (2003a) and *Excellence and Enjoyment: a strategy for primary schools* (2003b) have both emphasised the important contribution of study support to young people's learning experience. These documents reaffirm the Department's objective that all schools offer study support within their overall plans by 2006, which is consistent with the Children's Green Paper (the Children's Act 2004) commitment to fully service extended schools including study support provision. Check out the latest news on the DfES Study Support website http://www.standards.dfes.gov.uk/study-support/ including: Study Support Funding 2004/2005; and the Green Paper *Every Child Matters*.

Working with visiting professionals

The great untapped energy and abilities of other visiting professionals from the community can enhance a school's curriculum and go some way to revitalise staff enthusiasm. The important message is that these visitors should be made to feel valued by the whole school community. There are many good examples such as suspending the school's timetable for a week to permeate intercultural activities across the curriculum. Trips to a gurdwara or a synagogue (Sikh and Jewish places of worship, respectively) can be made educationally exciting by inviting people from such faiths to raise initial awareness. In three primary schools, for example, rituals and celebrations formed a project where multicultural dance focused on Chinese New Year celebrations. A visiting musician, dancer and cultural artist from China enchanted teachers and pupils alike with the sounds of her Ku-cheng, a Chinese harp. In one county, several secondary schools had planned the entire term's curriculum round an arts project. In another two secondary schools, there was collaboration of Year 8 classes focusing on a language week.

Other examples of working with visiting professionals include cross-curricular, cross-phase, cross-art-forms projects, technology weeks, a composing project with a symphony orchestra and classical singer, traditional folk songs revealing social history, and projects with sculptors and photographers creating knowledge and pride of place as well as new skills for pupils and teachers. In all this, energy, commitment, creativity, collaboration, co-operation and celebration were produced in abundance from all.

Working with the Ethnic Minority and Traveller Achievement Grant (EMTAG) teachers

Beginning teachers need to be aware of the role of such specialists as the Ethnic Minority and Traveller Achievement Grant (EMTAG) teachers. The author has specific experience in this area as a past advisory teacher for intercultural education in developing an intercultural support programme permeating a whole school. This involved leading, guiding, teaching and supporting teachers in the classroom to develop the curriculum which was more inclusive, holistic and diverse in its approach. There were activities to support classroom teachers through workshops to develop an antiracist approach to science, days of INSET on 'Arts across the World' to raise cultural awareness, governor training on issues of ethnicity and gender and through short- and long-term projects and residencies developing dance and drama programmes, exhibitions and performances. The success of such initiatives was seen through the creativity of teachers in making learning exciting, fun and relevant to a wide variety of pupils and, ultimately, owning the project or ideas which enhanced the curriculum.

On a practical basis, in every curriculum subject there are opportunities to engage pupils by showing respect for their cultural and personal identities. Here, issues of inequality and injustice can be explored using role play, developing knowledge and understanding of the history and development of one's own cultural traditions and of the ways in which these both foster and constrain one's own personal identity. There has been much borrowing, mingling and mutual influence over the centuries between different countries and cultural traditions (Richardson 1990). This gives the beginning teacher an opportunity to develop in their pupils an ability to learn from different cultural experiences, norms and perspectives, and to empathise with people with different traditions. Equally important is to develop in pupils the willingness to challenge instances of prejudice, intolerance and discrimination of any kind.

In art, with the support of teachers, visiting artists and minority ethnic staff can develop a range of resources stressing cross-cultural borrowings and influences. In English, fiction, drama and poetry can be drawn from a range of genres, times and places. In geography, pupils can be shown practical ways of making global connections and interdependence, whereas in history, British history can be taught within a world perspective, related to events in other countries. In mathematics, activities could be developed to reflect the multi-ethnic and multicultural nature of modern societies. In personal, social and health education (PSHE), there are opportunities for reflection on events in the school itself, including bullying and racial name calling. Here, beginning teachers can stress techniques and methods of conflict resolution which pupils themselves can use. Many more ideas can be found in the handbook produced by the Runnymede Trust (1993). See also Cole *et al.* (1997) and Hill and Cole (1999).

Beginning teachers then need to be aware of the role of these specialist teachers and where their support can best fit in the curriculum. Perhaps the EMTAG teachers could join the school planning meetings or see the half-termly plan to offer suggestions on how targeted support can be offered. Experience of working with such support staff and other agencies suggests that beginning teachers have to be flexible to mutually arrange dates and times of their meetings as these professionals may also have to visit other schools.

Working with the Traveller Education Service

The work of the Traveller Education Service (TES) according to the Ofsted report (1996) is generally of a high standard. The education for traveller children in one Midland county is provided by the West Midlands Consortium Education Service for Travelling Children. Advisory teachers from this establishment have very successfully run courses for BA Primary (QTS) students for a number of years at the author's initial teacher education (ITE) institution. In one example, an advisory teacher for the travelling children noted that her/his work with gypsy and traveller families involved an holistic service provision, and she or he was not thinking in isolation about accommodation, health care, education and welfare. A family constantly and erratically moved on and disrupted is not in a good position to prioritise preventative health care or education. The role of the travellers' advisor then is to sit down and plan with the different agencies, teachers and in consultation with the Gypsy and Traveller community, the best and most cost-effective solutions. Beginning teachers will need to understand and plan strategies with other teachers and support staff for the teaching and learning of all pupils, including the travelling pupils. In the Ofsted report (1996) the need for schools to openly acknowledge and give positive images of the different nomadic communities is emphasised.

As stated earlier, developing good relationships with parents is an essential role of a school. Beginning teachers can develop good practice when meeting and working with new parents, particularly those from the Gypsy/Traveller community, in these ways. Families will expect beginning teachers to be reliable, positive and sympathetic to their needs and to respect the confidentiality of any information they may give you. It may be that other people's values, life-style and experiences may differ from those of beginning teachers, but will be equally valid. Be aware of cultural differences, gender roles, child rearing, expectation for education, family responsibilities and work patterns affecting young people. Parents themselves may have little or no experience of school or pre-school opportunities and may not read or write well, if at all. Pens, pencils, books, paper, toys may not be available in the home. School premises may be daunting and educational terminology not readily understood. Children may not start school until age six, seven, eight or even older and parents may be reluctant to part from children, especially the youngest and the value of early years education may not be recognised. (For further information, contact the West Midland Consortium Education Service for Travelling Children, The Graiseley Centre, Pool Street, Wolverhampton, WV2 4NE.)

Working with Special Educational Needs Coordinators (SENCOs)

Knowing how to plan collaboratively with SENCOs and SEN support teachers requires an understanding of their roles. Beginning teachers will need to be familiar with the layout and purpose of an Individual Education Plan (IEP). Sometimes the TAs work more closely with children with special educational needs and may well have important contributions to make to their IEPs. Including these colleagues in your planning signals your recognition of their valuable support.

The need for each learning support colleague to know what they are going to do everyday is an important management function of beginning teachers These adults should know, through regular patterns of meetings, where they are going to be, which pupils they will be working with, which activities are set out for them and how they are going to set about using those activities and where they are going with them.

Bilingual and multilingual learner support

Deployment of bilingual and multilingual adult support for bilingual and multilingual pupils requires the same sensitivity and tact by beginning teachers as shown to any other adult. Indeed, bilingual and multilingual staff should be enabled to work in all areas of a school's programme. Bilingual and multilingual staff play a vital role in promoting learning and need to be supported in the work they do with pupils and families. Bilingualism and multilingualism is a positive benefit to all for educational, social, economic and family reasons. Indeed, the

TTA and other agencies in consultation with teachers and various community groups need to urgently consider the role of Asian languages and the way the National Curriculum renders them less important than European ones.

Some practical strategies of working with bilingual and multilingual staff offered by Siraj-Blatchford and Clarke (2000) include:

- encouraging bilingual and multilingual staff to add to all school resources as well as bilingual and multilingual resources

- encouraging bilingual and multilingual staff to plan group times in both languages every day

- translating signs and notices around the school and placing these next to the English ones

- making sure the physical environment reflects the home languages and cultures of the pupils

- using photographs in the classroom to create a challenging and exciting activity, full of potential for language work

- involving pupils in the experience of preparing for and meeting a visitor which can be a rich source of pleasure and interest and give many opportunities for language work.

There should be many chances to develop skills across different language levels like casual talk, response to visual and aural stimuli, listening to and telling unscripted stories and letter writing.

Teamworking and team building

A learning organisation is characterised by a culture of learning, reflection, self-improvement and a relaxed atmosphere. New ideas are listened to positively and there is a high level of discussion about learning and learners (see Senge 1993; Hadfield *et al.* 2000). As beginning teachers gain experience in their teaching career they may become a subject leader.

Developing good interpersonal relationships is therefore very important in leadership and management at all levels. Beginning teachers may find that much energy is spent on issues like team building, counselling, disaffection, stress or overwork.

Effective teams do not happen by chance, they have to be deliberately created and systematically managed and nurtured. As a member of a team, beginning teachers need to be concerned with feelings and consciousness as well as with structures. Effective team building is facilitated by getting to know individuals, to know their strengths and to know how you can work together. All these require free flow of information and meetings which are well organised and where there is sharing of responsibilities. Tensions arise when certain members of the team do not contribute their share equally or there is a misunderstanding of each member's roles and responsibilities. Sometimes a task explained to a member of the support staff is not made clear or he or she misunderstands what beginning teachers require, leading to undue anxiety, which must be sensitively and patiently resolved.

Shaw (2001) notes that learning assistants feel valued when working collaboratively and find it is better for learning if there is a good team supporting a pupil or pupils. She also found that pupils feel secure if the adult team is strong, especially in presenting a united front in maintaining discipline in the class. Team working between teachers and support staff takes time to be established and may even require changes in the classroom structure and organisation towards more collaborative ways of working. Shaw (2001) observes that where there are open plan sections connected to different key stages, it is more likely to facilitate adults and teachers working more effectively in teams. The quality of communication between team members is crucial in order to maintain continuity for pupils. Flexibility in deploying learning support staff might be a way forward.

Schools operate partly on the basis of teams. Examples include working alongside other colleagues in a co-operative team teaching situation. Good examples have been noted by the author where EAL specialists, bilingual and multilingual teachers and instructors and SEN specialists have planned and taught some sessions. Teachers and other adults who belong to these groups are expected to act collaboratively with each other in order to meet school or team objectives. Collegiality places emphasis on teamwork where the talents of all team members can be harnessed.

Conclusion

To conclude, TAs and other adults are very important people when used effectively in schools. To produce good practice, beginning teachers must appreciate the role of these supporters and try to encourage school managers to provide support, guidance and sound training for them. It is equally important for experienced staff to go on supporting beginning teachers, who at times may be feeling vulnerable. Lastly, as support for their school, TAs and other professionals must be considered 'not just part of the staff, but are part of a team' (DfES 2002b: 3), and beginning teachers have a decisive role to enable this to happen for the benefit of all pupils. Improving practice when working with TAs can be conducted by carrying out an audit of current practice (see DfES 2002 teaching assistants' web page which can be accessed via www.teachernet.gov.uk). So for example, TAs can be trained to deliver literacy sessions as part of a whole-school literacy initiative. When undertaken with care and sensitivity, this can develop and motivate colleagues to get better at what they are doing (DfES 2002b). The implications for *Every Child Matters* and the *Workforce Reform* agenda are profound and will require an awareness and understanding of issues contained within these documents so that the impact on beginning teachers is carefully worked through with experienced professionals within the school and beyond.

The author would like to acknowledge the very great help of Ms Malini Mistry, an experienced infant school teacher, in providing a range of examples of good practice of working with beginning teachers and other adults.

References

Ainscow, M. (2000) 'Poor tactics lets down mums' army', *Times Educational Supplement*, 31 March, 24.

Association of Teachers and Lecturers (ATL) (2003) Report (October). 26(1), 10–11.

Balshaw, M. (1999) *Help in the Classroom*, 2nd edn. London: David Fulton.

Bell, L. (2000) 'The management of staff: some issues of efficiency and cost effectiveness', in Coleman, M. and Anderson, L. (eds) *Managing Finance and Resources in Education*. London: Paul Chapman.

Booth, T., Ainscow, M., Black-Hawkins, K., Vaughan, M. and Shaw, L. (2000) *Index for Inclusion*. Bristol: Centre for Studies on Inclusive Education (CSIE).

Bush, T. (1994) 'Theory and practice in educational management', in Bush, T. and West-Burnham, J. (eds) *The Principles of Educational Management*. Harlow: Longman.

Children Act 2004 http://www.everychildmatters.gov.uk/key-documents (accessed January 2005).

Cole, M., Hill, D. and Shan, S. (1997) *Promoting Equality in Primary Schools*. London: Cassell.

Coleman, M., Bush, T. and Glover, D. (1994) *Managing Finance and External Relations*. Harlow: Longman.

Crowther, D., Dyson, A. and Millward, A. (1998) *Costs and Outcomes for Pupils/students with Moderate Learning Difficulties in Special and Mainstream Schools*. Research Report RR89: London: Department for Education and Employment.

Department of Health (2004) *National Service Framework for Children, Young People and Maternity Services*. http://www.dh.gov.uk/PolicyAndGuidance/HealthAndSocialCareTopics/ChildrenServices/ChildrenServicesInformation/fs/en (accessed February 2005).

DfEE (1998) *Teachers: meeting the challenge of change*. London: The Stationery Office.

DfEE (2000) *Working with Teaching Assistants, a Good Practice Guide*. London: The Stationery Office.

DfES (2002a) *14–19: extending opportunities, raising standards*. http://www.dfes.gov.uk/14-19greenpaper/foreword.shtml (accessed January 2005).

DfES (2002b) *Working with Teaching Assistants, a Good Practice Guide*. London: The Stationery Office.

DfES (2003a) *A New Specialist System: transforming secondary education*. London: The Stationery Office.

DfES (2003b) *Excellence and Enjoyment: a strategy for primary schools*. London: The Stationery Office.

DfES (2004a) *Every Child Matters*. London: The Stationery Office.

DfES (2004b) *National College for School Leadership Priorities*. Letter by Ruth Kelly, 20 December. London: The Stationery Office.

Hadfield, M., Chapman, C., Curryer, I. and Barrett, P. (2000) *Building Capacity. Developing your school*. Nottingham: National College for School Leadership (NCSL).

Hill, D. and Cole, M. (1999) *Promoting Equality in Secondary Schools*. London: Cassell.

Hoyle, E. (1986) *The Politics of School Management*. London: Hodder and Stoughton.

McPherson, A. (1997) 'Measuring added value in schools', in Harris, A., Bennett, N. and Preedy, M. (eds) *Organisational Effectiveness and Improvement in Education*. Milton Keynes: Paul Chapman.

Mortimore, P., Mortimore, J. with Thomas H. (1994) *Managing Associate Staff: innovation in primary and secondary schools*. London: Paul Chapman.

Noble, R. E. (2002) 'An analysis of the cost effectiveness of the use of support staff at St Peter's Junior School'. MBA assignment, University of Leicester, Educational Management Development Unit, Northampton.

Ofsted (1996) *The Education of Travelling Children – a Survey of Educational Provision for Travelling Children*. London: Ofsted.

Payne, A., Christopher, M., Clark, M. and Peck, H. (1995) *Relationship Marketing for Competitive Advantage: winning and keeping customers*. Oxford: Butterworth-Heinemann.

Richardson, R. (1990) *Daring to be a Teacher*. Stoke-on-Trent: Trentham Books.

Runnymede Trust (1993) *Equality Assurance in Schools: quality, identity, society – a handbook for action planning and school effectiveness*. Stoke-on-Trent: Trentham Books.

Scott, P. (1989) 'Accountability, responsiveness and responsibility', in Glatter, R. (ed). *Educational Institutions and their Environments: managing the boundaries*. Milton Keynes: Open University Press.

Senge, P. (1993) *The Fifth Discipline*. London: Century Business.

Shaw, L. (2001) *Learning Supporters and Inclusion*. Bristol: Centre for Studies on Inclusive Education (CSIE).

Siraj-Blatchford, I. and Clarke, P. (2000) *Supporting Identity, Diversity and Language in the Early Years*. Buckingham: Open University Press.

Stokes, D. (1996) 'Relationship marketing in primary schools', in *Proceedings of the 'Markets in Education, Policy, Process and Practice' Symposium*. Southampton: Centre for Research in Education Marketing, University of Southampton.

Sweeney, D. (1999) 'Liaising with parents, carers and agencies', in Cole, M. (ed.) *Professional Issues for Teachers and Student Teachers*. London: David Fulton.

Teacher Training Agency (TTA) (2004) *Qualifying to Teach: professional standards for Qualified Teacher Status and requirements for initial teacher training*. London: TTA.

Tett, L., Caddell, D., Crowther, J. and O'Hara, P. (2000) Parents and Schools: partnership in early years' education. (www.leeds.ac.uk/educol/documents/00001681.htm) (accessed January 2005).

Commitment to professional development

Valerie Coultas

Those awarded Qualified Teacher Status must understand and uphold the professional code of the General Teaching Council for England by demonstrating . . . [that] they are able to improve their own teaching, by evaluating it, learning from the effective practice of others and from evidence. They are motivated and able to take increasing responsibility for their own professional development.

(TTA 2004: 7 Section 1.7)

Learning objectives

To promote understanding of:

- how to become a self-critical, reflective practitioner
- the importance of collaborative planning and teamwork
- how to develop classroom management skills and subject knowledge
- how to use professional development to improve teaching and become a creative teacher.

Introduction

AN EFFECTIVE TEACHER IS SOMEONE who sees herself or himself as a learner. Teachers who evaluate and change their own practice to benefit their pupils are rewarding colleagues to work with. They make teaching a highly creative experience. Often the most useful lesson observations can be those carried out by a teacher who is a peer, someone who has to battle with similar problems. By planning lessons collaboratively, focusing on the same topic/text or the same type of pedagogy, and then evaluating these lessons together, it will help improve a teacher's practice. It is through close collaboration, shared evaluation and team teaching that teachers can make breakthroughs and deliver the most successful lessons. A colleague can often notice a detail in the instructions that has been missed out in a lesson that is team taught because they are paying close attention to pupil responses. Even the most experienced teachers can benefit from this process of collaboration.

It is far more positive to have these discussions with colleagues than to wait for an inspector to point out your errors. If teachers start teaching with this view of classroom practice, they will automatically evaluate lessons. An energetic professional teacher is self-critical and creative. Once a teacher adopts this approach to teaching they will never lose it. This view of teachers values the voice of the teacher and sees the teacher as an agent of change within the school.

Teamwork

Many schools encourage this kind of collaboration through teamwork in departments and joint planning between teachers in different phases. Teamwork takes place formally and informally in schools. The best schemes of work are often produced and evaluated collectively. This formal teamwork is excellent practice. Sometimes it is through a one-to-one discussion with a line manager during, for example, a feedback from a lesson observation that useful advice will be offered. Sometimes useful advice can be offered to a line manager in a support and supervision interview. Often it's the informal discussion with a colleague at break or after school that leads to a new approach in teaching.

However, the attempt to impose quantitative targets on those discussions by the Government through performance-related pay fails to comprehend the essence of good teaching which is teamwork and intellectual collaboration. A department or a school's results are not good because of isolated, inspired individuals but because good practice is shared, knowledge and expertise are valued, and colleagues and managers give positive support and advice to staff when required. Teachers are not working on production lines in industry. They are nurturing, training, educating and developing young people. Their intellectual energy is encouraged by good advice, good leadership and shared values – not through the imposition of individual targets. The teacher is a creative professional, not a skilled technician implementing the advice of government departments. The new pay schemes that are being suggested threaten some of the structures in schools that actually support teamwork, for example abolishing management allowances for pastoral responsibilities.

The Government's search for quantitative, measurable data to prove success can often dismiss qualitative improvements in schools. Education cannot be reduced to the acquiring of skills; the ticking boxes agenda is reductionist. As Caroline Benn (2001) suggests, the 'limited target culture' can have the effect of losing sight of the broader aims of education and the emotional and moral aspects of learning. Fortunately many practitioners are aware of this and have attempted to set individual targets that are more holistic and relate to broader educational and training needs.

Targets for improvement

It is suggested that teachers should identify areas for their own development and set targets for improvement. Schools are encouraged to base this on evidence from results. It may be that this will involve closely analysing exam results at the end of a key stage of a group that you have taught in order to evaluate your success. Sometimes your school will ask the subject co-co-ordinators or heads of subject to produce yearly comparisons of results. This overall comparison can help you evaluate your results, for example by comparing predicted levels or grades with final results. Looking closely at how individual pupils perform, linked to discussions with other teachers, will give you ideas about how to improve your teaching. The figures must be analysed and discussed to give this process real meaning.

But the qualitative evaluations with pupils are just as important, although often less valued by the male managerial 'quantitative analysis is best' culture that has been fostered by recent governments. This could involve an evaluation with all the pupils at the end of a unit or course using their individual self-assessments. Or it could involve a more in-depth discussion with a particular group to get feedback. The response of the pupils themselves to a unit of work or a course is often a key indicator of successful teaching and it can help you to make adjustments to improve the content, the pedagogy or focus more closely on particular skills the pupils need. Such an assessment, a qualitative judgement or piece of research, is of particular value to the teacher. It shows the pupils that you value their opinions and it is useful for precise subject targets. If whole departments engage in this process it means that the course will continually improve. The process of identifying areas for development individually can therefore be assisted by an in service education and training (INSET) session, a departmental or phase discussion led by a team leader or a line management review. But as a learning teacher you will come to those discussions with an awareness of where you have done well and how you can improve. You will even suggest themes for INSET to ensure that staff development serves your needs.

A teacher should also seek to improve their subject knowledge and build on areas of specialism. It is vital that teachers not only have secure knowledge of the subjects they teach but that they are aware of the new developments in those subjects, for example the new frameworks for teaching literacy and numeracy (DfEE 1998) and the debates these have generated. There are also areas of specialism within a subject that teachers may wish to become more familiar with. For example in a core subject, such as English, there are many possible subdivisions – oracy, ICT, media studies, poetry, drama, non-fiction writing and research. To gain greater expertise in one of these areas could be a goal that strengthens your teaching.

Equality and equal opportunity

In primary and secondary schools it may be a key stage or pastoral issues where you wish to specialise. An important area of knowledge the beginning teacher will have to develop relates to equality and equal opportunity issues. This is relevant to how you teach and how you build relationships with pupils and colleagues. A teacher must ensure they can identify and address all the different needs in the classroom. Lesson planning needs to address pupils with special needs, bilingual needs and high attainers. Even though setting is more common in secondary schools, the teacher cannot assume that all pupils in a particular set have the same ability. They must also be aware of how to involve boys and girls in the lesson. A teacher can ensure that boys do not dominate oral work by preparing pupils to answer questions and asking particular pupils to answer on some occasions. They can use drama to engage all pupils and writing frames/planning activities and clear time limits to ensure boys actually do some extended writing.

It is important that teachers have a sophisticated understanding of equal opportunity issues as these issues are constantly alive within the classroom and teachers must be aware of all the different social divisions to mediate effectively between them. This includes all forms of sexism, towards boys and girls, and the need to combat racism and homophobic bullying. You must also recognise the divisive effects of social class, and the way in which the formal middle-class values of schools often undervalue the skills of working-class pupils. Further, you should counter any discrimination based on disability. You must also show by the way you use praise and how you choose pupils to help you that you value all pupils equally, regardless of race, gender, class, sexual orientation or disability. You are a role model for the pupils and they will watch what you do and compare it with what you say.

As Cole (2002: 3–4) has argued, these social divisions 'are not inevitable features of any society' but they are a product of socialisation. Children can respond in contradictory ways to these issues. Often they will challenge these divisions quite spontaneously because their socialisation is incomplete. On other occasions they will also reproduce these social divisions very crudely. Teachers can intervene in this process to educate children very effectively if they understand equality and equal opportunity issues. For a wider discussion of the breadth of these professional issues related to equality see Cole *et al.* (1997); Cole (1999, 2005); Hill and Cole (1999, 2001a).

Classroom management

For many teachers new to the classroom a key area will be the issue of classroom management. This is often the primary concern of a beginning teacher and it is an area where they feel they have the least training. A teacher will gain a lot of good ideas by observing good practice in their own school but two useful guides with particularly practical advice on classroom management and good advice on handling challenging pupils have been written: these are Marland (2002) and Blum (1998). The latter text is useful for understanding how positive behaviour policies and praise can be used very effectively in turbulent classrooms. The beginning teacher would benefit from learning more about the idea of positive or assertive discipline, as it is one of the most important and practical theories that teachers have developed to handle disruptive behaviour. While it is formally subscribed to by many, the importance of rewarding good behaviour is often underestimated in practice, particularly in secondary schools.

As a teacher in charge of PSHE at an inner London school, in the Inner London Education Authority, I was involved in a Year 9 careers and sex education course that taught staff and pupils the ideas behind assertive behaviour. In a series of drama lessons, in separate all-boy and all-girl groups led by male and female members of staff, pupils learnt about aggressive, assertive, manipulative and passive forms of behaviour and how we had a choice about how we behaved: how we could learn to say no, distinguish between flattery and compliments and give and receive criticism. These lessons led onto a discussion of sexual/racial harassment and bullying and then into the sex education and anti-sexist careers guidance. These lessons were carefully designed to tap into the psychological, physical and social stage of development of the 13/14-year-olds. I used these assertiveness training sessions in several other school contexts and they were always extremely successful. All teachers and pupils should be taught about assertiveness to improve techniques in behaviour management and relationships in schools.

Since the Thatcher era there has been an increase in selection in secondary schools. The decision to develop specialist, Faith schools and City Academies will not only continue but as Hattersley (2002) argues will actually extend this process and dismantle the comprehensive system. This has meant that many teachers working in schools that have a more socially disadvantaged intake now face challenging behaviour in all their classrooms. Such schools are also under constant pressure to raise standards and compete with schools who have creamed off the less disadvantaged pupils where the behaviour is, in general, less challenging. Thrupp (2000), in an article reviewing the school improvement agenda, has listed some of the possible negative effects of this kind of pressure on such schools. In this article he argues that this 'over-optimistic view of schools improving against the odds' could mean that the school improvers fail to question the 'further polarisation of school intakes by educational quasi-markets' (p. 2). He also suggests that they 'downplay the importance of state support for disadvantaged schools by putting too much emphasis on their ability to be self-managing' (p. 2).

For the beginning teacher strategies to improve their classroom management skills will be a top priority, particularly in these challenging environments. All schools should have induction programmes to assist new staff and allow them time to observe other colleagues to gain knowledge of the range of strategies that can be used to address the needs of these pupils. Team teaching is also a valuable way to mentor and build confidence among new staff. I would argue that in challenging schools new staff and beginning teachers need more time to observe and teacher tutors should be given time to really tutor.

Pedagogy

The methods that you use in the classroom are very important if you wish pupils to really learn something new each lesson. Didactic teaching methods are still relied on by large numbers of teachers, particularly in secondary schools, but there are a lot of young learners who find this a difficult way to remember what they are told. Many teachers fear losing control or lack the preparation time that is required to plan the more interactive lessons. But all pupils need to be actively involved in the learning process to really make academic progress, particularly the pupils who are less motivated. Collaborative talk before writing is essential for bilingual and SEN pupils but it also improves the writing of all pupils. Lessons need to be planned that have an interactive element at their core (Coultas 2001 'Oracy across the curriculum', report distributed to staff at Selhurst High School). Primary school teachers can ensure this through joint planning for group work. But in secondary schools, where teachers may teach 150 children a day and follow a broad scheme of work, staff can often avoid planning interactive lessons and rely on teacher talk or even copying large junks of text from the OHP, the blackboard or the whiteboard.

There are many strategies that can stimulate pupils' interest and engagement in lessons. The key element of a successful lesson is that the pupils really engage with the learning and that usually takes place when they collaborate on a relatively shorter task, when their imaginations are sparked. One example from last year that comes to mind is a class discussion about flying after reading the first few chapters of *Harry Potter and the Philosopher's Stone*. The question on the board was: 'What if we could all fly?' The pupils had to discuss this using three columns: the plus points, the minus points and the interesting points. I expected a 10–15 minute discussion at the most. But the pupils would not let the discussion go. Hands kept on going up to give more ideas – traffic jams in the sky, new kinds of maps, how exactly we would be able to fly – the speculations were endless and the discussion went on for nearly 45 minutes.

Widening styles of teaching and addressing the multicultural identity of the pupil population was an area of expertise that really flourished during the life span of for example, the Inner London Education Authority. A London-wide authority with large numbers of advisory teachers was able to assist teachers in experimenting with collaborative and pupil-centered materials and to produce literature based on the pupils' writing. A whole host of new literature was made available to teachers and much of it is still used in schools. Professional associations such as the National Association of Teachers of English (NATE), the National Oracy Project (1992) and training centres such as The English and Media Centre have continued to promote styles of teaching that focus on collaborative and child-centered forms of pedagogy. The child-centred approach to teaching was an important feature of PGCE teacher education courses prior to the Thatcher era. Teacher education for primary and secondary teachers emphasised the importance of real talk in the classroom and the links between talking with confidence and writing with confidence. This approach recognised the alienating features of teacher talk for working-class pupils and suggested ways of establishing real dialogues between teacher and pupil – through anecdote, group work, visiting speakers, investigation, research and discovery. The National Curriculum, informed by the Cox Report (DES and the Welsh Office 1989), gave equal status to speaking and listening alongside reading and writing.

The National Literacy Strategy (DfEE 1998) has some good advice about the modelling of oral work, reading and writing. It also usefully develops the idea that every lesson needs to be literacy-aware. But there is a danger in aspects of the strategy that it could reinforce old-fashioned didactic methods of teaching English. If teachers are forced to study short, separate texts and decontextualised grammar exercises, this could become a new version of the comprehension textbooks that made some English lessons so tedious in the early 1960s. Wyse and Jones (2001) point out that in primary schools the literacy and numeracy strategies have left little opportunity for 'creative and unpredictable aspects of development such as talk' (p. 193). They are concerned that talk takes on 'a functional quality;

a means by which the skills of reading and writing may be enhanced' (p. 193). They recommend that teachers of all subjects allow talk to become 'open, exploratory, tentative, questioning, insightful and collaborative' (p. 195). The new QCA documentation (2003) *Speaking and Listening* and *Excellence and Enjoyment* (DfES 2003) have gone some way to address the imbalances in *The National Literacy Strategy* and give primary schools more flexibility in curriculum planning. An approach which encourages pupil-led talk has long been the hallmark of good teaching and learning and will continue to be a goal for the most creative teachers. To explore and experiment with different forms of pedagogy will be a vital goal for any beginning teacher.

There are also some interesting new developments in this area of pedagogy in the debate surrounding Able and Gifted pupils and the present discourse on thinking skills, accelerated learning and the different types of learner – kinaesthetic, auditory and visual learners (Smith 1996; Eyre 1997). Kinaesthetic learners are people who learn best through movement or touch. Auditory learners learn best through sound, and visual learners store images in their brain. Some researchers, such as Noble *et al.* (2001), have suggested that boys 'form a preponderance of kinaesthetic learners' (p. 100), that they are 'active and athletic', they 'learn best through doing what is being taught' (p. 100) and that 'if there is a dearth of kinaesthetic techniques' boys will fall behind 'into a vicious circle of under-achievement' (p. 101). Gardiner (1993) has also developed the idea of multiple intelligences. These theories underline the importance of teachers using multi-sensory learning styles.

It is important also to think carefully about how adults can acquire new knowledge. It cannot be assumed that all teachers learn in the same way or wish to be trained in the same way. It is up to each individual to define their own needs and learning styles as graduate teachers. Some teachers, as graduates with high levels of concentration, like to be lectured and told clearly what is expected of them at a training session. Others prefer to be involved in a much more active way in new proposals and initiatives. Some staff prefer to be given documentation before a session begins. Yet others gain knowledge and expertise from colleagues in similar roles in other schools. Another way of acquiring knowledge within school is through action research projects. I have initiated several of these projects – on gender and literacy, on oracy and teaching styles – and carried out literacy audits/work sampling in different schools. I have used samples of pupil evaluations of oral work to demonstrate how the pupils gain in enjoyment and enthusiasm for learning through collaborative based talk and how this increases their self-awareness. I recognise this as a valuable way of teachers acquiring expertise, learning more about the institution they teach in and the needs/interests of the pupils. This is an approach which operates on a grass-roots, co-operative model of teaching and on a belief that schools work best when teachers are allowed to have free souls to enquire and develop good practice.

Professional development

A beginning teacher must have initiative, seek out and make use of sources of professional development. As an INSET Coordinator, I assisted my colleagues by passing on the relevant training information. But individual teachers can also access the National Grid for Learning, join subject associations and attend network meetings to find the relevant forms of training to address their individual needs.

It is not only participation in training that defines the self-motivated teacher. It is also the ability to evaluate and use professional development opportunities appropriately that is vitally important. In work as in schools it is how we apply knowledge that marks us out. The teacher who tries out new techniques quickly after the training will incorporate that knowledge and adapt it to suit their situation. Some schools encourage each individual member of staff to evaluate their training through the provision of some kind of structure – a discussion with your line manager or an evaluation form. If not, the individual should develop their own records and process of evaluation to ensure that training is used constructively. Staff who keep a professional development portfolio will find this useful when applying for promotion. It is often surprising how much expertise exists among staff in any one school. Schools sometimes seek advice from consultants and experts from outside the school on the assumption that there is not a lot of knowledge on that subject within the school. Yet knowing your staff and where real knowledge and expertise lies and how to use it is a feature of good management and good teachers. I have often been surprised how willing overworked and stressed staff are to share expertise and assist other colleagues for formal and informal training. As with pupils, teachers should approach other staff carefully with specific requests for assistance and always give staff a lot of notice of extra demands. This applies to assistance with all routine duties as well as INSET. It can refer to making requests of your line manager to assist you or even your head teacher. Using the expertise of those around you is therefore a key indicator of the teacher who is a learner.

Being able to respond positively to praise, advice and criticism is also a crucial feature of a good practitioner. Having taught in two very tough London boys' schools and other challenging schools, I can attest that it's hard to accept some of the abuse that can come from pupils, nor should a teacher tolerate any disrespectful remarks. But when a colleague or pupil makes a thoughtful criticism it's worthwhile stepping back and deciding whether the criticism has any truth in it.

'Is there anything I can improve on here?' is a question the beginning teacher can ask him- or herself. Perhaps part of the criticism can be acknowledged while part of it may be unfair. Likewise with praise – too often we are too stressed or embarrassed and fail to acknowledge praise with a confident and positive response. Yet a motivated teacher knows that we can only survive in schools with the trust, help, support, advice and criticism of our colleagues/pupils and that it is this collective spirit and sense of purpose that makes teaching a worthwhile profession.

The teacher's role is a nurturing one towards the young. The best teachers ensure that they build good relationships with the pupils they teach in many subtle and important ways. Although a teacher has to deal with a class as a group, a successful teacher is also able to communicate with pupils as individuals. A teacher not only has to be available for one-to-one discussion with pupils but also has to interact with colleagues. To be available for and willing to assist your colleagues is an intrinsic skill required of all teachers, regardless of their status or position within a school. In my experience the more challenging the behaviour of the pupils, the greater the need for teachers to share their expertise and be available for each other. Knowledge of the individual child's background can be vital to understanding behaviour and academic progress. Having led several academic teams in different schools I know how important it is that staff understand school procedures if they are to follow them accurately. Staff who ask detailed questions about how exactly a section of a scheme of work breaks down in practice or who are able to admit that they don't fully understand what their role as tutor involves, assist all new staff. This is the same with whole-school issues in staff meetings. Teachers who fail to articulate their difficulties and concerns are far less likely to be following the school and department policies so consistently as those who acknowledge their need for help.

One of the negative features of re-structuring 'failing' schools in the 1990s was that staff were prevented from asking questions and reflecting on new policies because of the pressure of continuous inspection and the fear of being labelled troublesome. This led to many good teachers, particularly some of the most altruistic ones, changing schools, careers or even opting for early retirement and voluntary redundancy, which added to the crisis of teacher supply, a particularly severe problem now in challenging inner-city schools. It became unfashionable for teachers to talk of the realities of social deprivation and the effects in schools because this became an apology for 'low expectations'. Instead Blair's brave new world of education demanded high expectations and an end to the idea that social class determined or even influenced academic achievement. Mackie (2000) has written a very personal account of the effects of this on the lives of pupils and teachers in these schools. The reality is that social class has always played and continues to play a vital role in determining educational achievement (Hill and Cole 2001b) and while all teachers must have high expectations for all, they must also have a realistic understanding of how social class affects educational achievement.

An excellent training programme I attended at Stoke Rochford suggested that all teachers should view themselves as 'managers' of the classroom and managers and leaders of others. This view of the classroom teacher is important as it emphasises the variety and breadth of knowledge and skills a teacher possesses. The teacher's role was to empower pupils and manage the classroom. As teachers we could also empower each other by the way we relate to each other in schools, sharing expertise and good practice.

Collaboration

When assistance is offered to the beginning teacher she or he should know how to use it appropriately. Having worked very closely with bilingual and SEN colleagues and learning support assistants I am very interested when they give me examples of staff who do not know how to receive and use support. If lessons have an interactive/pair or group work element, teachers should always provide a role for another adult as they can easily target one group or the teacher can target a group and they can circulate. Reading aloud can always be made more enjoyable for the pupils when different adults participate. If it is planned support, teachers or support staff can read with a group or individuals or prepare a reading for the class with a particular group. Specialist staff are often willing to prepare materials for particular pupils if the classroom teacher makes the task clear. Collaboration with support staff is much easier when the support is a regular feature of a lesson each week and the relationship between the two adults has time to develop. When SEN and EAL staff are allocated to departments or year groups the collaboration is greatly improved as the support staff have a clear overview of the curriculum.

A second adult, who is there to help, is always welcome in my classroom. The very presence of another adult makes me feel more relaxed and able to be more adventurous in my teaching. There are often unusual spin-offs from lessons that are taught by two adults. Recently after a brief row with a colleague over cover I was sent a supply teacher to team-teach my lesson by way of apology. The teacher enthusiastically joined in the lesson on war poetry where the pupils were asked to draw a collage of pictures to illustrate the poem 'Dulce et Decorum Est' by Wilfred Owen in a unit on war poetry. The teacher not only joined in the reading of the poem aloud but he also drew his own sketches of the poem to the delight of the pupils around him. They were very good sketches. The next lesson

I used those sketches on an OHP to revise the poem and take the pupils into the next exercise.

The pupils and the staff had a good feeling about that lesson. The assistance of another adult can be of great benefit to the pupils and the teacher. There is often a more democratic ethos in a classroom where the teaching is shared on a more long-term basis and more independent learning can take place. Even short-term assistance, to remove a troublesome child or quieten down a noisy group, is also sometimes required and teachers should learn to welcome that assistance and not be fearful that it diminishes their authority.

Conclusion

The teacher who is a learner can always contribute to the development of other colleagues. Your enthusiasm for your subject or favoured forms of pedagogy may motivate both students and colleagues. Your belief in the value of teaching and education as a source for the enrichment of society can inspire others. Your belief that education can be a source for change towards building a more egalitarian society will motivate pupils and colleagues alike. Your practical advice and explanations of how to overcome difficulties and persevere will always be of value to your colleagues. Creative teachers can adapt, amend, and integrate new ideas about teaching. Beginning teachers, fresh from university, can enrich schools by looking at them with new eyes, and can contribute new ideas, approaches and insights. As teachers and learners, our minds should never be closed to learning something new.

References

Benn, C. (2001) 'A credible alternative: some tasks for the future', *Education and Social Justice*, 3 (2) (Autumn), 2–5.

Blum, P. (1998) *Succeeding and Surviving in Difficult Classrooms*. London: Routeledge.

Cole, M. (1999) 'Professional issues and initial teacher education: what can be done and what could be done', *Education and Social Justice*, 2 (1), 63–6.

Cole, M. (2002) 'Introduction: human rights, education and equality', in Cole, M. (ed.) *Education, Equality and Human Rights: issues of gender, 'race', sexuality, disability and social class*. London: Routledge/Falmer.

Cole, M. (ed.) (2005) *Education, Equality and Human Rights: issues of gender, 'race', sexuality, disability and social class*, 2nd edn. London: Routledge/Falmer.

Cole, M., Hill, D. and Shan, S. (eds) (1997) *Promoting Equality in Primary Schools*. London: Cassell.

Coultas, V. (2001) Oracy Across the Curriculum: Selhurst High School. Unpublished paper.

Department of Education and Science (DES) and the Welsh Office (1989) *English for Ages 5–16* (The Second Cox Report). York: National Curriculum Council.

Department for Education and Employment (DfEE) (1998) *The National Literacy Strategy – Framework for Teaching*. London: DfEE.

Department for Education and Skills (DfES) (2003) *Excellence and Enjoyment: a strategy for primary schools*. London: The Stationery Office.

Eyre, D. (1997) *Able Children in Ordinary Schools*. London: David Fulton Publishers.

Gardiner, H. (1993) *Multiple Intelligences: the theory in practice*. New York: Basic Books.

Hattersley, R. (2002) 'Education, education, education: a commitment reviewed', *Education and Social Justice*, 4 (1) (Winter), 2–6.

Hill, D. and Cole, M. (eds) (1999) *Promoting Equality in Secondary Schools*. London: Cassell.

Hill, D. and Cole, M. (eds) (2001a) *Schooling and Equality: fact, concept and policy*. London: Kogan Page.

Hill, D. and Cole, M. (2001b) 'Social class', in Hill, D. and Cole, M. (eds) (2001) *Schooling and Equality: fact, concept and policy*. London: Kogan Page.

Mackie, J. (2000) 'The death of the inner London comprehensive', *Education and Social Justice*, 2 (3) (Summer), 2–5.

Marland, M. (2002) *The Craft of the Classroom: a survival guide*. Oxford: Heinemann Educational.

National Oracy Project (1992) *Thinking Voices: the work of the National Oracy Project*. London: Hodder and Stoughton.

Noble, C., Brown, J. and Murphy, J. (2001) *How to Raise Boys' Achievement*. London: David Fulton Publishers.

Qualifications and Curriculum Authority (QCA) (2003) *Speaking and Listening*. London: QCA.

Smith, A. (1996) *Accelerated Learning*. Stafford: Network Educational Press.

Teacher Training Agency (TTA) (2004) *Qualifying to Teach: professional standards for Qualified Teacher Status and requirements for initial teacher training*. London: TTA.

Thrupp, M. (2000) 'Compensating for class: are school improvement researchers being realistic?', *Education and Social Justice*, 2 (2) (Spring), 2–11.

Wyse, D. and Jones, R. (2001) *Teaching English, Language and Literacy*. London: Routledge/Falmer.

8

Statutory frameworks relating to teachers' responsibilities

Jeff Nixon

Those awarded Qualified Teacher Status must understand and uphold the professional code of the General Teaching Council for England by demonstrating . . . [that] they are aware of, and work within, the statutory frameworks relating to teachers' responsibilities.

(TTA 2004: 7 Section 1.8)

Learning objectives

To raise awareness and understanding of:

- the concept of a teacher's duty of care
- the statutory framework relating to teachers' conditions of service
- regulations/guidance on the welfare of the child, special needs and health and safety
- legislation relating to equality and equal opportunity issues.

Introduction

THERE ARE THREE ELEMENTS TO the concept of a teachers' duty of care: the common law aspect, the statutory consideration and the contractual obligation. The 'common law duty' was highlighted in *Lyes v Middlesex County Council* in 1962 (Local Government Review 1963) where the 'standard of care' expected of a teacher was held to be that of a person exhibiting the responsible mental qualities of a prudent parent in the circumstances of the school, rather than the home. It has been acknowledged that a teacher's duty of care to individual pupils is influenced by the subject or the activity being taught, the age of the children, the available resources and the size of the class. This can be clarified further by adding the proviso that, even though others may disagree, if it can be shown that the teacher acted in accordance with the views of a reputable body of opinion within the profession, the duty of care will have been discharged. The definition of the 'common law' duty of care may become even more sharply focused as progress is made to reduce the size of classes and with the establishment of the General Teaching Councils (GTCs) for England and Wales.

Since September 2000 there has been established a GTC for England and a separate one for Wales; Scotland has had one since 1965. The GTCs have key powers over entry to the profession and the manner in which the profession conducts itself which will clearly impact upon individual teachers in relation to any issues that would fall into the category of misconduct. The GTCs will not have the powers that relate to pay and conditions; these issues will continue to be dealt with by the Review Body procedures.

With respect to the 'statutory duty of care', the Children Act 1989, Section 3; subsection 5 defined the duty of care as doing 'what is reasonable in all circumstances of the case for the purpose of safeguarding and promoting the child's welfare'. Teachers who are entrusted with the care of children during the school day have this statutory duty. The Children Act stresses the paramount importance of the wishes and needs of the child, reflecting the law's current more child-focused approach. Rather than the old-fashioned idea that a child was owned by its parents and this parental authority of property rights was delegated to teachers during the school day, the child's ascertainable needs and wishes should be taken into account by the teacher and considered in the light of the child's age and level of understanding. The teacher needs to assess the risk of harm that could arise to a child in particular circumstances, and to consider the safeguarding of the child and the promotion of the child's welfare and interest. This approach is clearly much more complex than the simplistic doctrine of the child as the property of the parents and demonstrates again how outmoded the term *in loco parentis* has become.

The new Children Act when it becomes law following the publication of the White Paper, *Every Child Matters* (DfES 2004a) will increase the trend already witnessed. It will also alter the way local authorities provide services for children and their parents. We have already seen some local authorities reorganise their provision and new departments have emerged from the previous education and social services departments; more and more we will see the development of Children, Families and Schools departments and the establishment of Children's Commissioners. Much of this proposed legislation has been motivated by the tragic case of Victoria Climbie. The legislation seeks to ensure that children like Victoria do not slip through any holes in local authority provision.

If the concept of the 'duty of care' appears to be a complicated matter when it refers to activities within the school, it becomes ever more complex when a teacher is engaged in leading or assisting with activities off the school site, such as educational visits, school outings or field trips. The law on negligence is particularly significant here; the legal liability of a teacher or head teacher for any injury which is sustained by a pupil on a school journey or excursion would be dependent upon the tests for negligence. If a child suffered an injury as a direct result of some negligence or failure to fulfil the duty of care, the employer of the teacher or head teacher would be legally liable. This is because employers have vicarious liability for the negligence of employees at work. Consequently where legal claims arise following an accident to a pupil, and there is a suggestion of negligence on the part of the teacher, the claim will most likely be made against the LEA as the employer of the teacher or the governing body in the case of Voluntary Aided, Foundation Schools, sixth form colleges or independent schools, if the teacher was, at the time of the accident to the pupil, working in the course of employment. It is, however, possible for teachers to be fined and, as recent cases have demonstrated, be subjected to custodial sentences particularly in relation to the breach of trust provisions of legislation.

Schoolteachers' conditions of service

What do we mean by conditions of service? In the 1920s and 1930s for example, a woman teacher could be dismissed if she got married or even kept company with men. She was not allowed to ride in a carriage or automobile with any man except her brother or father. She had to be home between the hours of 8 p.m. and 6 a.m., unless in attendance at a school function, and could not leave town without first obtaining the permission of the Board of Trustees. The contract also laid down a non-negotiable dress code which included the prohibition of make-up and stipulated that she should not be seen in places such as ice-cream stores (Teacher's Contract 1923: Women In Education).

Eighty years later, for those teachers employed in LEA-maintained schools, national conditions of service are derived from two basic sources. The first is the *Schoolteachers' Pay and Conditions Document* (DfES 2004b), often referred to as the 'Blue Book'. This sets out working time, professional duties and conditions of service. The second is *Conditions of Service for Schoolteachers in England and Wales* (Council of Local Education Authorities/Schoolteacher Committee (CLEA/ST) 1985; revised edition, August 2000) (the 'Burgundy Book'). This covers national agreements between local education authorities and the teachers' organisations, including such issues as sick pay, sick leave, maternity pay and periods of notice.

Much of what happens in schools is, however, subject to local interpretation. In addition, initiatives may occur either at local or national level which change certain aspects of the teacher's job or may simply emphasise one or a number of items in the conditions of service package at a particular time; for example, the administration in different schools of in service education and training (INSET) days – the so-called 'Baker Days'. These are named after Kenneth Baker who, as Secretary of State for Education and Science, introduced them in the Teachers' Pay and Conditions Act of 1987 (DES 1987). The Act does not specify where or when the INSET days need to be taken, so some schools have operated sessions known as 'twilight training', whereby INSET is carried out during the school's academic year. This is often with the agreement of the staff concerned, with some schools converting days designated as 'Baker Days' into days of school closure. However, if this is the case the school must provide the statutory 190 days of education for all pupils. Teachers are required to be available for work in school for 195 days in any school year, although during the Golden Jubilee Year in 2002 this was reduced by one day for both pupils and teachers.

There may also be local agreements, on issues not covered elsewhere. These may be better or worse than conditions agreed nationally. On the positive side, for example, some LEAs operate a maternity leave and maternity pay agreement that is better than the national one. On the negative side, there exist in the aided or voluntary sector and now in Foundation Schools – formerly Grant Maintained Schools (where the governing body is the employer of teachers) – conditions of service that may not be in teachers' best interests. In Church schools, for example, it is not uncommon to see a clause in the contract of employment that states that the employee should not engage in any activity that may bring the Church into disrepute. This is frequently subject to interpretation at local level within the parish. Here one can see shades of the 1920s contract, with teachers in such schools rarely realising the position they are in until the local parish notable starts asking questions. Beginning teachers should also bear in mind that there are three different types of contract: permanent,[1] temporary and fixed term. In addition, during the induction year the beginning teacher's contract only becomes permanent once the year has been successfully completed.

The 'Blue Book': *Schoolteachers' Pay and Conditions Document* (STPACD) in England and Wales

Prior to this system being introduced, negotiations on pay and conditions of service took place in the Burnham Committee and the Council of Local Education Authorities/Schoolteacher Committee (CLEA/ST), respectively. The Burnham Committee was abolished under the provision of the Teachers' Pay and Conditions Act 1987, whereas CLEA/ST still exists but rarely meets. An Order that provided for conditions of employment to be incorporated into teachers' contracts also came into force in 1987 (HM Government 1987).

The conditions of service elements of the Order dealt with teachers' duties and working time only. They contained little safeguard against the excessive workload that was being imposed upon teachers. The Order sets down a contractual requirement that teachers can be reasonably directed to perform certain duties by the head teacher for up to 1265 hours across the 195 days of service in any one year. It also specified a list of required professional duties. These cover teaching, related activities, assessments and reports, parental consultation sessions, appraisal, review of further training and development, educational methods, discipline, health and safety, staff meetings, cover for absent teachers, public examinations, management and administration.

The Workforce Reform agenda

As part of the remodelling agenda outlined in the Government's White Paper *A Time for Standards* (HM Government 2002), a number of significant changes have been incorporated into the Blue Book; these are being introduced progressively over the next couple of years. The parties to these amendments to the conditions of service element of the Blue Book make claims that the workload of teachers will be dramatically reduced; however, the largest teachers' organisation, the National Union of Teachers (NUT), has remained outside these discussions and has been excluded from discussions on Upper Pay Spine (UPS 3) progression and the future shape of management allowances in schools. The debate on all of this continues and the major stumbling block centres on whether schools should be able to employ non-qualified staff to supervise/teach whole classes.

The changes in the Blue Book stemming from the remodelling agenda are outlined in Section 4 of the 2004 edition of the STPACD (DfES 2004b). In 2003 a list of administrative tasks was drawn up which teachers could no longer be 'routinely required' to perform. Three tests are outlined to assist schools in determining whether teachers should carry out such tasks. These are:

- Does it need to be done at all?
- Is the task of an administrative or clerical nature?
- Does it call for the exercise of a teacher's professional skills or judgement?

If the answers to the first two questions is yes and the answer to the third is no, then the task should be transferred away from teachers.

A Work/Life Balance section has been added to the Blue Book; this is about helping teachers combine work with their personal interests outside school. The section emphasises the aim of reducing bureaucracy, limiting the time outside 1265 hours to what is regarded as reasonable, keeping a check on the number and length of after-school meetings and encouraging schools to develop Work/Life Balance policies. The evidence on this element would suggest schools and teachers have a long way to go in making significant reductions in the average working week, currently in excess of 50 hours during term time.

From September 2004 two new contractual changes on providing cover for absent teachers came into effect:

- A limit on the amount of cover that can be provided by an individual teacher (38 hours per year per teacher).

- An amended duty on head teachers to ensure cover is shared equitably . . . and of the desirability of not using a teacher at the school until all other reasonable means of providing cover have been exhausted, (this would include the use of non-qualified cover supervisors).

A no detriment clause is included in this part of the Blue Book to cover those schools and teachers where the amount of cover provided is already less than the 38 hours. The interpretation of how this clause will work in practice is currently the subject of intensive debate in staff rooms.

From September 2005 every school must introduce a minimum of 10 per cent Planning, Preparation and Assessment (PPA) time for all teachers. Again a no detriment clause is provided to protect teachers who are already in receipt of more than this amount. The consequences of this provision will mean greater strain on over-stretched school budgets. While welcome, PPA time will only work effectively if schools are given extra resources to pay for the extra staff that will need to be employed. Head teachers will also be entitled to guaranteed PPA time commensurate with their teaching time.

Finally, from September 2005 teachers will no longer be required routinely to invigilate external examinations including SATs (Standard Assessment Tests). The opening sentence of this section of the Blue Book boldly announces that invigilating examinations is not a productive use of teachers' time. As with the other elements of the remodelling agenda the aims are ambitious and far reaching, however, there are elements within this that are very worrying encapsulated in the question many parents and carers will pose: is my child being taught by a qualified teacher today?

The 'Burgundy Book': *Conditions of Service for Schoolteachers in England and Wales*

The 'Burgundy Book' deals with sick pay and sick leave, maternity pay and maternity leave and notice. It also refers to legislation affecting teachers' conditions of service with respect to redundancy payments, unfair dismissal, sex discrimination, trade union membership and activities, time off work, race relations, health and safety at work, premature retirement and medical fitness to teach (including those medical conditions when teachers would be suspended from teaching duties on the grounds of ill-health).

Three other sections of the 'Burgundy Book' are also worthy of note. These are the model procedure to resolve collective disputes, facilities for trade union representatives and the 1968 School Meals Agreement. This agreement was a major breakthrough for teachers in that it allowed teachers the freedom to take a lunch break away from the children and the school. Teachers could no longer be required to undertake supervision at lunchtime and that aspect of the conditions of service package remains intact to the present day. There is not much employment law beneficial to the workforce that has survived over 35 years. The 1968 School Meals Agreement was thus an historic landmark for teachers and, in my view, remains so.

Grievance and disciplinary procedures

The 'Burgundy Book' places an obligation on employers (LEAs and governing bodies in relation to Foundation Schools, Voluntary Aided Schools, sixth form colleges and City Technology Colleges and schools in the independent sector) to provide teachers with copies of procedures governing the resolution of grievances and discipline. Since Local Management of Schools (LMS), governing bodies have usually adopted procedures recommended by the personnel sections of LEAs. It can be argued that all such procedures form part of a teacher's contract of employment and if they are not followed, this could readily give rise to a claim for breach of contract.

Since new regulations on making claims to Employment Tribunals (ETs) were introduced from the beginning of October 2004, the use of grievance procedures and disciplinary appeal procedures will play an increasingly significant role prior to cases ever coming before an ET. In short, an applicant will have to demonstrate that all existing internal procedures have been exhausted before the case is listed for a hearing in tribunal. The most significant impact will be to reduce the number of claims that ever reach an ET hearing; in addition, the new regulations make it almost impossible to secure a successful decision when claims for constructive dismissal are lodged.

Local agreements

The third component of the conditions of service package for teachers is contained within whatever local agreements have been negotiated within the LEA or the school (e.g. Foundation, Voluntary Aided or sixth form college); it is unlikely that negotiated local agreements will exist in the independent sector, as recognition of the teaching unions and associations is likely to be problematic. However, since the introduction of the right for unions to be recognised under certain specific circumstances, there have been a few instances of union recognition developing in the independent sector. Local agreements normally cover matters not covered in the 'Burgundy Book', such as time off other than for sickness and maternity leave. Entitlements or guidance to head teachers and governing bodies in exercising discretion on leave of absence covering bereavement, a relative's illness, weddings, study leave, moving house and other circumstances are all dependent on local agreements. There will not always be a right to time off for these matters and it may not always be paid leave. The decision on leave of absence may be delegated to the head teacher. This has particularly been the case since the introduction of LMS. However, the ultimate decision on the right to leave of absence will rest with the employer, which in most cases will be the LEA.

Other aspects of teachers' conditions of service that are determined locally are the precise timings of the school day. There are considerable variations between the key stages. The amount of contact time in an infant school, for example, may be around five hours, whereas in a secondary school it may be up to 5 hours 45 minutes. It is left to the school to decide the precise timings of the day, the timing of breaks, the length of morning and afternoon sessions and the length of the lunchtime.

The changing face of conditions of service

Market forces applied to the education service have had a serious effect on the conditions of service of schoolteachers and on their salaries. It inevitably means local variations within the national framework; sometimes this local interpretation at school level can work to the advantage of teachers, sometimes not. However, the evidence would suggest that the workload of teachers is still excessive.

What is specifically required is a limitation on the current paragraph 67.7 within the STPACD 2004. This paragraph effectively means that a teacher's working time is open-ended in terms of performing the professional duties of the job. In practice, this means that teachers work regularly on average in excess of 50 hours per week during term time. The whole aim of the remodelling agenda is to assist serving teachers to reduce their workload; however, an equally important aim is to make teaching as a profession more attractive to prospective teachers. As the age profile of teachers becomes older this increasingly takes on a greater significance. Within the next five years a huge number of teachers will be eligible for retirement when they attain 60 years of age. The question for the Government both then and now is whether those who retire will be easily replaced by another generation of teachers; the evidence suggests that a severe teacher shortage is almost upon us so it is essential people are attracted to the profession and, what is more, once in it they stay in it for a significant period of time.

The Education Reform Act of 1988 (HM Government 1988) changed conditions of service considerably. This provided for local management of schools (LMS), giving governing bodies much more control and seriously eroding the power of the head teacher and the LEAs. The Act also made provisions for schools to opt out of LEA control and become grant maintained. This has subsequently been amended within the Schools Standards and Framework Act (HM Government 1988); so that former grant maintained schools are now back under the umbrella of the LEA although as most are Foundation Schools, the governors are still the employer. The overall effect was to loosen the influence LEAs had on schools and consequently potentially worsen the conditions of service of teachers at local level.

More recently in 2004 there has been an attempt to worsen the sick leave and sick pay provisions for teachers. The National Employers' Organisation for School Teachers (NEOST) in discussions with the teacher unions failed to reach a negotiated agreement even after the matter was referred to the Advisory, Conciliation and Arbitration Service (ACAS) (1998). Subsequently, the assistant secretary of NEOST issued Bulletin No 493 in October 2004 to all education authorities covered by the Burgundy Book. This bulletin encouraged LEAs and other employers to introduce the proposed changes into the contracts for all newly appointed teachers, thereby creating a two-tier system within the national framework. To their credit several LEAs have not agreed to do this; however, this does demonstrate the level to which the employers are prepared to descend in order to worsen certain aspects of teachers' conditions that are regarded as generous.

The profession needs the confidence to take control of its own destiny. The role of the newly established General Teaching Council (GTC) will need to be seen in the context of an education system, however, which a number of commentators (e.g. Cole 1998, 2005; Hatcher 1998; Allen *et al.* 1999; Hill 2001; Rikowski 2001) have suggested is witnessing burgeoning privatisation. In order to protect and advance the conditions of service of schoolteachers, a major role of GTCs and, of course, the teacher unions, should be to resist this trend.

The welfare of the child

The new guidance issued in 2002 (TTA 2002: 9) specifically mentions confidentiality and states that beginning teachers need to develop an ability to judge when they may need to seek advice. Two specific examples are cited: child protection and confidentiality. It is important for all teachers to be aware that it is frequently not possible to give a pupil an undertaking that everything that is said in a conversation between a teacher and a pupil can remain confidential. Should the teacher be given information by a pupil that would be covered by child protection procedures, then the teacher would have to pass on that information either to the head teacher or the designated child protection officer. If the teacher remained unsure about any aspect of such a conversation with a pupil, then, clearly, advice should be sought from an appropriate colleague. Teachers may also need to seek advice when requests are made for formal assessments or when providing information under the *Special Educational Needs Code of Practice* (DfES 2001b).

Appropriate physical contact and restraint

DfEE *Circular 10/95, Protecting Children from Abuse* (DfEE 1995) provides guidance about physical contact with pupils or students. Appropriate points of that guidance have now been incorporated into Section 550A of the Education Act 1996 (discussed later in this chapter). The relevant paragraphs of the circular are quoted here. These were drawn up after consultation with the teacher organisations.

It is unnecessary and unrealistic to suggest that teachers should touch pupils only in emergencies. Particularly with younger pupils, touching them is inevitable and can give welcome reassurance to the child. However, teachers must bear in mind that even perfectly innocent actions can sometimes be misconstrued. Children may find being touched uncomfortable or distressing for a variety of reasons. It is important for teachers to be sensitive to a child's reaction to physical contact and to act appropriately. It is also important not to touch pupils, however casually, in ways or on parts of the body that might be considered indecent.

Employers and senior staff have a responsibility to ensure that professional behaviour applies to relationships between staff and pupils or students, that all staff are clear about what constitutes appropriate behaviour and professional boundaries, and that those boundaries are maintained with the sensitive support and supervision required. That is important in all schools, but residential institutions need to be particularly mindful of this responsibility, as do individuals in circumstances where there is one to one contact with pupils, for example, in the teaching of music or extra-curricular activities.

Teachers are considered to occupy a position of trust in relation to pupils and this may appear to be an obvious point to make; however, under the terms of the Sexual Offences (Amendment) Act 2000, a criminal offence is committed when a teacher embarks upon a relationship of a sexual nature with a pupil who is under the age of 18 years (DfEE 2000).

The offence can result in a custodial sentence upon conviction; any teacher who was convicted of such an offence would undoubtedly be placed on List 99, which is maintained by the DfES, and which contains the names of all those people who have been prohibited from working with children and young people. At the time of writing (December 2004) schoolteacher Justine Rowe has been sentenced to 12 months imprisonment, banned from working with children and has been put on the Sex Offenders Register for ten years for having a lesbian relationship with a girl of 16.

Schools may find it helpful to agree in consultation with the LEA or Area Child Protection Committee (ACPC) a code of conduct for staff to reduce the risk of allegations being made. Some LEAs have already drawn up such codes that are recommended to schools. Where a school agrees such a code, it should be made known to parents/carers to help avoid any misunderstandings.

There have been recently a number of well-publicised cases that relate to teachers, child protection and misconduct cases. Some of these have concentrated on teachers being the subject of false or malicious allegations made by parents/carers and/or children. The length of time teachers are suspended from duty while child protection procedures are applied has also given cause for concern, so much so that a number of Regional Co-ordinators were appointed during 2001 to ensure procedures are not subject to any unnecessary delay to avoid teachers who are under investigation being left in a state of 'limbo'. Clearly, LEAs and governing bodies have responsibilities to protect children from harm and they need to be vigilant in their approach to these responsibilities. However, there is also a duty of care towards the individual teacher who is the subject of any enquiry and LEAs, head teachers and governing bodies must not forget this. All too often the needs of the teacher, who is away from the school community because of the suspension while the investigation is conducted, are considered not to be a priority, furthermore the teacher's absence from the school community leads to rumour, gossip and often unfounded speculation. This frequently makes it very difficult indeed to reintegrate the teacher even when the investigation either exonerates the individual or permits a return to the school community after the disciplinary procedures have concluded.

The GTCs also have roles to play in relation to teacher misconduct and competence issues. The establishment of the GTCs means that the teaching profession is much more self-regulatory although for certain serious criminal convictions, and being placed on the Sex Offenders Register would be one such example, a person's right to teach can be taken away directly by the DfES.

Whereas before the introduction of the GTCs all misconduct cases were referred to the Teacher Misconduct Unit and decisions about whether a teacher could continue to practise were taken by that Unit, in consultation with the Secretary of State, now less serious cases of misconduct and appeals relating to the failure of the Induction period will be dealt with by the Professional Conduct Committee of the GTC. In much the same way as doctors and lawyers can be 'struck off' by their professional bodies, the GTCs will have the power to de-register a teacher, subject, of course, to the usual rights of the teacher concerned making representations to the GTC.

Since 1998, provisions contained in Section 4 of the Education Act 1996 have clarified the position in relation to the use of physical force by teachers. The relevant section of the Act, S550A, defines the powers of members of staff to restrain pupils or students. Staff can use such force as is reasonable in the circumstances for the purpose of preventing the pupil from doing or continuing to do any of the following:

(a) committing any offence;
(b) causing personal injury to or damage to the property of any person (including him or herself); or
(c) engaging in any behaviour prejudicial to the maintenance of good order and discipline at the school or among any of its pupils, whether that behaviour occurs in a teaching session or elsewhere.

These circumstances apply where a member of staff of a school is:
(a) on the premises of the school; or
(b) elsewhere at a time when, as a member of staff, he or she has lawful control or charge of the pupil concerned.

(DfEE 1998: para. 10, p. 4)

The use of corporal punishment is excepted from these provisions as it was abolished in the maintained sector in August 1986.

The term 'member of staff' is defined as any teacher who works at the school, and any other person who, with the authority of the head teacher, has lawful control or charge of pupils at the school. 'Offence' is qualified by the caveat that under a certain age a child may not be capable of committing an offence.[2] The interpretation of this section of the law, therefore, is open to conjecture; the initial assessment and judgement of the teacher and the subsequent course of action adopted will be critical in assessing whether the amount of force used is reasonable. This will also be dependent upon a number of variables such as the age and size of the pupil and how much the teacher knows about the pupil. Other variables may be relevant: for example, whether the pupil concerned suffers from any pre-existing medical condition that may or may not have been known to the member of staff concerned. Restraining, by use of physical force, a pupil who suffers from brittle bone disease, for example, may not be considered a reasonable option in the circumstances.

Before the implementation of the Act, force was allowed in an emergency only: where pupils placed themselves at risk of physical injury, where pupil actions placed others at risk of physical injury and where damage to property could be limited by the use of restraint, without endangering the physical safety of pupils, staff or members of the public. The new provisions make clear that teachers and other authorised members of staff are entitled to intervene in other, less extreme, situations.

There is no definition in the Act of what constitutes 'reasonable force'. The interpretation of this is crucial for teachers and others defending their actions. It must be emphasised that the use of any degree of force is unlawful if the particular circumstances do not warrant it. The degree of force should be in proportion to the circumstances and seriousness of the behaviour or consequences it is intended to prevent. The level and duration of the force used should be the minimum necessary to achieve the desired result, such as to restore safety.

In some circumstances it will, of course, be inadvisable for a teacher to intervene without help, particularly where a number of pupils are involved and where pupils are older and more physically mature. Unless this was considered, the teacher might be at risk of injury and clearly this should be avoided.

Although the new provisions do not specifically mention the failure to take appropriate action, in circumstances which merit the use of reasonable force, such failure could be regarded as seriously overreacting. This means that it is no longer possible to argue that it is a safer option for a member of staff to do nothing or to take very limited action, when to take some action would restore safety. As far as a teacher's duty of care is concerned, an omission can be significant if there were to be a subsequent claim for negligence. Having said that, a teacher would not be expected to intervene to restore safety, at all costs, to the personal safety of the teacher concerned. It is a matter for professional judgement that may need to stand up to detailed analysis and justification at a later time.

In 1994, the DfEE provided specific guidance on the physical restraint and education of children with emotional and behavioural difficulties (EBD) contained in Circular 9/94 (DfEE 1994). Schools are required to have clear written policies on controls, restrictions and sanctions that can be used in dealing with EBD pupils and a positive approach is encouraged where intervention by teachers is based upon reward rather than punishment.

There is an acknowledgement in the circular, however, that difficulties in relation to EBD pupils are likely to be more severe and occur more frequently than with other children. Circular 9/94 advises:

> Physical contact and restraint should never be used in anger, and teachers should seek to avoid any injury to the child. They are not expected to restrain a child if by doing so they will put themselves at risk. Brief periods of withdrawal away from the point of conflict into a calmer environment may be more effective for an agitated child than holding or physical restraint. Parents with children in special schools should be told how restraint is being exercised. Children who require complex or repeated physical management should have a prescribed, written handling policy. Staff dealing with them should be trained in proper and safe methods of restraint.
>
> (DfEE 1994: 37, 38)

Section 550A of the Education Act 1996 applies equally to EBD children.

The NUT recommends that all incidents of restraint should be logged in a record book provided for that purpose and regularly monitored by a senior member of staff. The record should be contemporaneous and sufficiently detailed to help in any later investigation or complaint. It is advisable to inform parents/carers of any recorded incident. Since September 1998, all schools are required to have a behaviour policy which may well include guidance on the use of physical restraint involving touching, pushing, pulling and holding. Teachers will need to be made familiar with the school's policy and ensure they act within its terms at all times.

Training in methods of restraint may be considered appropriate for some staff and for certain types of school; however, the training provided should be appropriate and suitable people should be involved in its provision. A few years ago a residential special school that had encountered a number of students, mainly adolescent boys, exhibiting aggressive and challenging behaviour, brought in some prison officers on a training day to give instruction in physical restraint. The whole staff, teaching and support staff received the training. Afterwards the incidence of restraint increased dramatically and the injuries to students also gave cause for concern. Physical restraint and punishment almost became synonymous in the school and it is not surprising that shortly after an LEA inquiry into the school and its climate of indiscipline, it was recommended for closure.

The Special Educational Needs and Disability Act 2001

In its advice to beginning teachers (NUT 2004), the NUT summarises the provisions of this Act (DfES 2001a), concentrating on the *Special Educational Needs Code of Practice* (DfES 2001b). It suggests that relevant teachers, in consultation with the SENCO, should devise interventions, additional or different to those provided by the school's usual curriculum. The *Code of Practice* established two straightforward levels of intervention: school action and school action plus. Only the latter category will require agencies from outside the school. The purpose of the legislation was to streamline the provision of education for children with special needs, and the parents of those children. Time will tell how successful this will be.

The Health and Safety at Work Act 1974

The Health and Safety at Work Act 1974 (HM Government 1974) is one of the major pieces of legislation of the 1970s. It was and still is 'enabling legislation' and, since the onset of more and more Directives from Europe, the whole health and safety arena has become more and more crowded with regulation, codes of practice and written recording of such matters as substances that are hazardous to health, dangerous occurrences and risk assessments. It would be impossible for teachers to be familiar with everything connected with the Act; it is far too extensive a field. However, certain elements of the legislation are very important for teachers, particularly Sections 7 and 8 of the Act. The main responsibility under the 1974 Act rests with the employer, who has to take reasonable care for the health and safety of employees and others who are on their premises. This includes not only the children, teachers and support staff, but also parents/carers and other visitors to the school, in particular, those making deliveries.

However, all employees have a duty under the Act to take reasonable care for the health and safety of themselves and others who may be affected by their acts or omissions at work. Consequently teachers have a duty to take reasonable care of both their own and their pupils' health and safety at school. The law also requires employees to act in a co-operative manner with respect to any guidance provided by the employer to assist in maintaining a safe working environment. For teachers, this means following carefully school-based or LEA guidance on policy and procedure, and ensuring they are familiar with such practices. It means in practice that teachers should act with reasonable care at all times and apply good sense to everything they do, including not taking any unnecessary risks or doing anything that is potentially dangerous to themselves, the children and parents/carers who may be helping out either in school or on out-of-school activities. There is a duty on all employees to report any hazards and potentially dangerous incidents at work; teachers should make themselves familiar with the reporting and recording system in their school (e.g. the accident report book). There may also be a need to report certain types of accident to the Health and Safety Executive for possible investigation, consideration of prosecution and recommendations to be implemented to avoid a similar occurrence. Occupational injuries should also be reported to the local office of the Department of Social Security; delay in reporting such injuries could result in benefits being lost in the short and long term. To facilitate all this, each school should have a trained and well informed health and safety representative. The unions do encourage members to take on such a role, and provide comprehensive training in the rights and responsibilities associated with such a role. However, the unions discourage members becoming health and safety officers as, under the Act, such individuals are much more liable legally for their acts and omissions; representatives are not liable for the things they do or do not do as representatives.

Health and safety representatives' responsibilities are towards the trade union members they represent only and their job is to ensure that information is made available, accidents and the aftermath are properly recorded and acted upon, investigations are carried out, where appropriate, and inspections of the premises are undertaken on a regular basis (at least once a term in school time). It is important for health and safety representatives to encourage everyone to report even what might seem to be a minor matter that may simply require cleaning up, or a small inexpensive repair. Seemingly minor matters can cause serious accidents. The most frequently recorded accidents in schools involve slipping, tripping and falling – usually because of a patch of wet or because rubbish on the floor has not been cleared away. Teachers themselves can contribute to their own accidents; the most common problem tends to be piling up furniture, attempting to mount displays or to change broken light bulbs on wobbly chairs or wobbly tables. The first questions anyone investigating such accidents will ask are why did the teacher not use proper equipment and, with respect to the light bulb, why, when it is not their responsibility, was a teacher changing a light bulb in the first place?

Teachers who undertake particular specialist activities, such as the instruction or teaching of swimming, trampolining, canoeing and rock climbing, are required to hold particular qualifications. There may also be a requirement within the qualification to regularly update the skills required in order to continue teaching and supervising the activity. Should there be any doubt about the need for an extra qualification or the need for updating, teachers should not take on the activity until the appropriate professional body or association concerned has been consulted. The health, safety and welfare of children in the care of teachers are a fundamental requirement. Parents/carers entrust their children to the schools and to teachers in particular; they do not expect children to come to any harm there.

Satisfying the duty of care absolves teachers from legal liability. However, sometimes accidents occur as a result of the fault of someone with no organising or supervising responsibility for the activity: for example, the bus company used for the trip. Should an accident occur where pupils and/or teachers sustain injury as a result of some defect in the vehicle, the bus company would of course be liable.

Some accidents are pure accidents, not reasonably foreseen and not the result of negligence on anyone's part, if no one is responsible then there can be no liability. Consequently liability goes with fault. In the case of a pure accident no one bears liability. Schools and LEAs will be covered in this eventuality by 'no-fault insurance'. Some LEAs act as loss adjusters for their own insurance procedures and settlement of a particular claim does not carry with it a notion of liability on the part of the LEA as employer. Recently an Appeal Court judge, deliberating on a case for damages following an accident, said something quite profound given the type of 'blame culture' we now encounter relentlessly in society. She said, 'Sometimes, some things happen that are, quite simply, nobody's fault.' We would all do well to heed these words of wisdom before rushing to the law to attempt to apportion blame.

Equality and equal opportunities

Sex, 'race' and disability discrimination

Under the Sex Discrimination Act 1975 (HM Government 1975) and the Race Relations Act 1976 (HM Government 1976), it is unlawful to discriminate against a person on grounds of sex or marital status, or on racial grounds. The latter includes 'race', colour, nationality, citizenship, ethnic or national origins. It is unlawful to discriminate against a person directly or indirectly.

Direct discrimination

Direct discrimination is where, in similar circumstances, a person is treated less favourably, because of his or her 'race' or sex than the way in which another person of the opposite sex or different 'race' would be treated. Direct discrimination takes many forms. In the treatment of pupils and students, for example, it may vary from crude remarks to subtle differences in assessment, expectation, provision and treatment. It may be unconscious or even well meaning; however, it is still unlawful. Racial or sexual harassment is also a form of direct discrimination. Rights exist on 'race' and sex discrimination when candidates apply for posts and during the interview and other selection processes. This means that short-listing and questions at interview must not contravene the legislation. The woman candidate who was asked at interview for the Head of Technology Department how she would deal with all the reactionary men who currently worked in the department suffered an incidence of sex discrimination on two counts: first, the terms of the question itself and second, the woman claimed that the question was discriminatory and sexist because the same question could not be put to a man and because it challenged her as a woman, rather than as a professional. She was the only candidate who was asked the question, as all the other candidates were men (NUT 1991a: 25).

Indirect discrimination

Indirect discrimination is more complex. It occurs when a requirement or condition, although applied equally, is such that a considerably smaller proportion of a particular racial group or sex can comply with it and when this cannot be objectively justified. The phrase 'objectively justifiable' means in an educational context that the condition or requirement cannot be justifiable on educational or other grounds. It has to be a question of examining the facts and the reason for the objective justification put forward in each and every case. An example of this is a case that reached the House of Lords (*Mandla and Mandla* v. *Lee and Park Grove Private School Limited* (1983) *Industrial Relations Law Reports* 109 HL) and involved the requirement to wear a cap as part of a school uniform. Although applied equally to all pupils and students, it had the effect of excluding Sikh boys from a particular school and this was not justifiable on educational grounds and, therefore, constituted unlawful indirect racial discrimination.

In schools, discrimination is specifically unlawful with respect to the terms of admission. Schools must not refuse to admit pupils or to employ staff on grounds of 'race' or sex. In addition, any arrangement that does not afford pupils equal access to benefits, facilities or services is also unlawful. Finally, it is against the law to exclude pupils from school or to subject them to any other detriment on grounds of sex or 'race'. The law makes an exception for single-sex schools although in doing so, it stipulates that the facilities available should be no less favourable than those in any other school in a given LEA.

The Commission for Racial Equality and the Equal Opportunities Commission have both issued Codes of Practice on the elimination of discrimination and organisations such as the NUT publish, from time to time, pamphlets and research findings on a variety of equal opportunities issues (see, for example, NUT 1988, 1989a,b,c, 1991a,b, 1992, 1995, 2002). Any complaints against schools or LEAs concerning discrimination can be made to the Secretary of State for Education and Skills or, if a legal redress is sought, one can go to the county court. Complaints by employees or potential employees can be brought, without any need for a qualifying period, to Employment Tribunals in cases that relate to sex and race discrimination.

The Race Relations (Amendment) Act 2000

Following the Stephen Lawrence Inquiry, the Race Relations Act 1976 was amended to assist public authorities in promoting race equality in all aspects of their work. The Commission for Race Equality (CRE) sent to all schools a draft guide of the new Act and *Race Equality Standards (Learning for All)* (Commission for Racial Equality 2000) providing advice on how schools are able to meet their statutory duties.

The General Duty section of the Act (Home Office 2000) has three parts:

- eliminate unlawful racial discrimination
- promote equality of opportunity
- promote good relations between people from different racial backgrounds.

In relation to schools this means that policies and statements covering admissions, assessments, raising attainment levels, curriculum matters, discipline, guidance and support, and staff selection and recruitment, should all have elements which address the three parts of the General Duty. Schools have to bear in mind that the size of the minority ethnic population does not matter; racial equality is important even when there are no minority ethnic pupils or staff in a school or local community.

Schools must have a written statement of policy for promoting race equality and, as soon as is practicable, arrangements for assessing the impact of policies on pupils, staff and parents, and a system of monitoring the operation of the policies paying particular attention to the levels of attainment of pupils from minority ethnic groups. The Race Equality Policy may be a clearly identifiable and easily available part of the school's policy on equal opportunities or the policy on inclusion; there should also be a clear link between the policy and the school's action plan or the School Improvement Plan.

Such policies and planning should become an integral part of the development of the school and its existing decision-making processes; the governing body, therefore, plays a vital role in ensuring that the school meets it statutory duties in relation to promoting racial equality. Parents, pupils and staff need to know what the policy says and what it means for them. The questions that schools will need to ask on this amended legislation would include:

- Does the school help all its pupils to achieve as much as they can and do pupils gain the most from what is on offer?

- Which groups of pupils are underachieving and what are the reasons for this?

- Are the policies of the school having a positive impact on pupils, parents and staff from different racial groups?

- How are differences explained and justified? Are there explanations and justifications that have a basis in non-racial grounds like difficulties in the English language?

- Are the aims of each policy addressing the different needs of different groups? Do these aims lead to action on specific points like extra tuition or preventative measures to obviate racist incidents?

- Does the school prepare pupils for living in a multicultural society, promoting racial equality and harmony, and preventing and dealing with racism?

In attempting to address these questions the school will at least begin the process of complying with the General Duty contained within the Act. More importantly, the school and the community it serves will be laying down guiding principles which will hopefully become the firm foundations for a more tolerant and fair society committed to equal opportunities for all.

The Disability Discrimination Act 1995

The Disability Discrimination Act (DDA) (HM Government 1995), introduced in 1995, addresses discrimination in employment and in the provision of goods and services. It abolishes the employment quota of 3 per cent for disabled people established under the Disabled Persons (Employment) Act 1944 (HM Government 1975) . This quota system, whereby employers had to employ a minimum percentage of registered disabled people, was introduced towards the end of the World War II when many service men and women were returning to the labour market and some had suffered disabling injuries during wartime service. The 1995 Act covers temporary and part-time staff as well as permanent and full-time staff.

Section 5 sub-section 1 of the Act states that:

> an employer discriminates against a disabled person if, for any reason relating to their disability, the employer treats them less favourably than he treats or would treat others not having the disability and he cannot show that the treatment is justified.
>
> (DDA 1995, cited in TUC 1996: 2)

Teachers need to be aware of this not only in relation to disabled pupils in their care and in the interests of fostering greater awareness on the part of all the children about the needs, perceptions and feelings of disabled people, but also in relation to the employment of disabled young people when they leave school and enter the world of work.

Moreover, schools need to be regarded as places of work for disabled people (both children and adults) and the 'reasonable adjustments' section of the legislation is particularly relevant in this regard. Employers have a duty to make such reasonable adjustments to the workplace, work equipment or organisation of work where disabled employees or applicants need them because of their disability. Victimisation is also unlawful under the Act and employers must not take action against any person (disabled or not) who uses the provisions of the Act or appears as a witness at a tribunal hearing or gives evidence during an internal hearing.

A disability is defined as 'a physical or mental impairment that has a substantial and long term adverse effect on the ability to carry out normal day-to-day activities' (DDA 1995, cited in TUC 1996: 3). An impairment is one that has existed for 12 months or more, can reasonably be expected to last 12 months or more, or can reasonably be expected to last for the rest of a person's life. The impairment can be related to mobility, manual dexterity, physical co-ordination, continence, and the ability to lift, carry or move everyday objects. It can also be connected to speech, hearing or eyesight, memory, ability to concentrate, learn or understand. Some impairments will need medication or specific equipment. People with a learning or mental disability are covered by the DDA particularly when there is a substantial or long-term effect on the ability to carry out normal day-to-day activities.

The Act does not apply to employers with fewer than 20 employees, so the only schools which are not covered by the provisions are very small Church schools or very small Foundation Schools where the governing body is the employer and the total number of employees who work at the school is less than 20.

Employment discrimination under the terms of the Act takes place when an employer treats a disabled person less favourably than others for a reason that relates to the disability of the disabled person. If the reason for less favourable treatment were not related to the disability then that would prevent a claim being pursued. However, the reason does not have to be the disability itself; if it is related to the person's disability, it is discrimination. For example, refusing to appoint a teacher with a facial disfigurement, not because of the disfigurement, but because it is claimed children might be frightened or upset, would still count as discriminatory.

Probably the most controversial area in the definition of discrimination is the part that deals with justifiable discrimination. The TUC is extremely unhappy about this concept and believes such discrimination can never be justified. As case law develops on this point and others, it may become clearer what this part of the legislation actually means in practice. In the meantime, negotiation and agreements on good equal opportunities policies, procedures and practices will have to be sufficient safeguards against employers using this part of the legislation to abrogate their responsibilities.

The Act applies to disabled applicants for jobs as well as to disabled employees. So the recruitment practices of governing bodies must be in keeping with the legislation. The selection of the best candidate must be based on an objective assessment of the candidate's ability to do the job and in many, if not all, cases the disability of any candidate will be irrelevant unless, of course, the 'reasonable adjustments' section of the legislation is relevant. Indeed this may only become applicable when an employer takes on an employee who is disabled in some way or an existing employee reports an impairment that has lasted 12 months or is expected to last 12 months or longer. Examples that are given about reasonable adjustments include:

making alterations to premises	providing training
reallocation of work	modifying or acquiring equipment or providing special instruction manuals
transfer to another job or site	
changing a disabled person's working hours	providing a reader or interpreter
permitting reasonable absence from work for rehabilitation assessment or treatment	providing a disabled person with supervision and guidance in fulfilling the requirements of the job

All these examples cover all employment, not just teaching.

The DDA is enforced by the employer's grievance procedure, and the Employment Tribunal system. Cases are beginning to be reported where disabled employees have successfully won several thousands of pounds in compensation, when tribunals have accepted that discrimination has occurred in terms of the provisions of the DDA. Much of the legislation is subject to interpretation, so teachers will need to seek advice and support in pursuing claims under the Act and will undoubtedly look to the unions for assistance with this as they do with other issues that relate to employment, conditions of service, educational and professional matters.

The Human Rights Act 1998

All workers in the UK have been covered by the Human Rights Act 1998 (HM Government 1988b) with the incorporation into domestic legislation of the European Convention on Human Rights (ECHR). This Convention and the legislation will develop over time so that account can be taken of case-law precedents and the way societies across the European Community change and evolve; those who wrote the Convention were keen for it to become 'a living instrument' which would act as a benchmark for making judgements about human rights issues. This would cover a wider range of discrimination issues than we have been used to in UK legislation and that is why it has been added to the list of legislation that beginning teachers should be familiar with and hopefully understand.

Equality issues for the future

Mike Cole in the Introductory chapter has dealt with the setting up of the Commission for Equality and Human Rights (CEHR) and the new equality legislation. Other more general questions relate to employment law: should workers be forced to retire at a particular age? We have seen recently the Government's proposals to increase the retirement age of teachers and other public sector workers to 65 years from 60 years; a lobby of Parliament took place in November 2004 on the issue of pensions in the public sector. Are schemes like the statutory redundancy payments formula, which are currently based on age and length of service, discriminatory if the law is changed to include a person's age as a factor in determining discrimination?

Conclusion

Becoming professional is one thing; remaining professional is another. The days when the acquiring of a certificate to teach for life (or up to 40 years) are gone. The rate of change is so rapid and dramatic that the beginning teachers trained in the early part of the twenty-first century may not be equipped to function effectively well into the new millennium unless, and this is the important part for government to understand, time is made available and built into the system for serving teachers to be given the opportunity for extensive professional development, education and training. Examples of good practice are already up and running with courses like the 'Keeping In Touch with Teaching' schemes. These are normally run by LEAs and are open to any teacher who wishes to return to the profession after a break in service, usually following absence for family reasons. There are also many successful returnees' courses that LEAs and training institutions organise.

There are also examples now of the unions offering members not only training in matters that relate to union work but, increasingly, courses that assist in the continuing professional development of members. The NUT is at the forefront of this development, and the TUC is keen to encourage union members to become 'Learning Representatives', and to work alongside and within the recently formed Learning and Skills Councils. For example, the South East Region of the TUC recently set up a Sussex Union Learning Forum to promote the concept of lifelong learning among union members.

Perhaps, in the education service, in order to prepare adequately for the future, we might look back to the recommendations of the James Report, written almost 35 years ago (James of Rusholme 1970). This important analysis of teacher education and the needs of the profession suggested a regular system of sabbatical terms or years dependent upon length of service. For example, a teacher with seven years' experience could look forward to a year's sabbatical that could provide valuable time for retraining and battery recharging. Money spent on that rather than on the introduction of the 'advanced skills teacher' would target resources in a more constructive and supportive way for the teaching profession and bring to the education service a precise strategy to improve the overall performance of practitioners, ensure there was adequate time for professional thinking and development and provide a substantial boost to morale, as well as making the teaching profession more attractive to potential recruits. While it may be true that 'everyone remembers a good teacher', a system must be devised whereby good teachers are not burnt out in a short time-scale. The implementation of this recommendation of the James Report is long overdue.

Notes

1 At the present time, 'permanent' only becomes significant after an employee has worked for an employer for a continuous period of one year. For this reason, some full-time union officials use the term 'ongoing' rather than 'permanent'.

2 The James Bulger murder case, in which two ten-year-old boys were found guilty of murdering two-year-old James Bulger, opened up a debate that is still continuing into the concept of the age of criminal responsibility. The age of criminal responsibility is currently ten-years-old; however, courts will consider cases on their merits taking account of range of factors including the public interest.

References

Advisory, Conciliation and Arbitration Service (ACAS) (1998) *Code of Practice for Time Off for Trade Union Duties and Activities*. London: HMSO.

Allen, M., Cole, M. and Hatcher, R. (1999) *Business, Business, Business: the New Labour agenda for education*. London: Tufnell Press.

Children Act 1989 http://www.hmso.gov.uk/acts/acts1989/ukpga_19890041_en_1.htm (accessed February 2005).

Cole, M. (1998) 'Globalisation, modernisation and competitiveness: a critique of the New Labour project in education', *International Studies in Sociology of Education*, 8 (3), 315–32.

Cole, M. (2005) 'New Labour, globalisation and social justice: the role of education', in McLaren, P., Sunker, H. and Fischman, G. (eds) *Critical Theories, Radical Pedagogies, and Global conflicts*. Lanham, Maryland: Rowman and Littlefield.

Commission for Racial Equality (2000) *Race Equality Standards (Learning for All)*. London: CRE.

Council of Local Education Authorities/Schoolteacher Committee (CLEA/ST) (1985) *Conditions of Service for Schoolteachers in England and Wales*, 2nd edn. (The 'Burgundy Book'). Revised edition 2000. London: Employers' Organisation for Local Government.

DES (1987) *Teachers' Pay and Conditions Act*. London: DES.

DfEE (1994) *Educating Children with Behavioural and Emotional Difficulties*. Circular 9/94. London: HMSO.

DfEE (1995) *Protecting Children from Abuse*. Circular 10/95. London: HMSO.

DfEE (1997) *Education Act 1996*. London: HMSO.

DfEE (1998) *Section 550A of the Education Act 1996. The Use of Force to Control or Restrain Pupils*. Circular 10/98. London: HMSO.

DfEE (2000) *Sexual Offences (Amendment) Act*. London: DfEE.

DfEE (2001a) *Special Educational Needs and Disability Act*. London: DfES.

DfES (2001b) *Special Educational Needs Code of Practice*. London: DfES.

DfES (2004a) *Every Child Matters*. London: The Stationery Office.

DfES (2004b) *Schoolteachers' Pay and Conditions Document*. (The 'Blue Book'). London: HMSO.

Hatcher, R. (1998) 'Labour, official school improvement and equality', *Journal of Educational Policy*, 13 (4), 485–99.

Hill, D. (2001) 'Global capital, neo-liberalism, and privatisation: the growth of educational inequality', in Hill, D. and Cole, M. (eds) *Schooling and Equality: fact, concept and policy*. London: Kogan Page.

HM Government (1944) *Disabled Persons (Employment) Act*. London: HMSO.

HM Government (1974) *Health and Safety at Work Act*. London: HMSO.

HM Government (1975) *Sex Discrimination Act*. London: HMSO.

HM Government (1976) *Race Relations Act*. London: HMSO.

HM Government (1987) *Statutory Instrument (schoolteachers pay and conditions)*. London: HMSO.

HM Government (1988) *Education Reform Act*. London: HMSO.

HM Government (1995) *Disability Discrimination Act*. London: HMSO.

HM Government (1998) *Schools Standards and Framework Act*. London: HMSO.

HM Government (1998b) *Human Rights Act*. London: HMSO.

HM Government (2002) *A Time for Standards*. London: HMSO.

Home Office (2000) *Race Relations (Amendment) Act*. London: HMSO.

James of Rusholme, Lord (1970) *Report of a Committee of Enquiry into Teacher Education and Training*. (The James Report). London: HMSO.

Local Government Review (1963) *Lyes* v. *Middlesex County Council* (1962) London: HMSO.

National Employers' Organisation for School Teachers (NEOST) (2004) Bulletin No 493 October.

National Union of Teachers (NUT) (1988) *Towards Equality for Boys and Girls: guidelines on countering sexism in schools*. London: NUT.

New Brunswick Teacher's Association (1995) 'Teacher's Contract 1923: Women in Education' *in New Brunswick Teacher's Association Newsletter*, March 1995.

NUT (1989a) *Job Sharing for Teachers: NUT guidelines*. London: NUT.

NUT (1989b) *Anti-racism in Education: guidelines towards a whole school policy*. London: NUT.

NUT (1989c) *Opening Doors: encouraging returners into teaching as a career*. London: NUT.

NUT (1991a) *Fair and Equal – Union Guidelines for Promoting Equal Opportunities in the Appointment and Promotion of Teachers*, 2nd Report. London: NUT.

NUT (1991b) *Lesbians and Gays in Schools: an issue for every teacher*. London: NUT.

NUT (1992) *Anti-racist Curriculum Guidelines*. London: NUT.

NUT (1995) *Research into the Issuing of Fixed-term and Temporary Contracts on a Full- or Part-time Basis with Particular Reference to Women*. London: NUT.

NUT (2002) *Relearning to Learn. Advice to teachers new to teaching children from refugee and asylum-seeking families*. London: National Union of Teachers.

NUT (2004) *Education, the Law and You: the main points*. London: The National Union of Teachers.

Rikowski, G. (2001) 'Schools: building for business', *Post-16 Educator*, 3, 14–15.

Teacher Training Agency (TTA) (2002) *Handbook on Guidance on QTS Standards and ITT Requirements*. London: DfES.

Teacher Training Agency (TTA) (2004) *Qualifying to Teach: professional standards for Qualified Teacher Status and requirements for initial teacher training*. London: TTA.

Trades Union Congress (TUC) (1996) *The Disability Discrimination Act, A TUC Guide*. London: TUC.

Name index

Subject index